IMAGES
of America

Child Labor in Greater Boston 1880–1920

On the Cover: Bootblacks pose in Bowdoin Square, Boston, in 1909. Nine boys, each with his own homemade boot-blacking box, are seen here. The boys walked the streets of downtown Boston, asking men if they wanted their shoes shined. The Boston School Committee required boy bootblacks to be licensed and wear a badge when working. (Library of Congress, Lewis Wickes Hine Collection.)

IMAGES
of America

CHILD LABOR IN GREATER BOSTON 1880–1920

Chaim M. Rosenberg and Linda Clare Reed

ARCADIA
PUBLISHING

ISBN 978-1-4671-2106-4

Published by Arcadia Publishing
Charleston, South Carolina

Printed in the United States of America

Library of Congress Control Number: 2013945882

For all general information, please contact Arcadia Publishing:
Telephone 843-853-2070
Fax 843-853-0044
E-mail sales@arcadiapublishing.com
For customer service and orders:
Toll-Free 1-888-313-2665

Visit us on the Internet at www.arcadiapublishing.com

*We dedicate this book to immigrants—past and present—
who bring variety and vitality to Greater Boston.*

Contents

ACKNOWLEDGMENTS

Out thanks go to our families for allowing us the time to pursue the study of child labor in Boston and surrounding towns. The photographs here come from the Lewis Wickes Hine Collection at the Library of Congress unless otherwise noted. The Hine photographs of laboring children across America—taken between 1908 and 1917—are a national treasure. Special thanks to the Prints Department, Boston Public Library, for permission to use photographs of the 19th-century Boston public schools and students. Aaron Schmidt sent the images to us electronically, saving us a trip to the library.

INTRODUCTION

In 1630, John Winthrop led a fleet of 14 ships of sail with 840 passengers "of various crafts and professions, some of whom were from the west of England; but the greatest part from the vicinity of London," to settle the Massachusetts colony. A number of the settlers made their way up the Charles River to Charlestown, where they found "several wigwams, a few English people, and one house with an old planter, who could speak the Indian language . . . they landed their goods at a well watered place . . . and here began to build a town," Winthrop's city upon a hill. From the earliest days of European settlement, children were expected to help their parents with the chores in the home and on the farm. Boston, as the capital of the Massachusetts colony, reached a population of 4,000 people in 1675 and 15,520 people by the year 1765.

The American industrial revolution began early in the 19th century, with cotton textiles made in factories powered by the flow of the Charles and Merrimack Rivers. Boston grew rapidly as the financial center and port of imports and exports. In his speech before the US House of Representatives on April 26, 1820, Sen. Henry Clay of Kentucky recounted his visit to the Boston Manufacturing Company in Waltham. Clay stated that it was better for children to be working than see them idle. Outside the House of Representatives were "crowds of little mendicant boys and girls [who] assail us every day . . . as we come and go out, begging for a cent. [If they] were employed in some manufacturing establishment, it would be better for them." In 1825, the senate of the Commonwealth of Massachusetts recorded that children in factories worked "12 or 13 hours each day, excepting the Sabbath, which leaves them little opportunity for daily instruction, [keeping them in] ignorance to all other concerns." It was necessary to set up schools "for the education of the laboring classes in the practical Arts & Sciences."

Seth Luther was one of the early American labor reformers and a champion of the downtrodden child. In 1833, he published the passionate *Address to the Working Men of New England*. If Henry Clay returned to the region, wrote Seth Luther, "We could show him some of the prisons of New England, called cotton mills. Instead of rosy cheeks, the pale, sickly, haggard countenance of the ragged child, haggard from worse than their slavish confinement in the cotton mills . . . The child is taken from his bed at four in the morning and plunged into cold water to drive away his slumbers and prepare him for the labors of the mill." To Seth Luther, American industry was following the pattern long established in Britain, where children "of very tender ages are compelled to work in mills for 12 to 14 hours, with only 30 minutes for all meals." In 1833, claimed Luther, of 57,000 persons employed in the cotton and wool mills of America, "31,044 are under 16 years of age, and 6,060 are under the age of 12 years." The mill owners made great profits while "the poor must work or starve . . . 13 hours actual labor is required each day, it is impossible to attend to education among children." Luther demanded that children work "only" 10 hours a day and that they attend school.

By 1845, Boston's population of 114,366 was largely of old Massachusetts stock. Lemuel Shattuck prepared the *Census of Boston for the Year 1845*. He divided the population of Boston into three classes. The Dependent Class was under 15 years of age—one third of the population—"because they are dependent on others for support." The Productive Class (aged 15 to 60) contained 60 percent of the total population, which did the work, while the small Aged Class (over 60 years) no longer worked. With epidemics and poverty rampant, early deaths were common. Four out of 10 children died before reaching five years of age. After finishing school, girls from well-off families did not work but stayed at home until they married. Less fortunate girls found employment in the textile mills or as domestic servants. Boston's census for 1845 recorded 5,706 domestics (4,984 females and 722 males) serving in Boston homes.

The Irish came before the Civil War, the girls and women to work as domestic servants and the men as unskilled laborers. Until 1880, Boston was still a walking city, with most of its residents living within two miles of the state house. During the 40 years after 1880, many thousands of Eastern and Southern European immigrants arrived, and the population of the city more than doubled to 748,060. Railroads and streetcars linked Boston with its suburbs and with the surrounding towns. The wealthy and the middle classes took advantage of rapid transportation to move away from the crowded city center. Residential communities sprang up around the railroad stations. People built their homes in the suburbs and nearby towns along the new streets that carried the electric streetcars. By 1920, the Boston metropolitan region had a population of nearly two million.

At the height of immigration, 4 out of 10 Boston residents were foreign born. As unskilled workers, manual laborers, or tailors, they occupied the lowest levels of the social and economic ladder. Driven from their native lands by poverty and political turmoil, the immigrants gravitated to the old Boston neighborhoods such as the South, North, and West Ends, making Boston an increasingly poor and immigrant city.

Boston schools began to fill with children of the immigrants. They differed from the native Bostonians in language, religion, and customs. Yet these children were eager to become Americanized and to do their part in helping their families. Francis Amasa Walker, president of the Massachusetts Institute of Technology, was not impressed by the mass migration and believed that the newcomers had "little mechanical insight, and almost no inventive power . . . We must teach the children of these men," pontificated Dr. Walker, "the use of tools, and we can do it in no other way than through the public schools. Cooking and sewing in the public schools can be made . . . as truly educational as the three R's." For the boys, "instruction of mechanical arts" should be implemented. Teaching job skills to immigrant boys and girls would "increase the interest of the pupils in their schoolwork" and make them useful to the economy of the commonwealth.

By 1900, Boston had 24,323 students in the three years of primary school, 31,608 in the six years of grammar school, but only 2,938 in the three years of high school. Only one child in six in Boston continued his education into high school. In 1908, when the city's population neared its peak, the number of school-aged children exceeded 111,000; most attended public schools, with 15 percent in private school, siphoning off students from wealthier families. Industrialization, mass immigration, and the move of the wealthy to the suburbs made Boston an industrial city with rundown tenements and complex social issues. To survive, the desperate immigrants sent their children to seek work early. Boston tried to stem the tide of school dropout by setting up trades schools to train boys as craftsmen and girls as domestic servants.

The Mechanic Arts High School opened in 1893 at the corner of Dalton and Belvidere Streets in the Back Bay. This all-boys school offered instruction in woodworking, forging, machine maintenance, printing, and drafting. The school aimed to train boys "for advantageous entry into industry on the business and directive side." Chapter 471 of the Acts of 1911 of the Commonwealth of Massachusetts codified "the laws relating to state-aided vocational schools." These schools sought to keep children in school by offering vocational training to those 14 years or older. The Boston Trade School for Boys opened in 1912 at 550 Parker Street, Roxbury, and trained boys to be skilled journeymen, such as mechanics, carpenters, plumbers, electricians, or painters. Girls' High School for Practical Arts taught dressmaking, cooking, millinery, knitting, and sewing. The Trade School for Girls at 620 Massachusetts Avenue, Boston, taught box making, catering, cutting and filling, dressmaking, millinery, and embroidery. Trade schools were "particularly attractive to girls whose chief interest is to earn money as soon as possible." By 1910, Boston public schools were bursting at the seams, with over 110,000 students accommodated in a network of elementary schools, eight inner-city high schools, and six suburban high schools.

Massachusetts was the first state to require children to attend at least three months of schooling a year and to limit the hours they could work in factories. Across America, children worked in the mills, mines, canneries, and farms. Newsboys, messenger boys, bootblacks, and child vendors were out in the streets from early morning to late at night. The girls found work as domestic servants, seamstresses, in the tenement industries, and in shops. Children were kept out of school to tend the fields and pick the harvest. Progressives feared that unskilled child laborers would land up in dead-end jobs without prospects to advance or acquire the knowledge to become responsible citizens. Without training and with only limited education, the fear was that these youngsters would turn to crime, further burdening the social fabric. Many children opted to leave school early without the benefits of the trade schools. In 1907, Boston alone issued 4,856 certificates to children aged 14 or 15 who wanted to quit school and go to work. In the 1910s, some 25,000 boys and girls in Massachusetts each year left school at ages 14–16 to start work. With the entry of the United States in World War I, the number of Massachusetts early school-leavers rose to 42,000 in 1917 and 50,000 in 1918. With older brothers off to fight the war, jobs were plentiful and the pay was good. In 1919, the city of Boston alone had 11,807 working children aged 14 or 15 years.

The national struggle to ban child labor was long fought. In 1938, the Fair Labor Standards Act regulated nationwide the age and hours of the employment of children. *Child Labor in Greater Boston, 1880–1920* shows how the efforts to keep children in school and out of the factories played out in Boston and surrounding towns.

One

Boston

Boston was settled in 1630 on the Shawmut peninsula. Fifty acres of land were set aside as Boston Common, initially for grazing cattle and later for use as a public park. Boston had a long tradition of child labor. Thomas Hancock, born in 1703, was apprenticed at age 14 to a Boston bookseller and bookbinder. In 1718, Benjamin Franklin, born on Milk Street, started work at age 12 as an apprentice printer to his older brother.

In 1713, the old state house was built for meetings of the Massachusetts Legislature. The population of Boston grew slowly, reaching 13,000 a century after its founding. In 1740, Peter Faneuil built his marketplace close by the town's seaport.

Boston played a key role in the events leading to the American Revolution. In 1768, British troops occupied the town to keep the order and to ensure taxes were collected. On March 5, 1770, Edward Garrick, a wig-maker's apprentice, insulted a British officer, leading to a confrontation known as the Boston Massacre, in which five people were killed. Tension mounted following the Boston Tea Party of December 16, 1773. On April 18, 1775, Paul Revere left Boston on his midnight ride to warn that British troops were marching on Lexington and Concord. Starting the following day, the colonists laid siege on the 13,000 British troops and their dependents stationed in Boston. On June 17, 1775, the colonists fought a heroic battle against the British in the Battle of Bunker Hill. The siege of Boston continued until March 17, 1776 (Evacuation Day), when the British troops departed in defeat by ship bound for Halifax, Nova Scotia.

Two hundred years after the city was founded, the population of Boston reached 61,393. In 1836, Massachusetts passed a law prohibiting children under 15 from working in factories unless they received at least three months of education each year. Swelled by immigrants from Ireland, Germany, and Eastern and Southern Europe, Boston's population from 1830 to 1930 grew over tenfold, reaching 781,188 residents. Immigrant children filled the schools and were soon eager to start work in Greater Boston's mills, factories, stores, and streets.

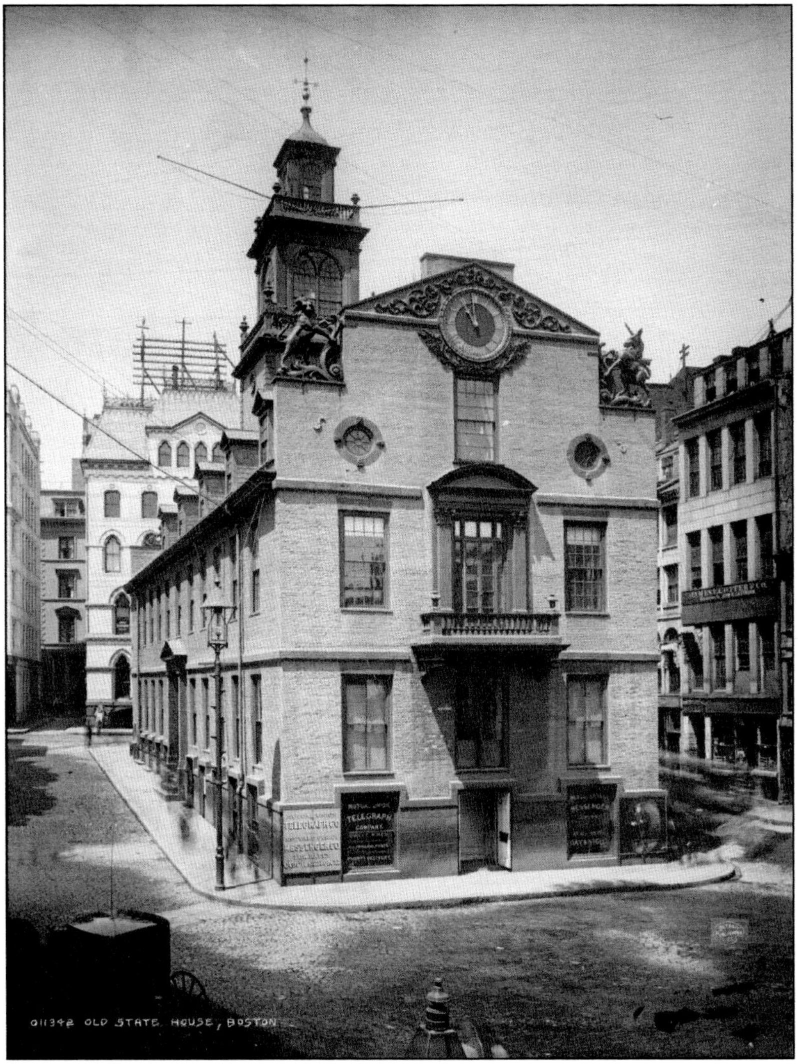

Built in 1713, the old state house in Boston was the seat of the Massachusetts Legislature. On March 5, 1770, the Boston Massacre occurred on Devonshire Street in front of the building. When this c. 1880 image was taken, the building housed tailors, merchants, and shipping agents. The telegraph companies at ground level sent out messenger boys at all hours, day and night.

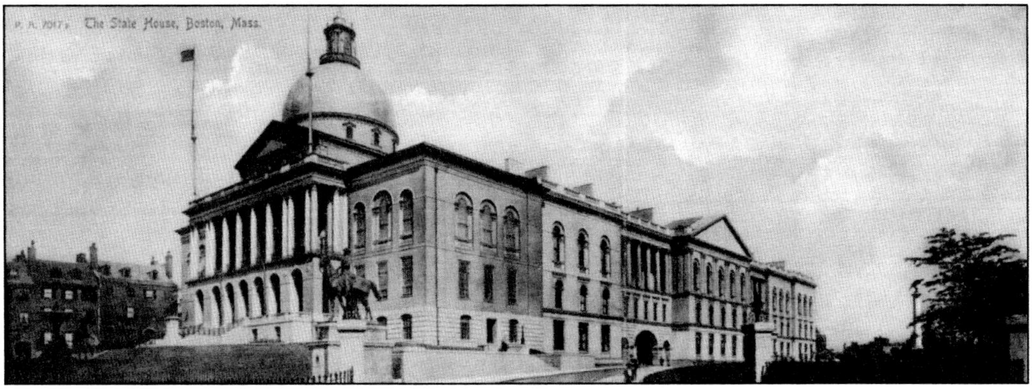

Shown here is the present Massachusetts State House as it looked in 1905. Built in 1798 on Beacon Hill, it faces Boston Common. The state house was designed by Charles Bulfinch and was inspired by Somerset House in London.

Faneuil Hall was built in 1742 as Boston's marketplace and meeting hall. The building was a gift to Boston by the merchant Peter Faneuil, of Huguenot birth, who traded with the Caribbean, Spain, and England. The c. 1880 image shows the marketplace. The famous building is capped by a grasshopper weather vane.

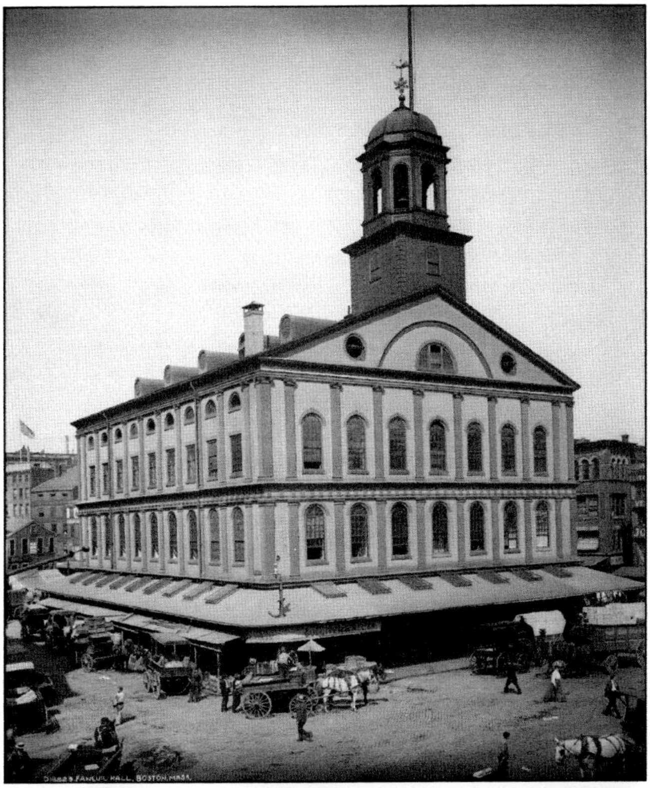

The Paul Revere House, at 19 North Square in Boston's North End, is seen in this c. 1880 image. The original house was built in 1680. Paul Revere was born in the North End and at age 13 started his apprenticeship as a silversmith. He is famous for his midnight ride on April 18, 1775, to warn that British troops were marching on Lexington and Concord.

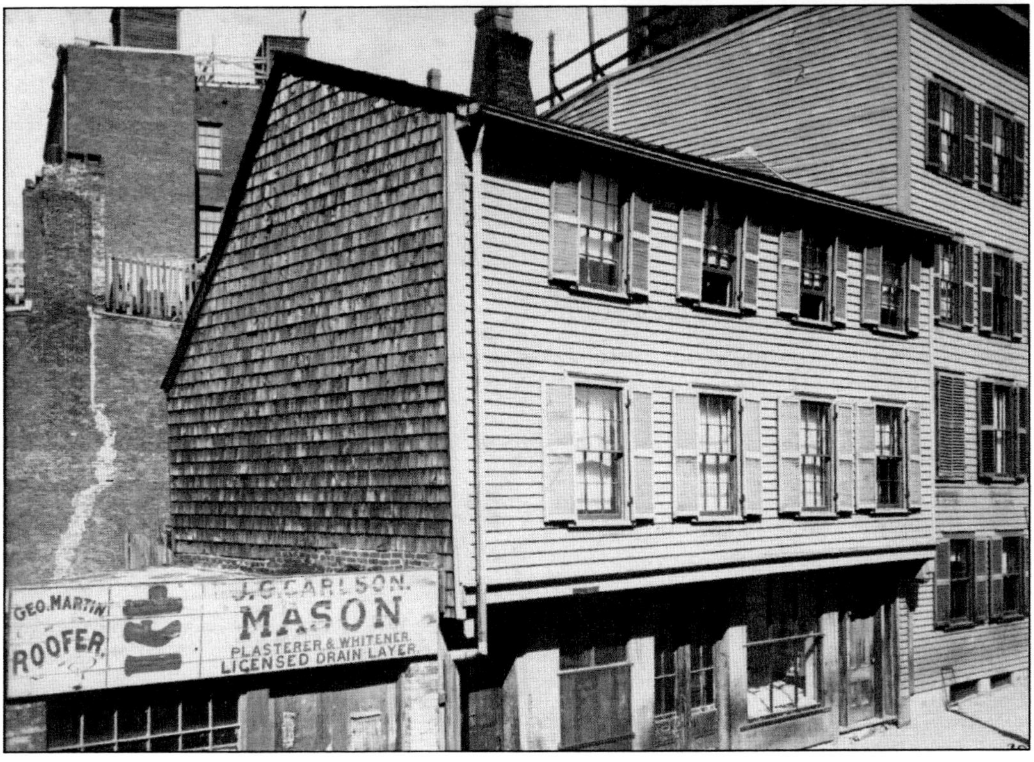

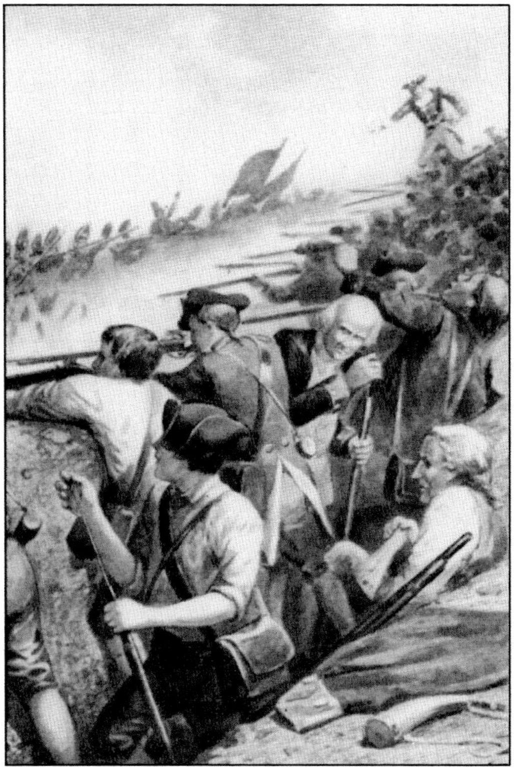

James Otis Kaler (1848–1912), a successful author of children's books, wrote a fictional series on the Minute Boys who served the cause of freedom during the American Revolutionary War. This illustration from *The Minute Boys of Boston* (1910) is by Louis Jesse Bridgman; it shows a Minute Boy fighting in the Battle of Bunker Hill.

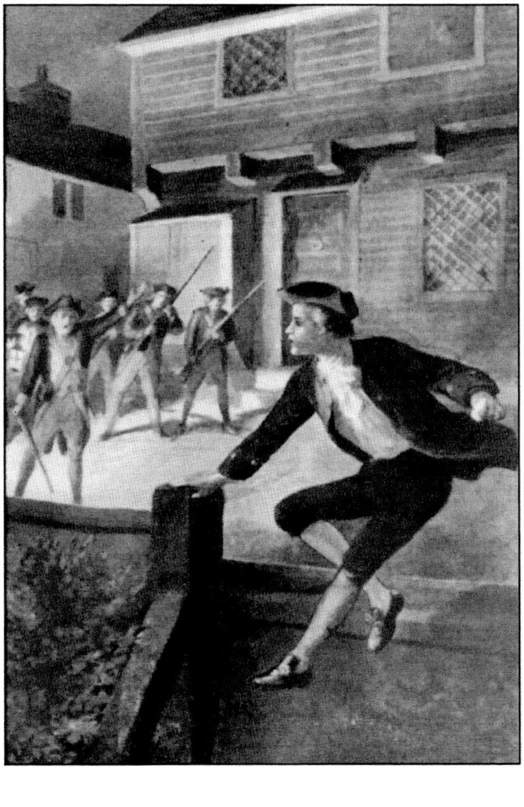

A Minute Boy is volunteering to do men's work and escaping from British troops in occupied Boston. The illustration is by Louis Jesse Bridgman, who lived from 1857 to 1931. (*The Minute Boys of Boston*. Boston: Dana Estes Publishers, 1910.)

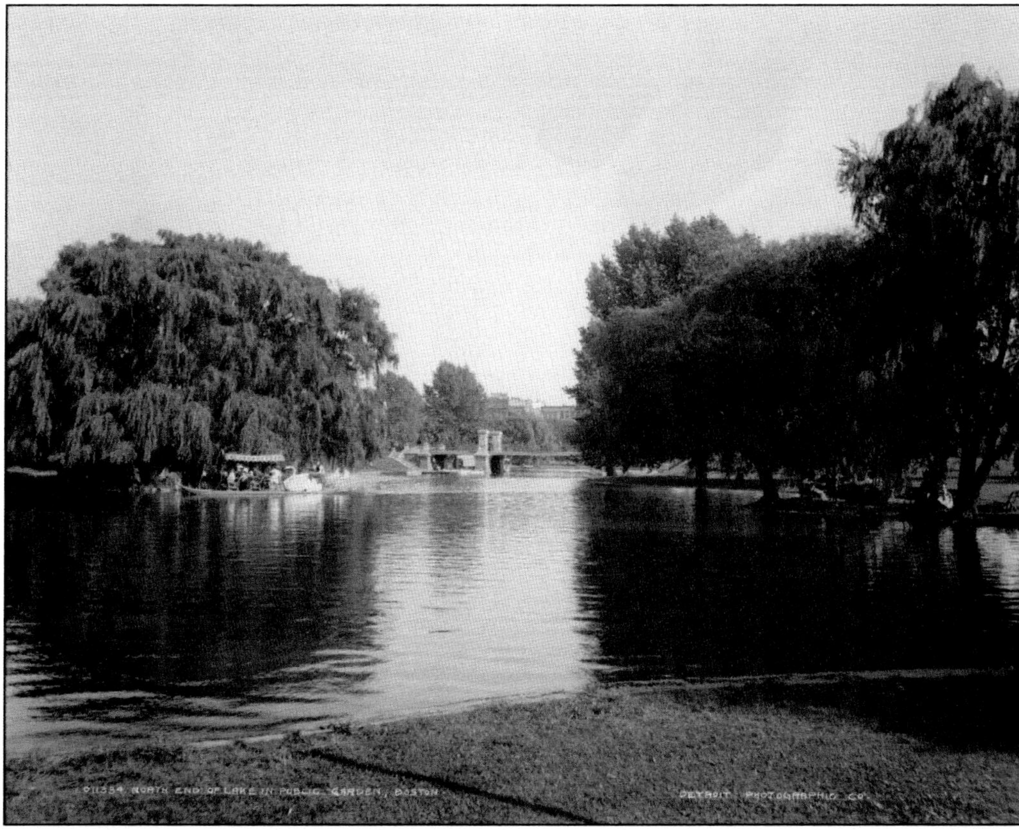

This c. 1890 photograph shows the lake and swan boats at Boston Public Garden, a scene virtually unchanged for well over a century. The botanical garden on 24 acres was started in 1857. The bronze statue of George Washington is by Thomas Ball. (Library of Congress, Princeton Photographs.)

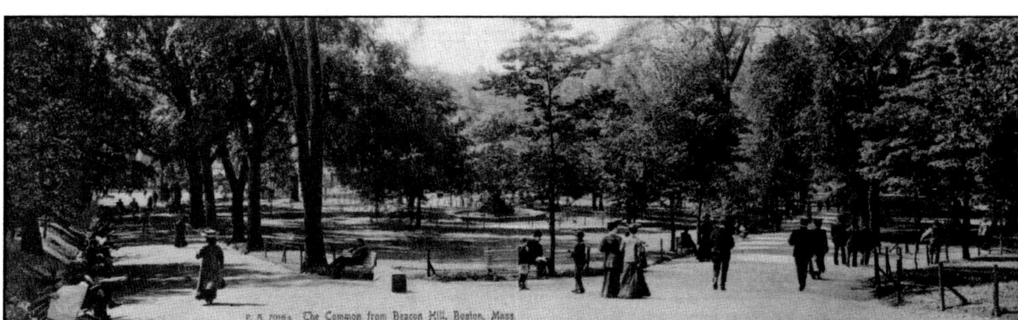

Shown here is a view of the Boston Common as it was early in the 20th century, a public place in the center of the city for strolling and relaxing. Established in 1634 as a cow pasture and later as a park, it served as a camp for British soldiers during the Revolutionary War. Boston Common is the oldest city park in the United States.

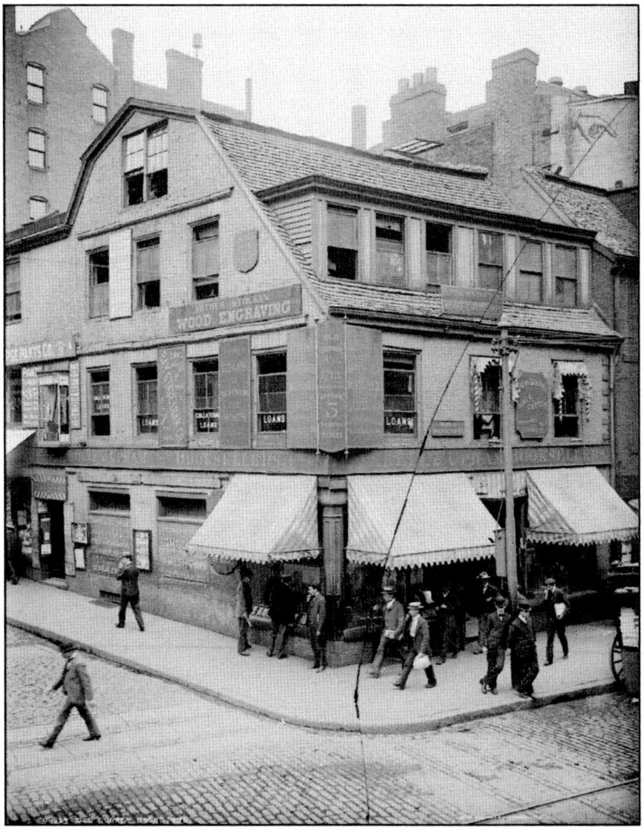

This brick building at the corner of Washington and School Streets was constructed in 1711 and served as an apothecary shop. A century later, it became known as the Corner Bookstore. From 1832 to 1868, it was the home of Ticknor and Fields, book publishers. This picture dates to around 1900.

In this 1909 image, a boy is acquiring the theater habit, checking on what is on show in the theaters along Washington Street. Boston then had several vaudeville and live theaters. In that year, the Boston Opera House opened. Seats in the second balcony cost 50¢. The best orchestra seats were $2.

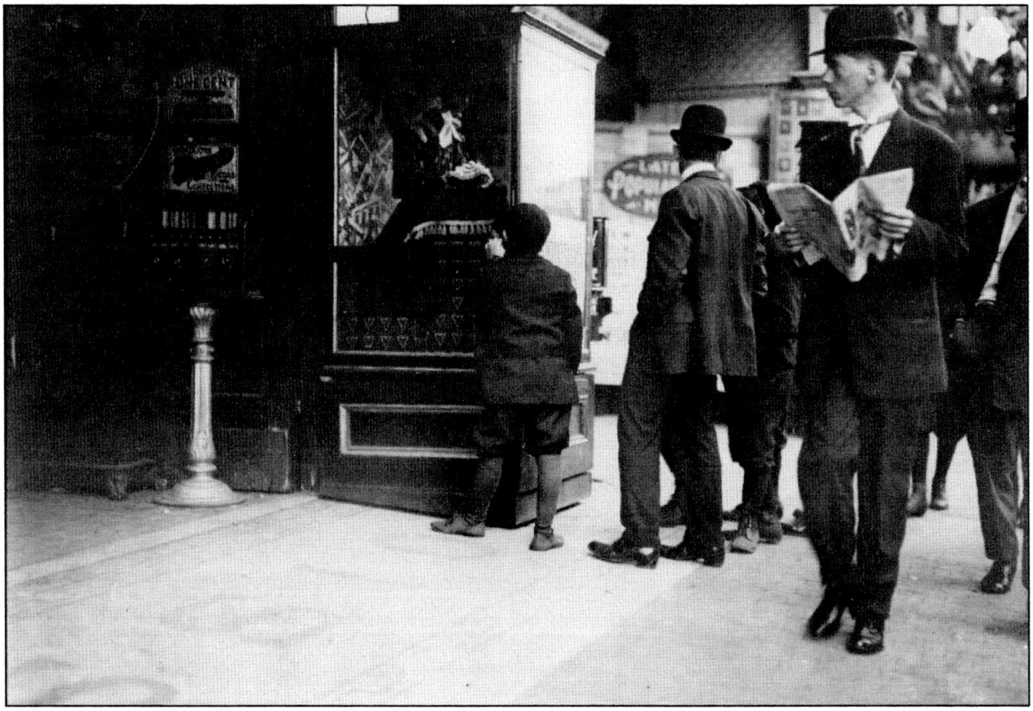

In this 1899 image is the Jewish Quarter of Boston as it appeared to the artist William Allen Rogers. The streets are filled with peddlers, pawnshops, clothing stores, and shoppers. Rogers was born in Ohio and was a student at the Worcester Polytechnic Institute. His illustrations appeared in *Harper's Weekly* and the *New York Herald*. (Library of Congress print and photograph collection.)

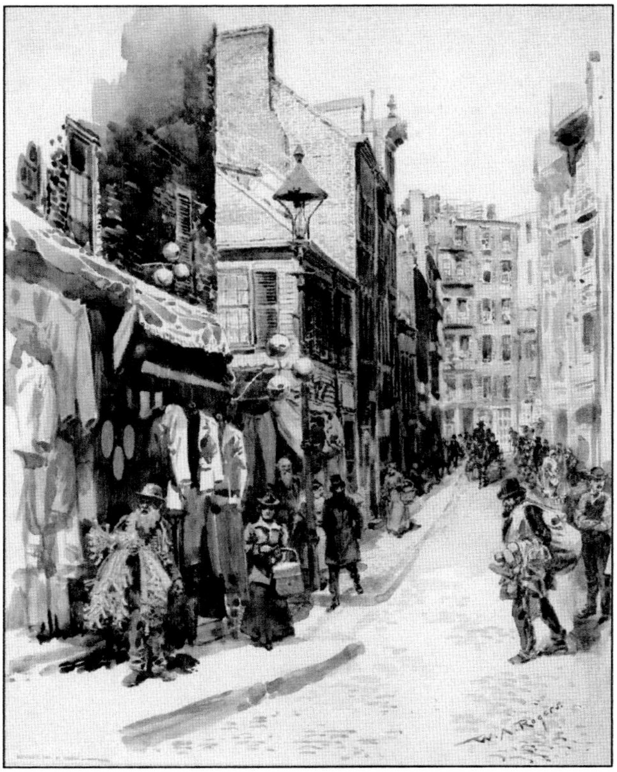

This c. 1920 picture shows the narrow cobbled streets of the North End, lit by gaslight and lined by wooden tenement houses, which were ill suited to house the dense population. In 1919, a molasses tank on Commercial Street exploded, killing 21 people and flooding the area. (Library of Congress photograph.)

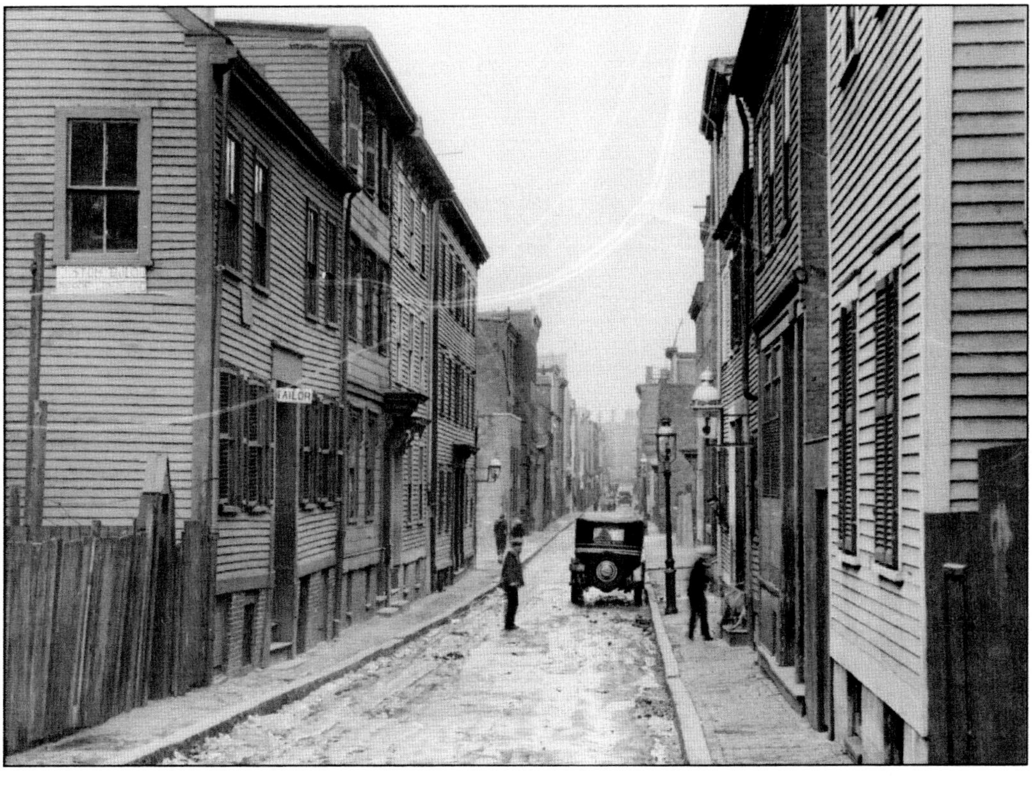

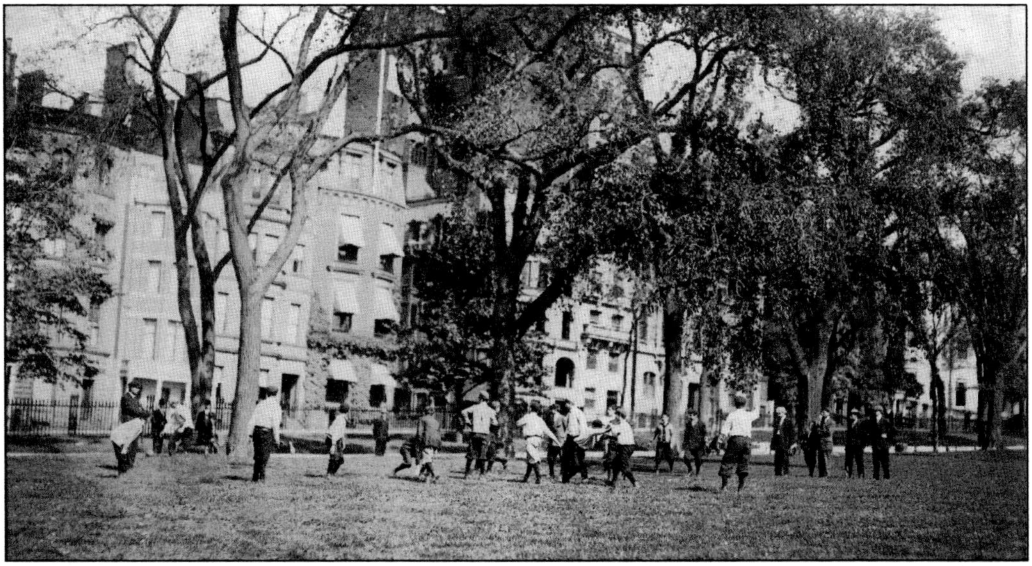

Boys play football on Boston Common in this 1909 image, showing the grand townhouses along Beacon Street, many of which date from 1828.

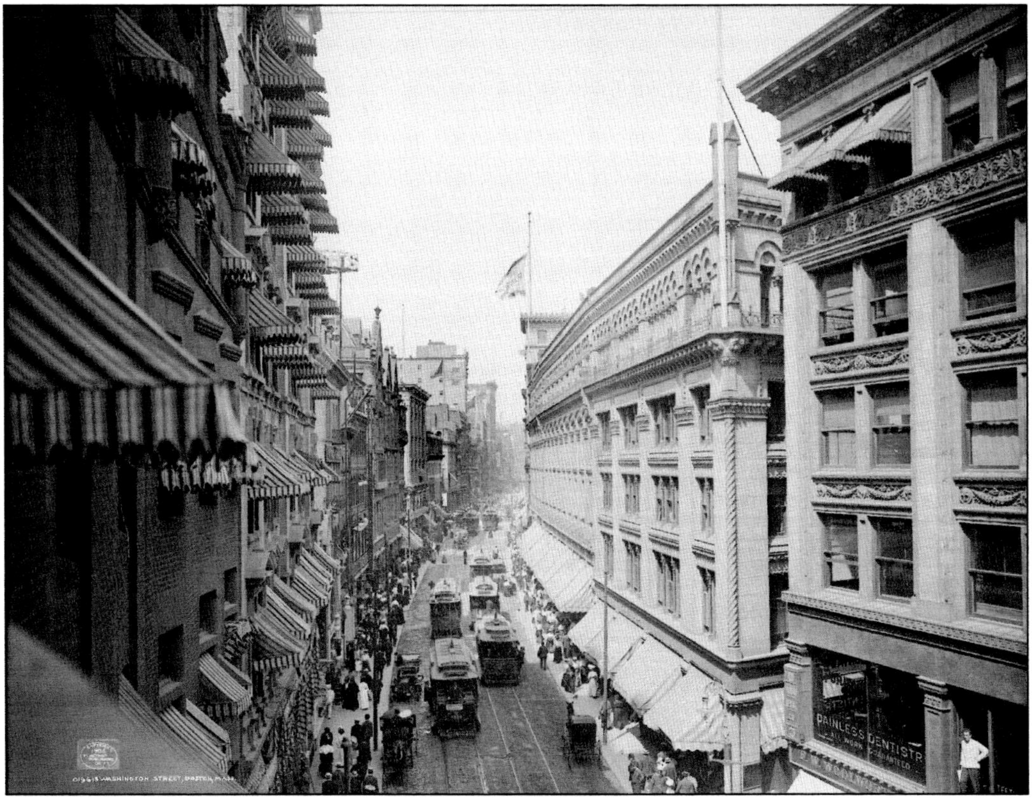

Washington Street was the commercial street of Boston. This 1906 picture shows the busy street, with electric trolley cars competing with automobiles and horse carts. The sidewalks are teeming with pedestrians, including boys and girls selling newspapers, vegetables, or fruits; shining shoes; or scavenging wood.

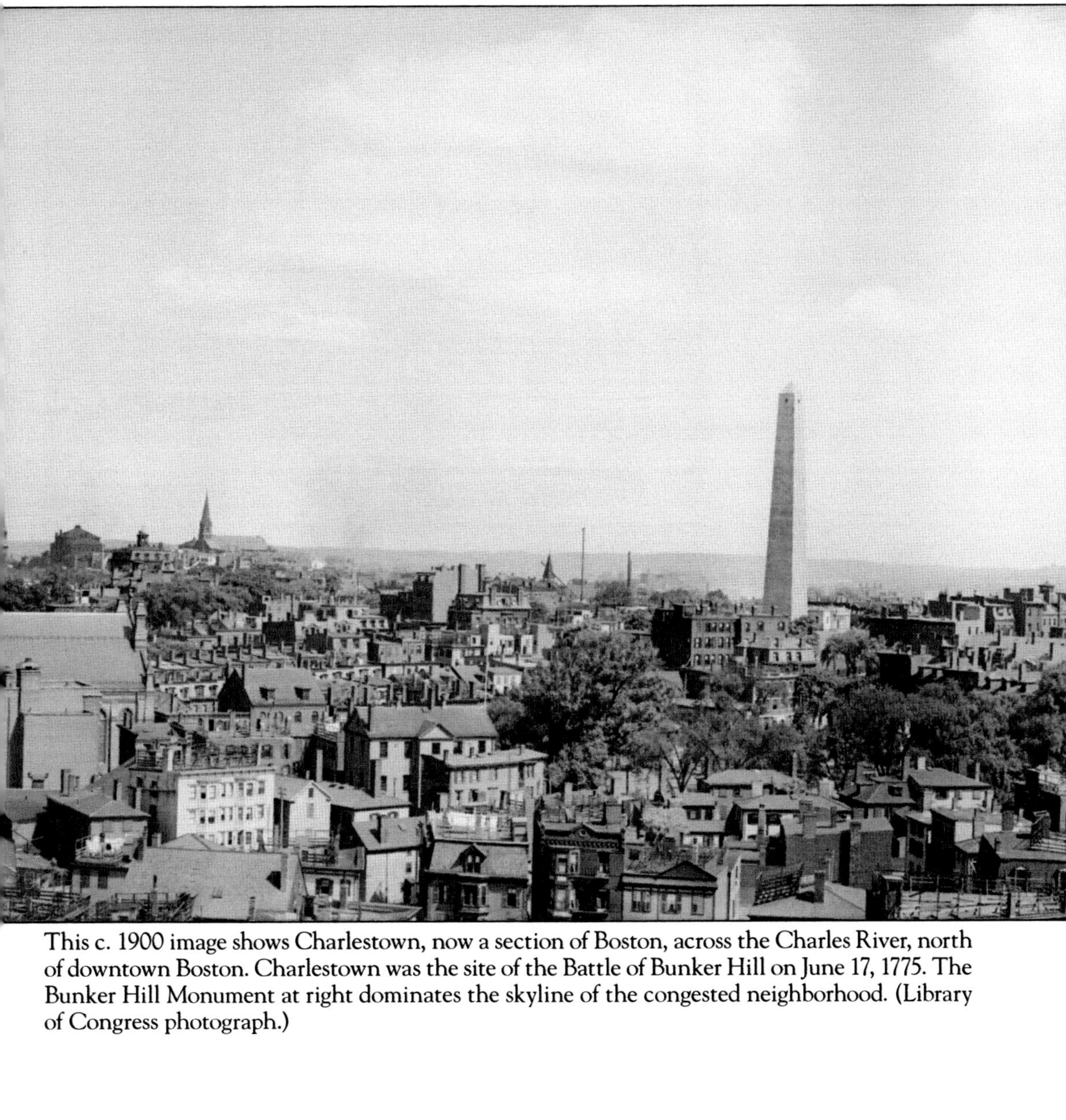

This c. 1900 image shows Charlestown, now a section of Boston, across the Charles River, north of downtown Boston. Charlestown was the site of the Battle of Bunker Hill on June 17, 1775. The Bunker Hill Monument at right dominates the skyline of the congested neighborhood. (Library of Congress photograph.)

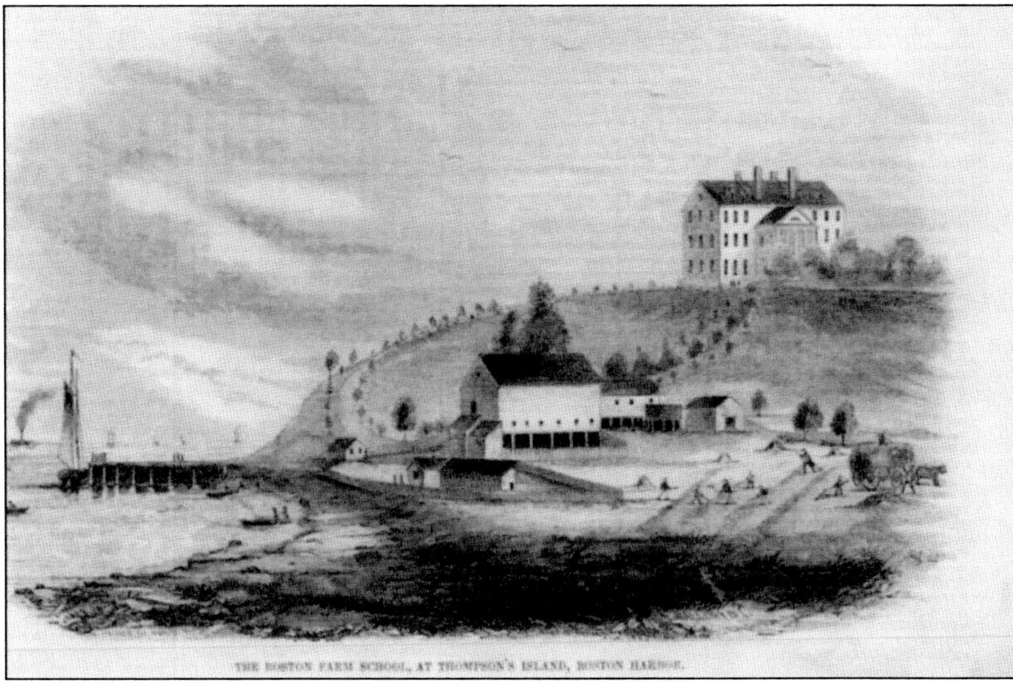

The Boston Asylum for Indigent Boys was established in 1814 to care for orphaned, poor, or abandoned children. With funding from Boston merchants and textile mill owners, the asylum moved to Thompson's Island in Boston Harbor, seen in this 1852 drawing, where it housed up to 300 boys.

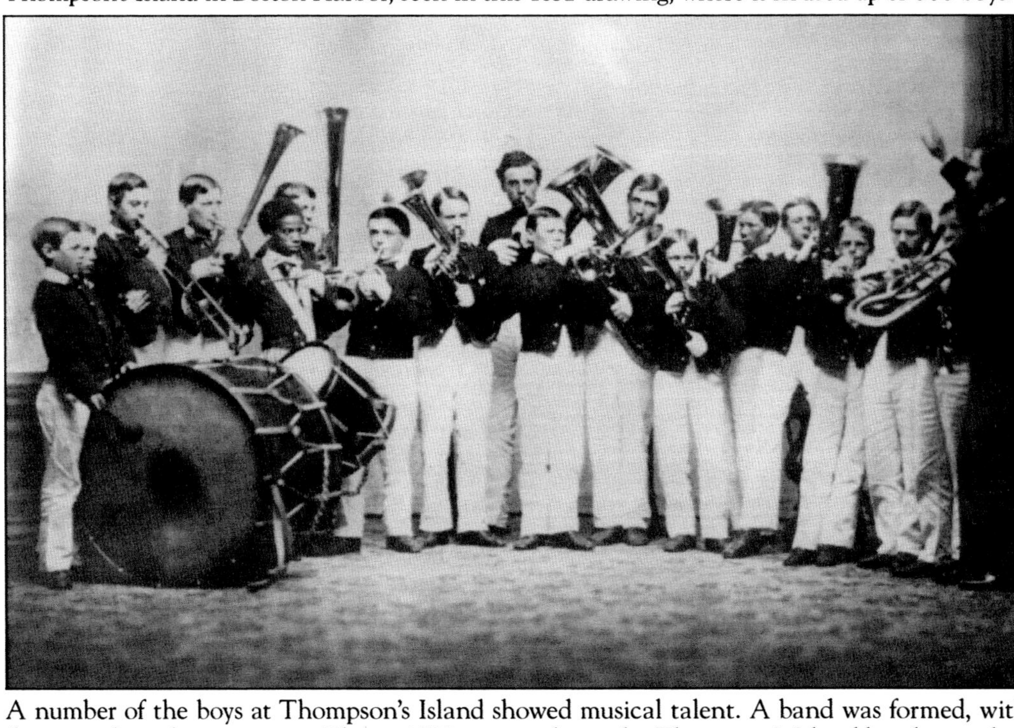

A number of the boys at Thompson's Island showed musical talent. A band was formed, with drums and wind instruments. This c. 1890 picture shows the Thompson's Island band, complete with instruments and uniforms. (Library of Congress photograph.)

The boys on Thompson's Island were educated through the Boston school system. In addition, they worked on the farm or did other chores around the island. Upon graduation, the boys became apprentices to tradesmen and farmers. (University Archives & Special Collections Department, Joseph P. Healey Library, University of Massachusetts Boston.)

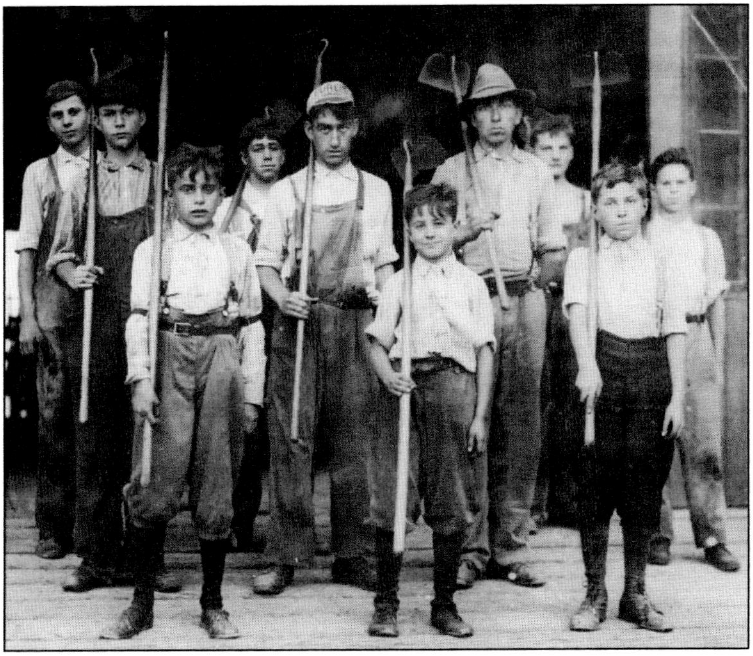

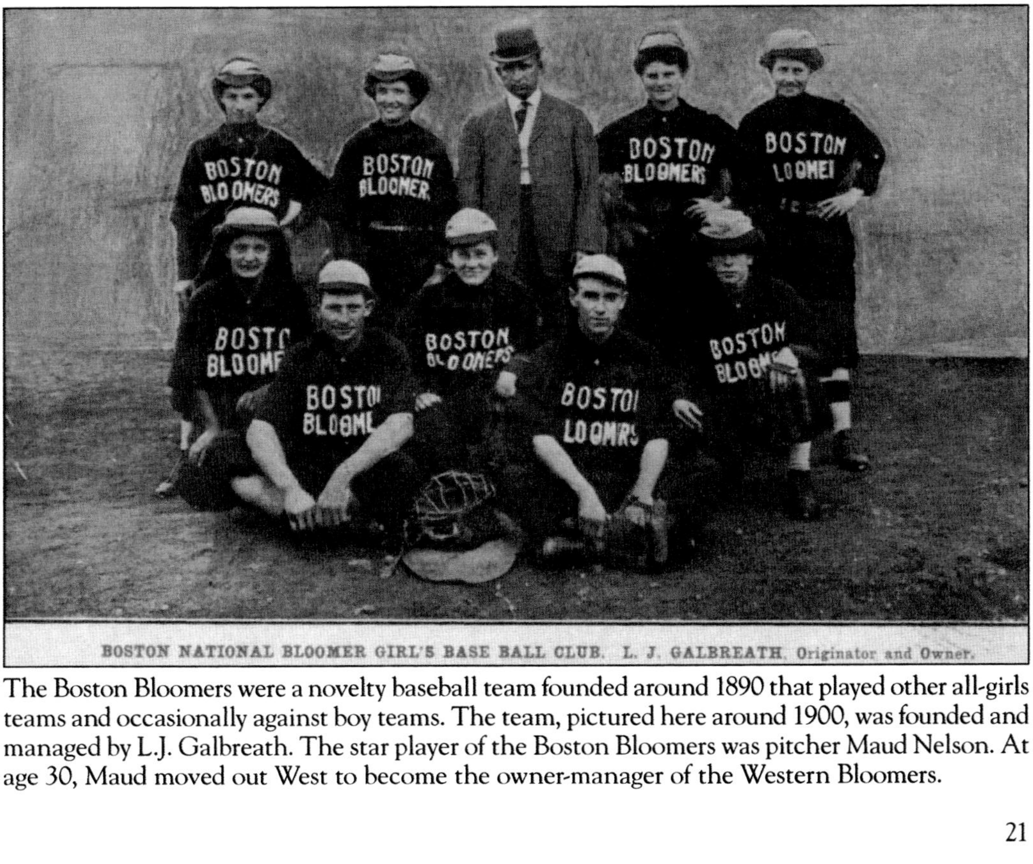

The Boston Bloomers were a novelty baseball team founded around 1890 that played other all-girls teams and occasionally against boy teams. The team, pictured here around 1900, was founded and managed by L.J. Galbreath. The star player of the Boston Bloomers was pitcher Maud Nelson. At age 30, Maud moved out West to become the owner-manager of the Western Bloomers.

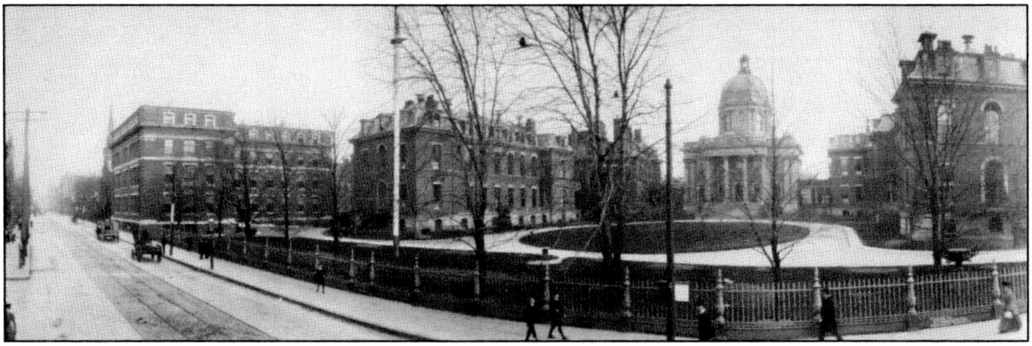

Boston City Hospital is shown in 1903. The public hospital, funded by the City of Boston, opened in 1864 and was "intended for the use and comfort of poor patients." The architect of the building on Harrison Avenue, in South End, was Gridley James Fox Bryant.

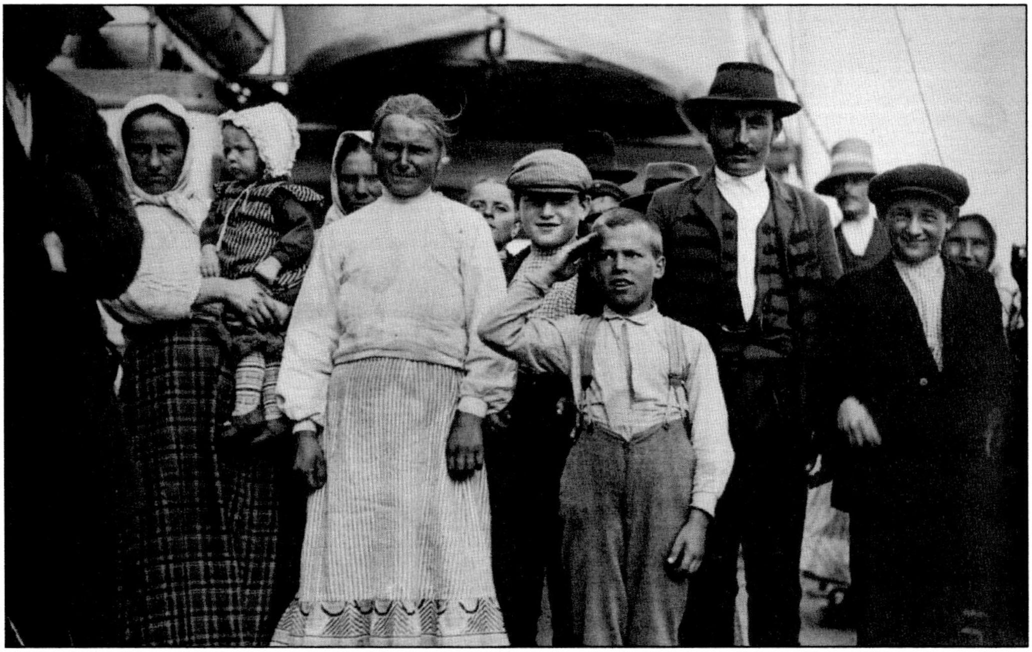

Hope springs eternal. Italian immigration to Boston began in the 1860s, with most of them settling in the one square mile of North End. At its peak, the crowded area contained 40,000 Italians, complete with their distinctive customs, food, ceremonies, and love of life.

Two

SCHOOLS AND STUDENTS

In 1635, the Boston Latin School, the first school in America, was established. Latin School taught boys English, Latin, Greek, mathematics, geography, and history to ensure they would be "fully prepared for the most respectable colleges." The following year, Harvard College opened across the Charles River in Cambridge and was America's first center of higher learning. All this when Boston was still a village. In 1642, the Massachusetts colony required that all boys be educated sufficiently "to enable them perfectly to read the English tongue and a knowledge of the capital laws." Girls were first accepted into public schools only in 1790. The venerable Boston Latin School remained the only high school in Boston until 1821, when English High School, "for young men of this city, who are not intended for a collegiate course of study," opened.

By 1845, Boston had set up a network of primary schools for children aged 5 to 7 and grammar schools for boys and girls 8 to 16. The children were taught English, reading, writing and composition, history, rhetoric, arithmetic, bookkeeping, algebra, and geometry. In 1852, English High School for Girls was established, followed by Girls Latin School in 1877. After age 16, no public education was offered to the girls, but boys had the choice of work or high school. Only one boy in six over age 14 continued his education.

In 1887, the superintendent of the Boston Public Schools noted that a classical education did not prepare most boys and girls for the future. "I would suggest," he wrote "that manual training be introduced after a boy or girl has passed the age of 14 years. . . . Put the boy at a trade and teach the girl to do domestic work." Massachusetts child labor laws of 1876 allowed children at 14 to opt out of school and go to work. The child had to show evidence that he was over 14 years old, had a satisfactory school attendance, could read and write English at least at the fourth-grade level, had the promise of a job, and was in good health. If all the requirements were met, a member of the school committee signed the employment form permitting the child to leave school and start work. Truant officers hired by the school department monitored the system and investigated false identities and tampered certificates.

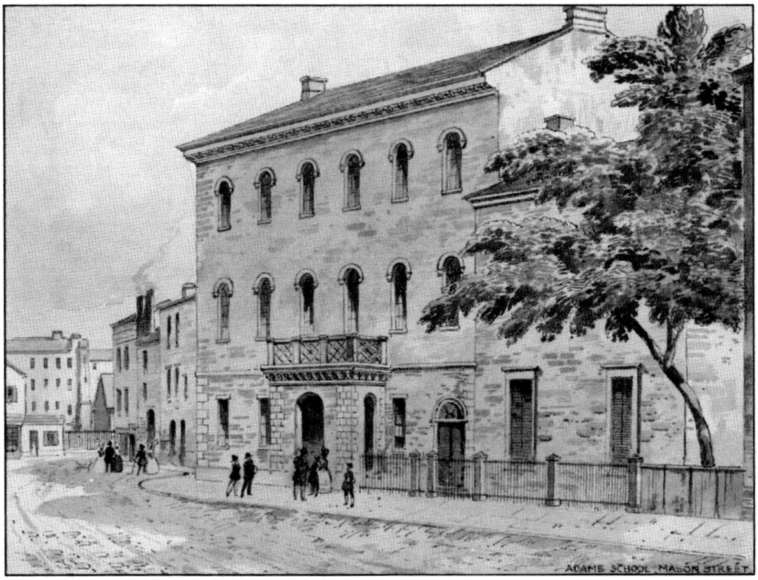

Adams School began in 1717 as a place to learn reading and writing. In 1848, the all-boys school moved to Mason Street, close to the Boston Common. (Boston Public Library.)

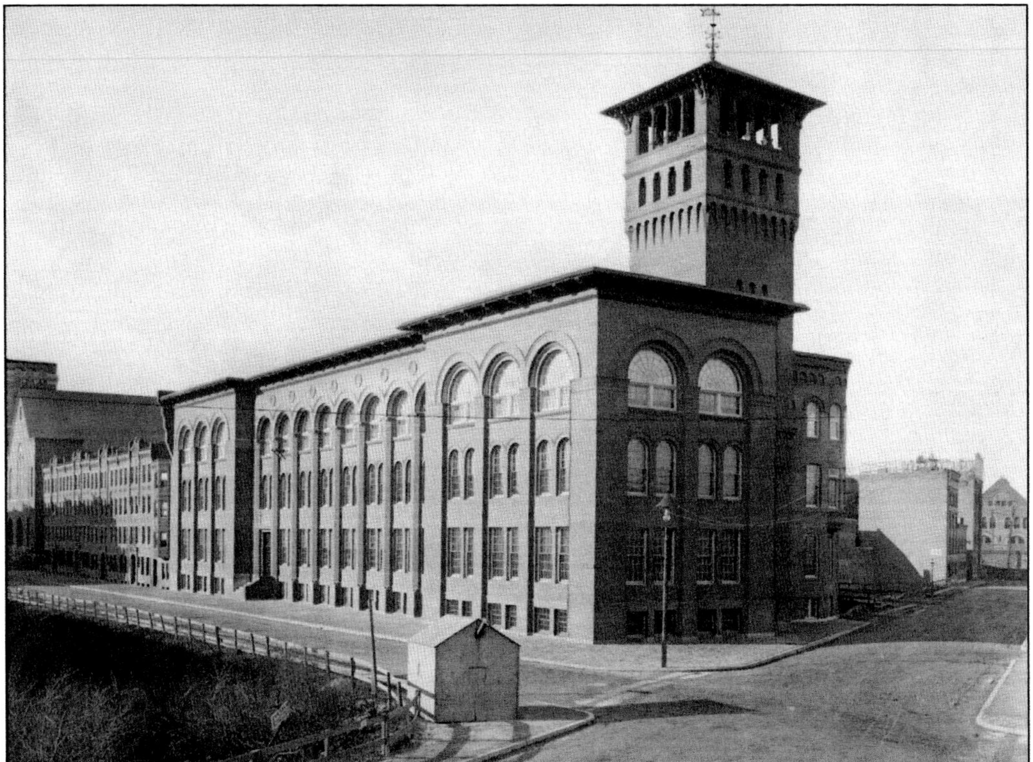

In 1883, the superintendent of Boston Schools, Edwin P. Seaver, prepared a plan to build a "system of manual training" for the children of Boston. The Mechanic Arts High School opened in the Back Bay in 1892 to teach carpentry, forging, machine shop practice, and mechanical drawing. The image above shows the building in 1893. Augustine H. Folsom was a commercial photographer based at 48 Allegheny Street, Roxbury. From 1890 to 1893, he took pictures of the Boston public schools. Many were displayed at the 1900 world's fair in Paris. (Boston Public Library, Folsom Collection.)

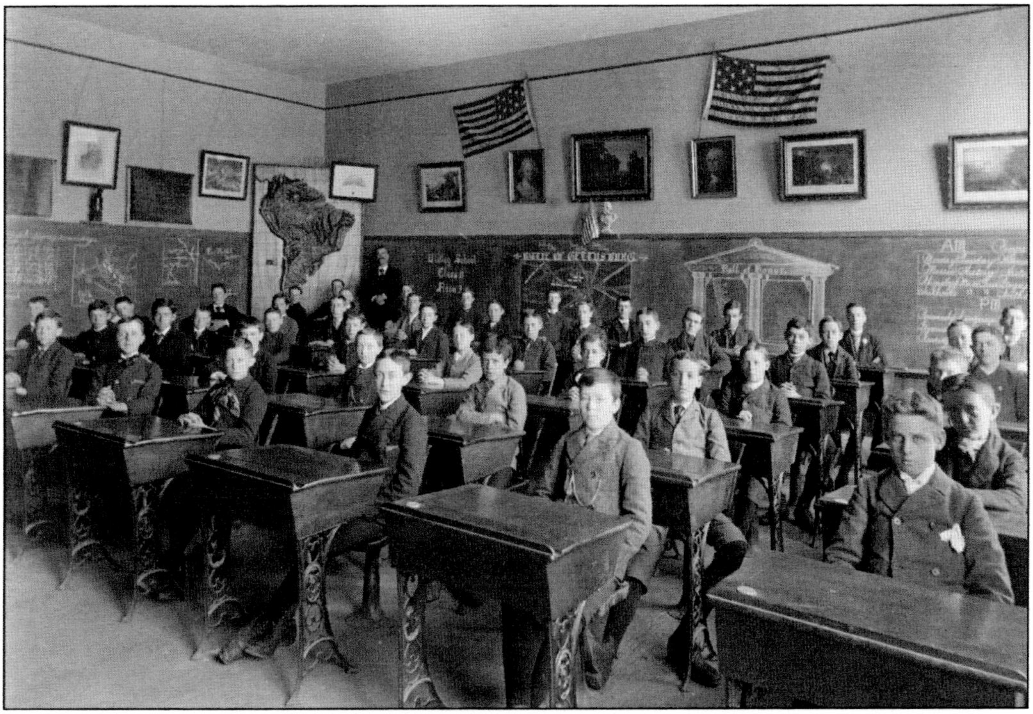

This 1893 picture shows neatly dressed students of class 2, room 3, of the Dudley School in Roxbury. There is a large map of South America, and the students are learning about the Battle of Gettysburg. The Dudley School is close to the historic Shirley-Eustis House, built between 1747 and 1751 for the royal governor of Massachusetts, William Shirley.

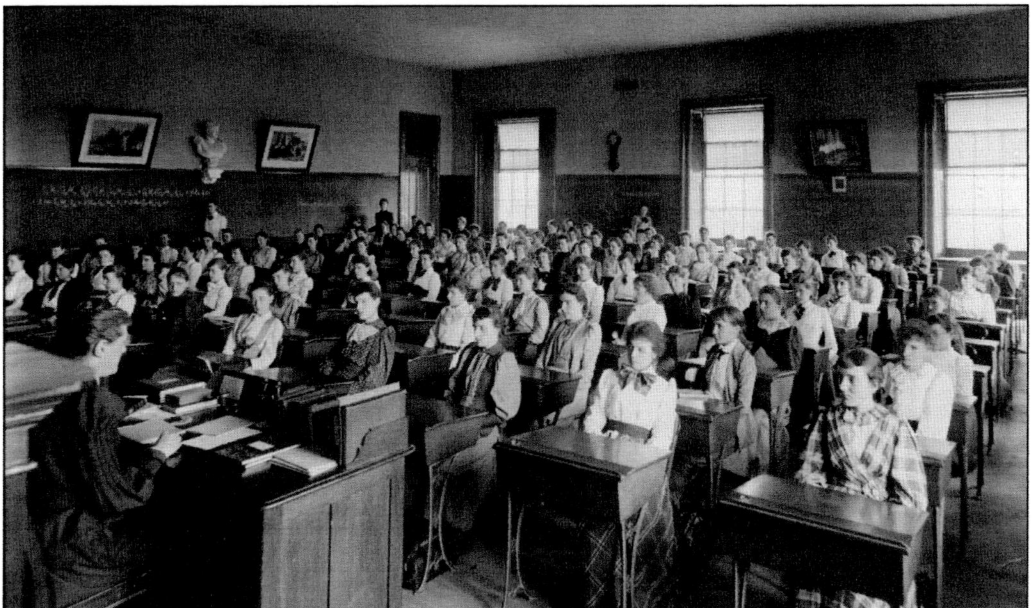

The image above shows the third-year class of the prestigious Girls Latin School in 1893. The school opened in 1878 on West Newton Street in Boston's South End. The class holds some 70 students. (Boston Public Library, Folsom Collection.)

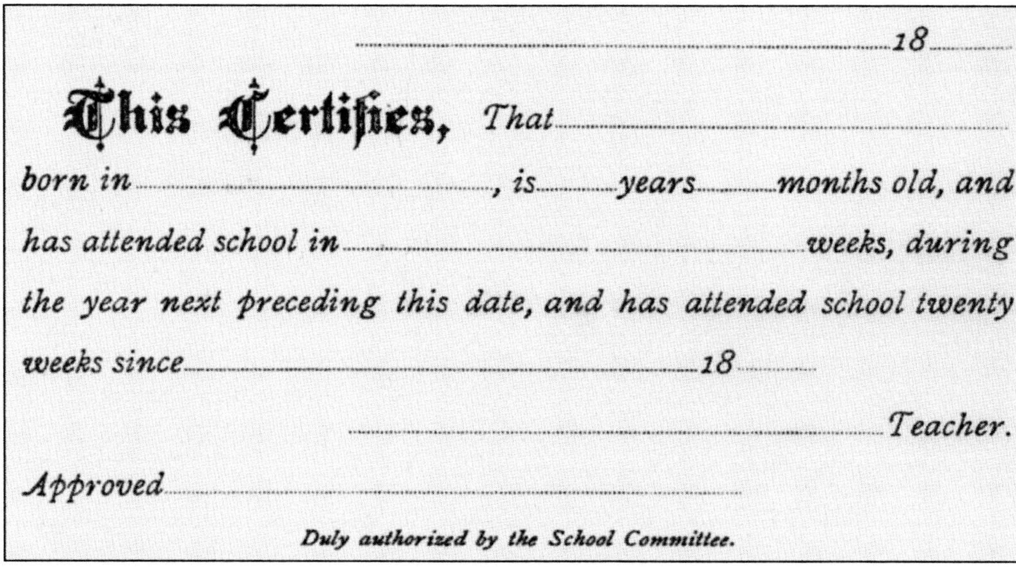

18

This Certifies, *That*

born in , *is* *years* *months old, and*

has attended school in *weeks, during*

the year next preceding this date, and has attended school twenty

weeks since *18*

Teacher.

Approved

Duly authorized by the School Committee.

Starting in 1842, Massachusetts law forbade children younger than 12 years from working more than 12 hours a day. Over the years the law was tightened to encourage children over 14 to stay in school rather than go to work. However, children of 14 or 15 years were permitted to leave school early if they had a job offer, were in good health, and could read and write at the fourth-grade level. This certificate for early school leaving, shown above, was first issued in 1876 and was completed by the teacher and then taken to the school committee for approval.

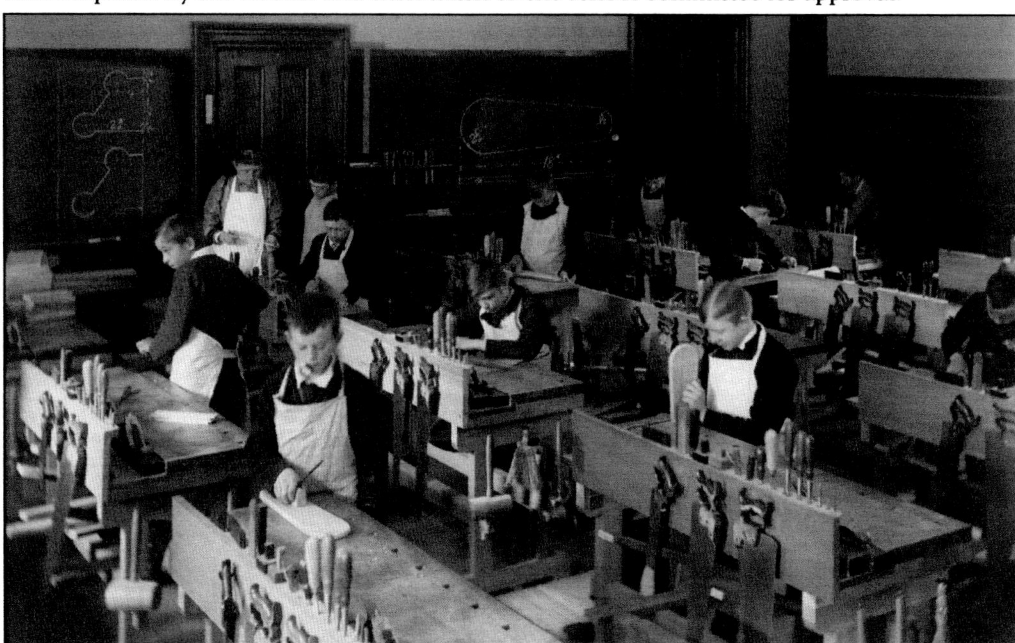

Boys in the Boston grammar schools learned from the fourth grade to use tools and different materials, such as wood and clay, as seen in this 1893 image. Making furniture, wood turning and whittling, and clay modeling encouraged self-expression and prepared children for future employment. The Boston Trade High School, at 550 Parker Street in Roxbury, opened in 1912 to prepare boys as carpenters, plumbers, painters, electricians, metal workers, and mechanics. (Boston Public Library, Folsom Collection.)

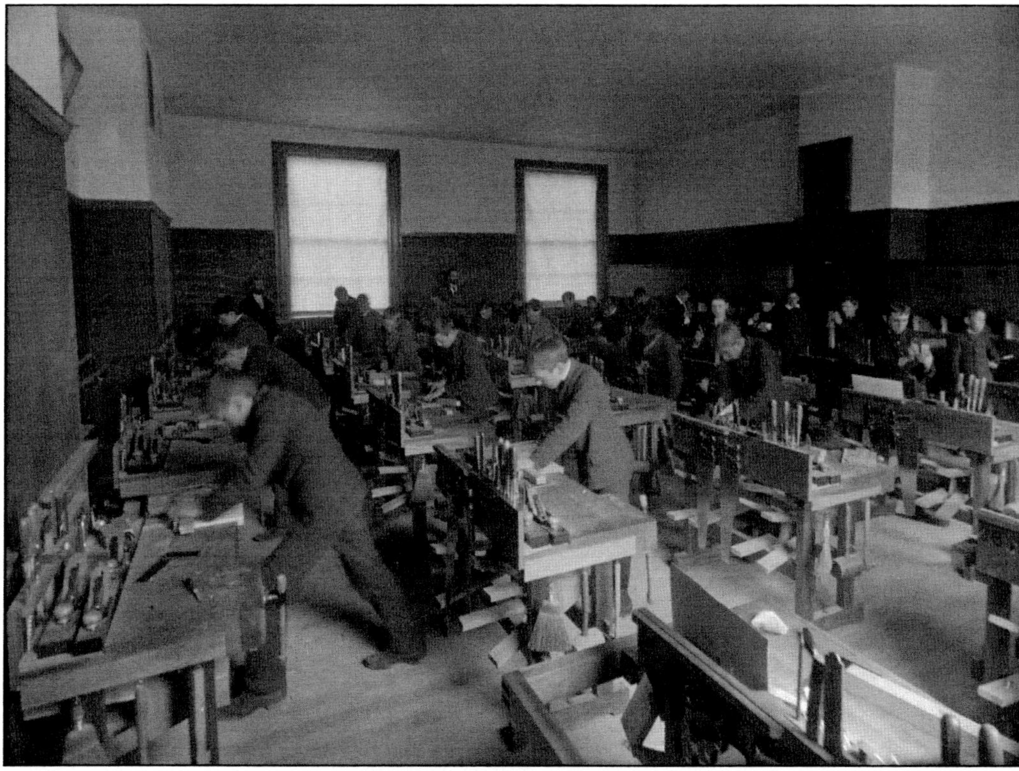

Shown here is a well-equipped carpentry workshop in a Boston school in 1893. The Sloyd system was introduced into the Boston schools late in the 19th century. Derived from the Swedish word for handicraft, the Sloyd system of education encourages self-expression through woodwork, clay molding, and paper folding. The student learns to use different tools and materials to design and create objects that express his individual talents.

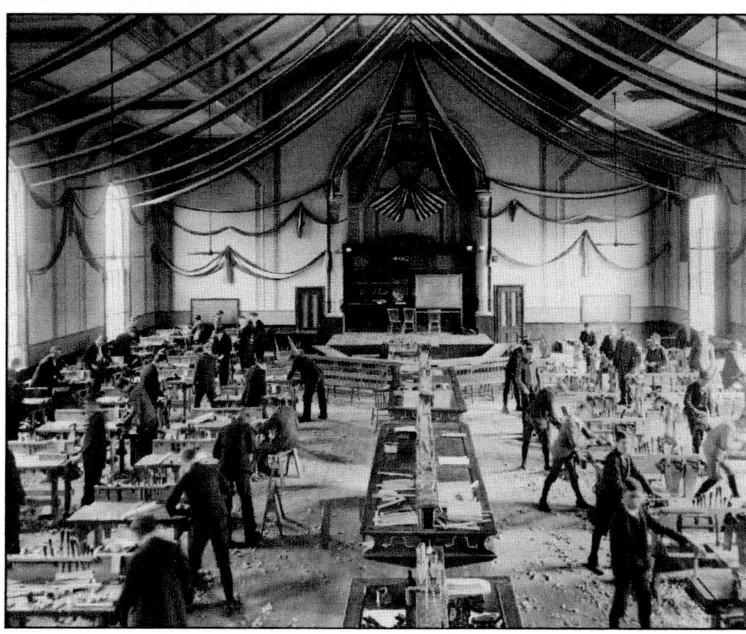

Dahlgren Memorial Hall at 306 E Street, South Boston, was used by veterans groups as well as by the Boston school department. Built in the 1880s, the hall was named for John A. Dahlgren (1809–1870), head of the US ordnance department during the Civil War. He is credited with designing cannons that were successfully used in naval battles. (Boston Public Library, Folsom Collection.)

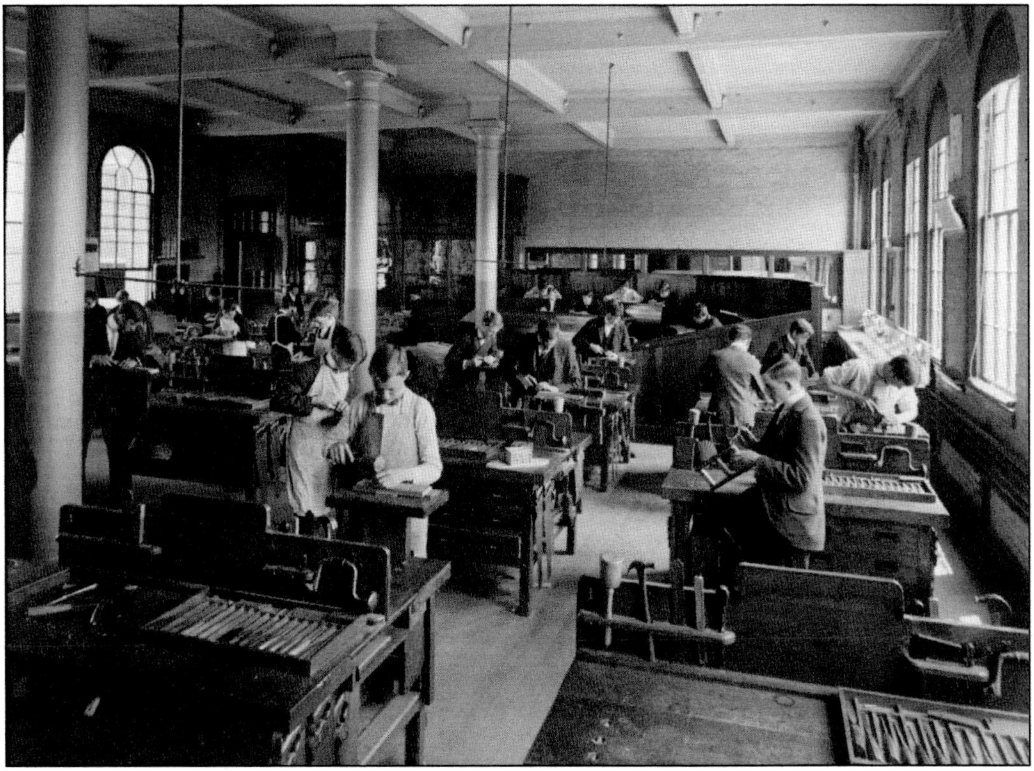

A woodworking class at the Mechanic Arts High School in Boston's Back Bay is seen in this c. 1895 image. Later, the school relocated to 205 Townsend Street, Roxbury, and was renamed the Boston Technical School. In 1992, it was renamed the John D. O'Bryant School of Mathematics & Science in honor of an esteemed teacher who died that year. (Boston Public Library.)

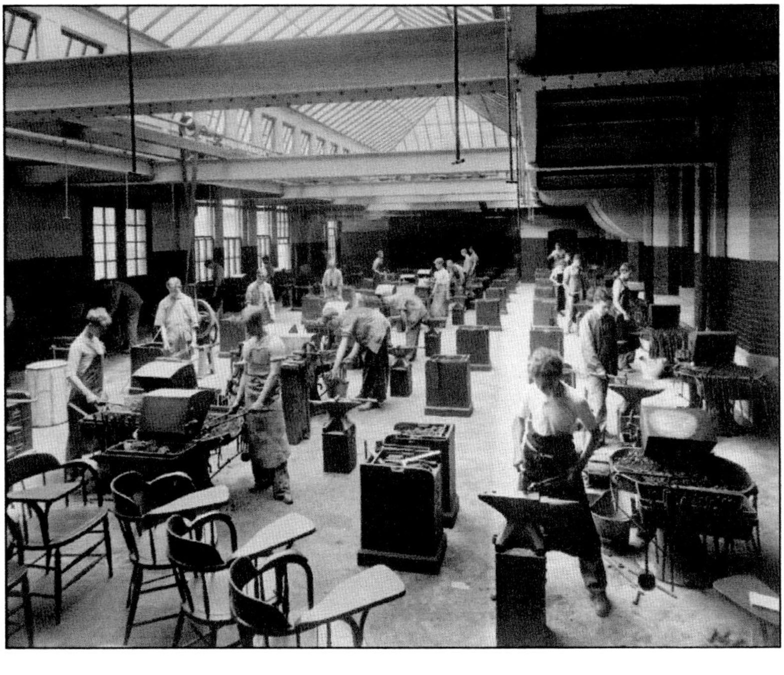

The picture shows the forge workshop at the Mechanic Arts High School in 1892. In the age of the horse and cart, these boys were trained as blacksmiths, using the hammer and anvil to make horseshoes as well as gates, railings, and agricultural tools. With the coming of power tools and the automobile, these skills would soon be obsolete. (Boston Public Library, Folsom Collection.)

Pauline Agassiz Shaw (1841–1917) was born in Switzerland as the youngest child of Louis Agassiz, who became a professor of zoology and geology at Harvard University. Pauline married the wealthy Quincy Adams Shaw. She founded the North Bennet Street Industrial School in Boston's North End in 1885 with the goal of teaching immigrants the skills needed for gainful employment. In addition to carpentry and cabinet making, the school offered courses in pottery, sewing, watch repair, and jewelry making. The North Bennet Street School was affiliated with Boston's school system.

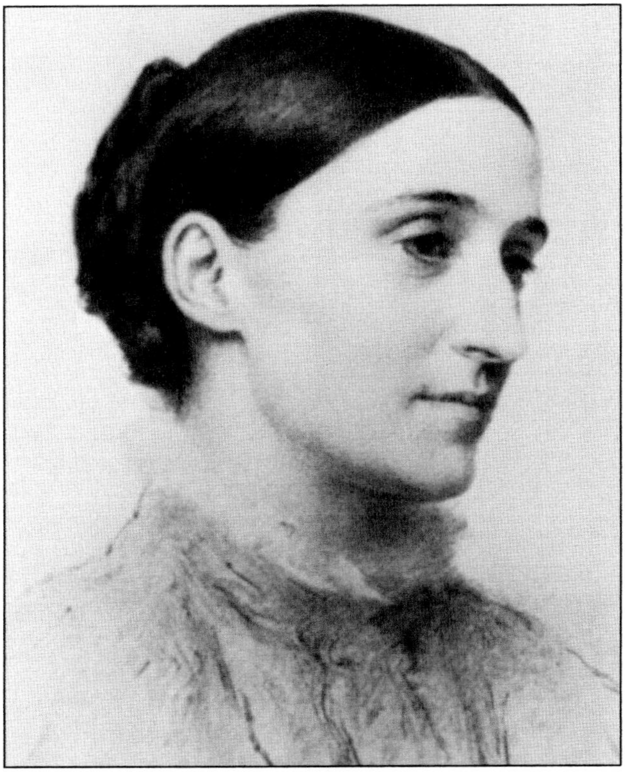

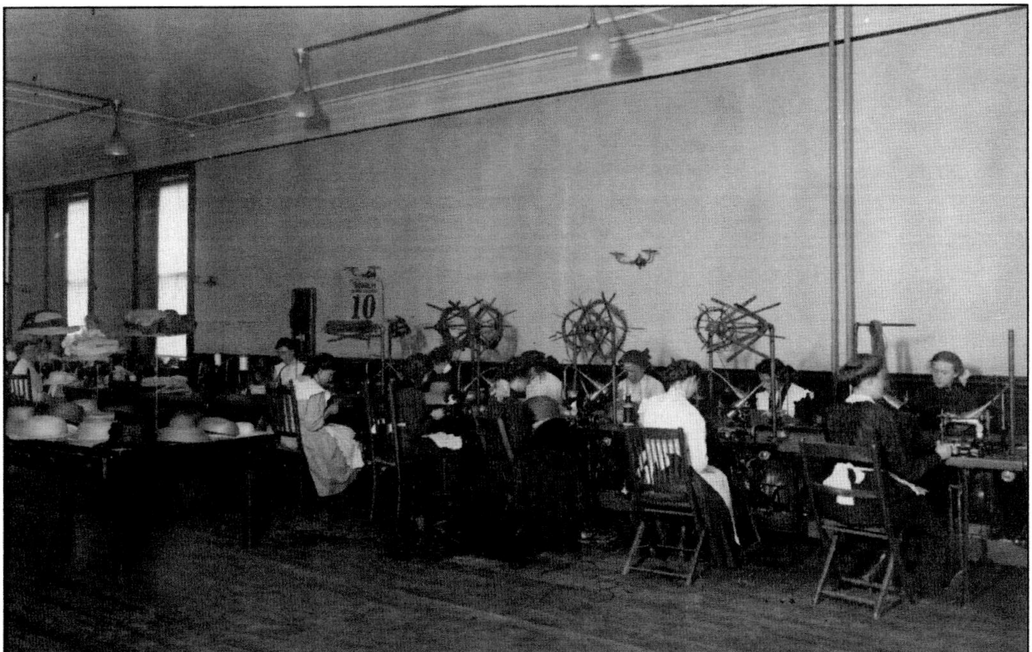

This picture shows straw hat making machines at the Trade School for Girls in 1893. The girls practiced by making doll hats and baskets, graduating to making hats of various sizes and shapes.

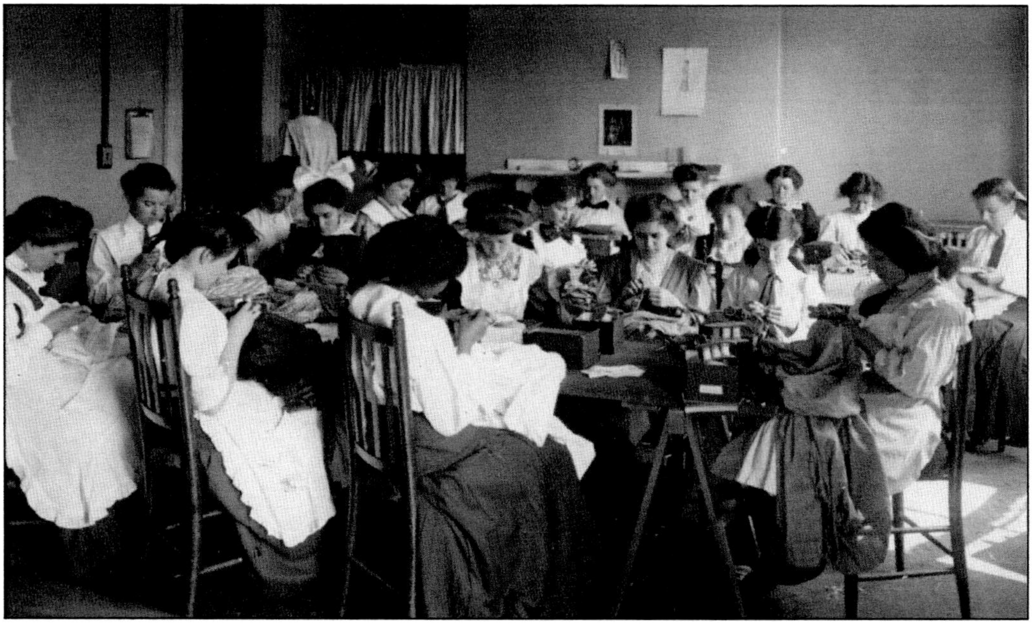

The girls first made aprons, then doll clothing, before moving on to clothing for children and adults in their hand-sewing class, shown here. Boston once had a thriving clothing industry, but the Great Fire of 1872 destroyed many of the factories. The industry was moving to New York, especially the Lower East Side, by the time of this image; these girls were being trained for jobs that no longer existed in Boston. (Boston Public Library.)

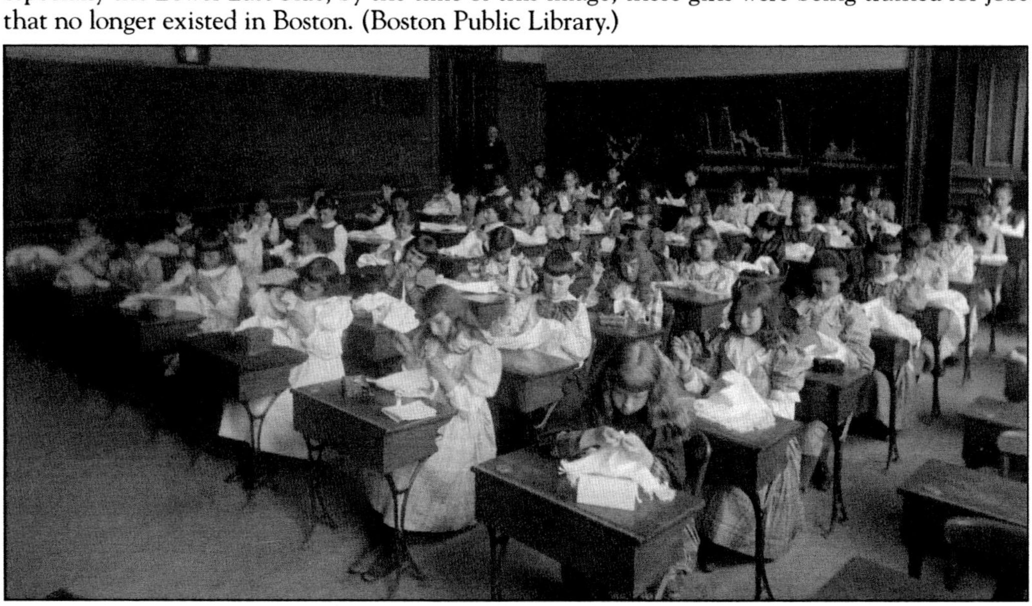

The Trade School for Girls at 620 Massachusetts Avenue, Boston, grew out of the efforts of the Massachusetts Association of Women Workers to prepare girls for employment. With support from the Massachusetts Commonwealth and the City of Boston, the Trade School for Girls opened in 1909 to train girls in box and hat making, sewing, dressmaking, millinery, cooking, and embroidery. A class is seen in this 1893 image. There were some 40 children to a class. Each year, the trade school sold the "fancy articles" made by the girls, such as handkerchiefs, laundry bags, and aprons. Gowns were sold for $12–$25, and underwear was priced at 50¢–$1.75.

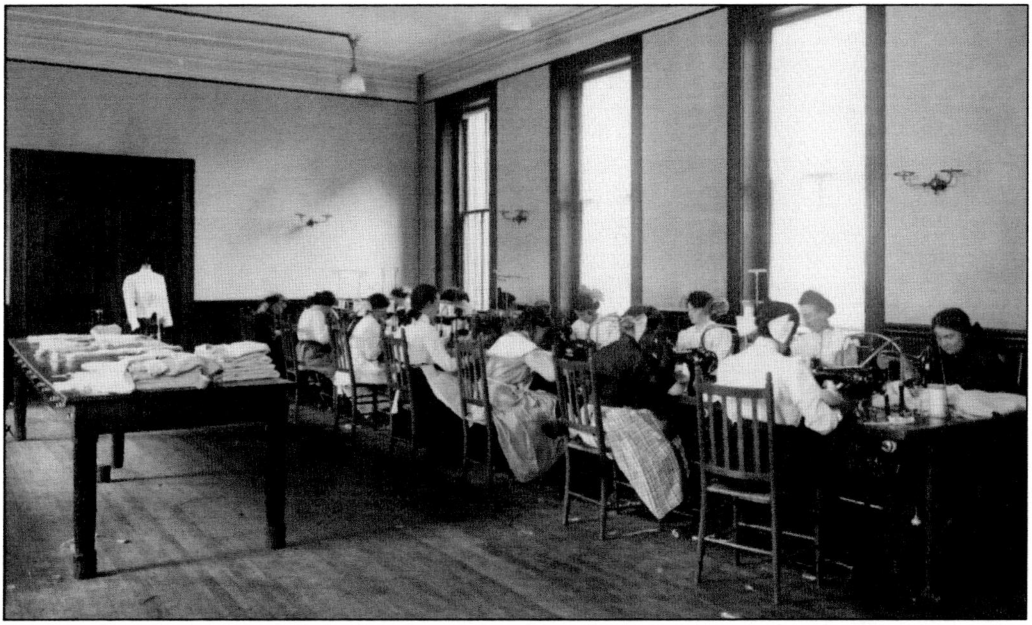

Students are seen learning to use power sewing machines in this image. First making hospital aprons and children's clothing, the girls learned how to use sewing machines with speed and accuracy. The school had a design department where the girls learned dress design and embroidery. In those days, the average working life of young women in the trades was less than five years before they left to marry and raise a family. The girls were also taught cooking, sewing, and laundering.

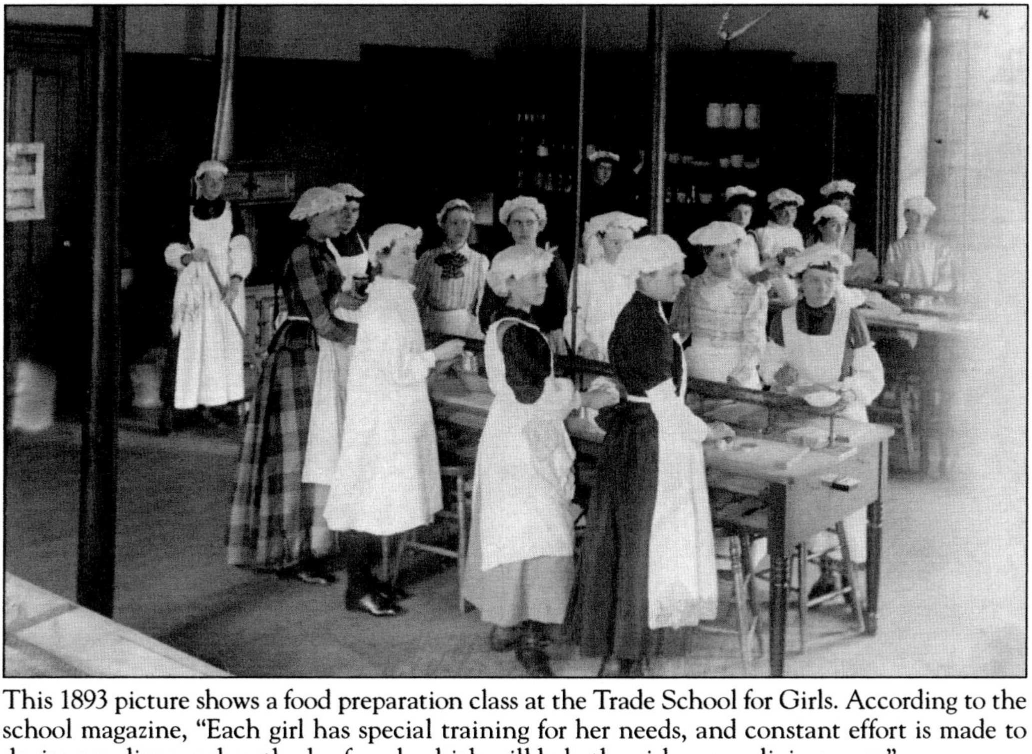

This 1893 picture shows a food preparation class at the Trade School for Girls. According to the school magazine, "Each girl has special training for her needs, and constant effort is made to devise new lines and methods of work which will help the girls earn a living wage."

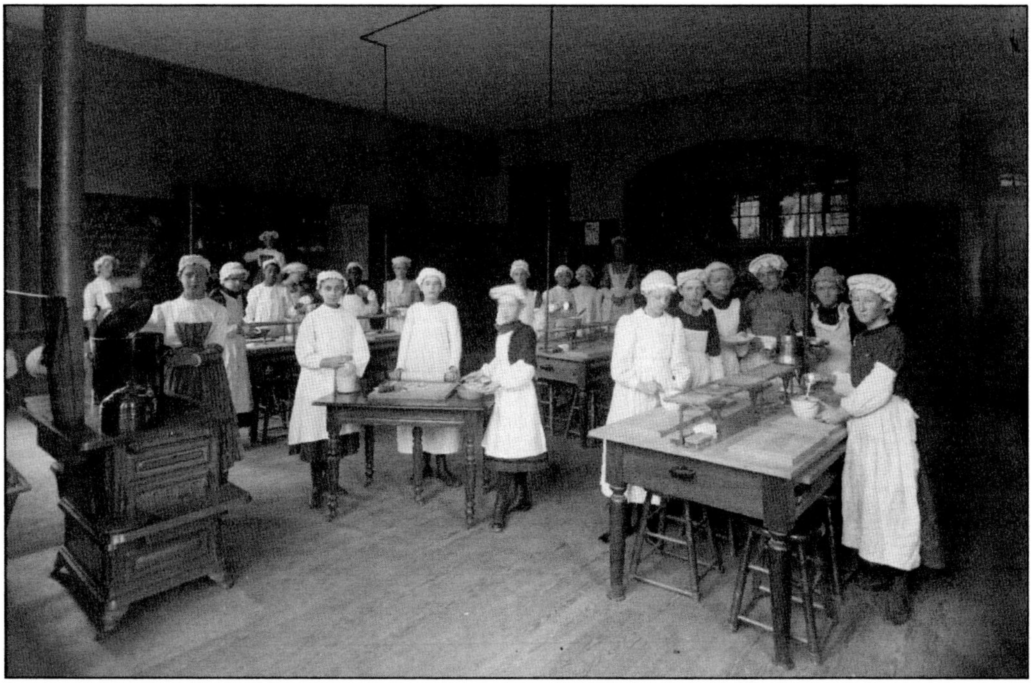

This image from 1893 shows a food preparation class at the Trade School for Girls. Note the coal-burning stove at left; the classroom was lit by gaslight. The average wage paid after graduation was $5.70 a week.

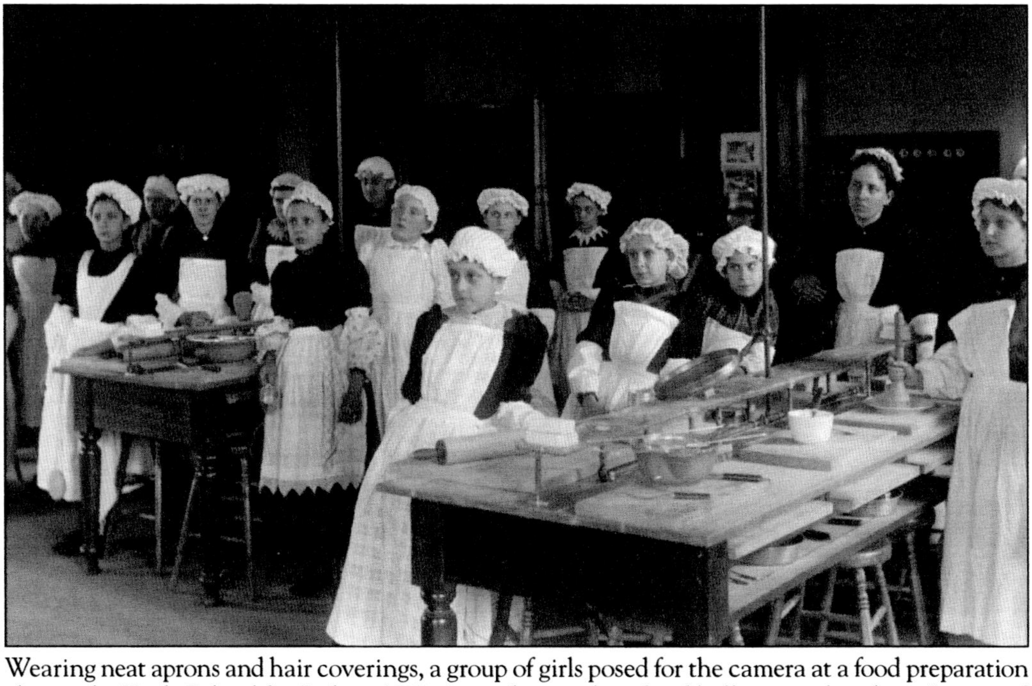

Wearing neat aprons and hair coverings, a group of girls posed for the camera at a food preparation class at the Trade School for Girls in 1893. According to the school bulletin, each girl was "prepared for some specific work which shall earn a living wage . . . and the girls are helped in every possible way to prepare for the highest vocation for any woman—the making of a happy home."

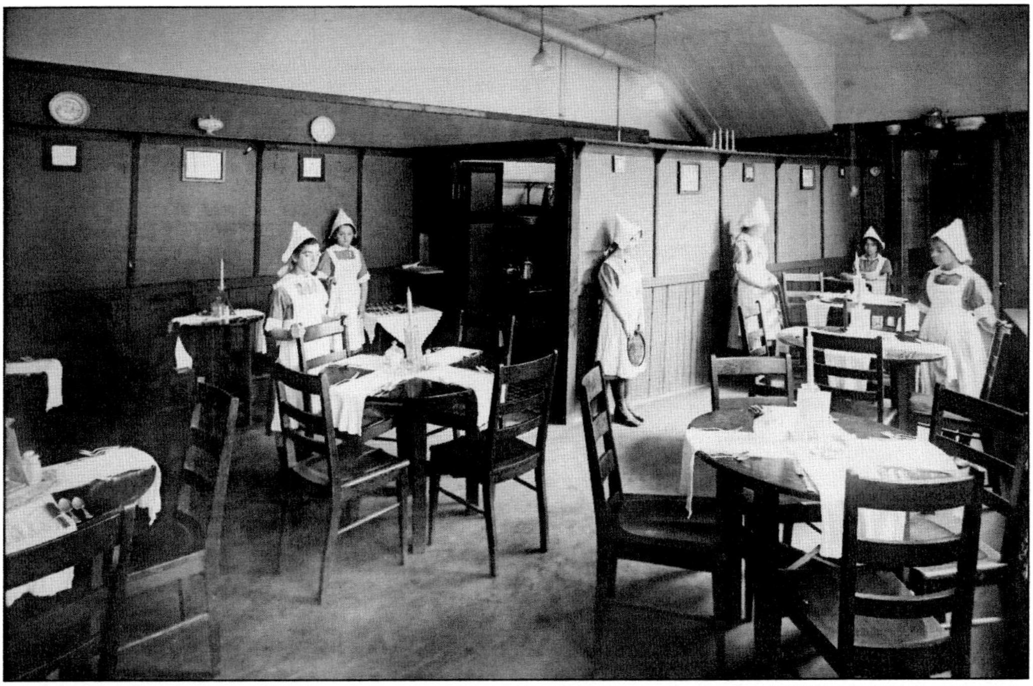

This 1910 image shows the lunchroom at the North Bennet Industrial School filled with girls learning to be waitresses. Situated in the North End, the school taught immigrant children skills for employment and helped them adjust to American ways.

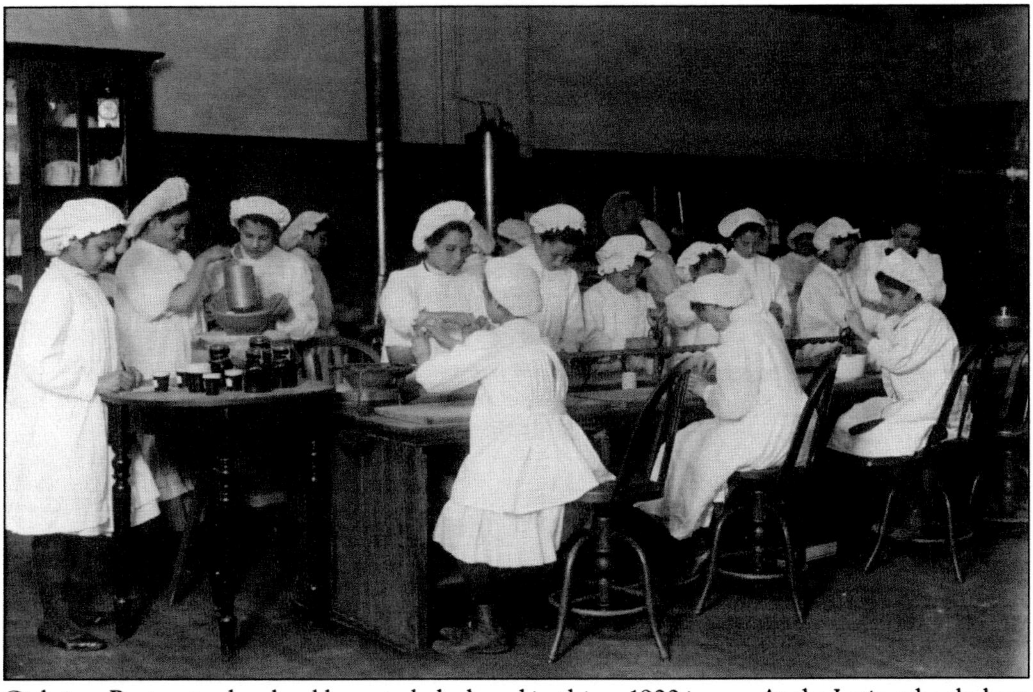

Girls in a Boston trade school learn to bake bread in this c. 1900 image. At the Latin schools, boys and girls studied languages, mathematics, chemistry, physics, and art. At the trade schools, girls learned waitressing skills, how to cook and bake, and how to make underwear, dresses, and hats.

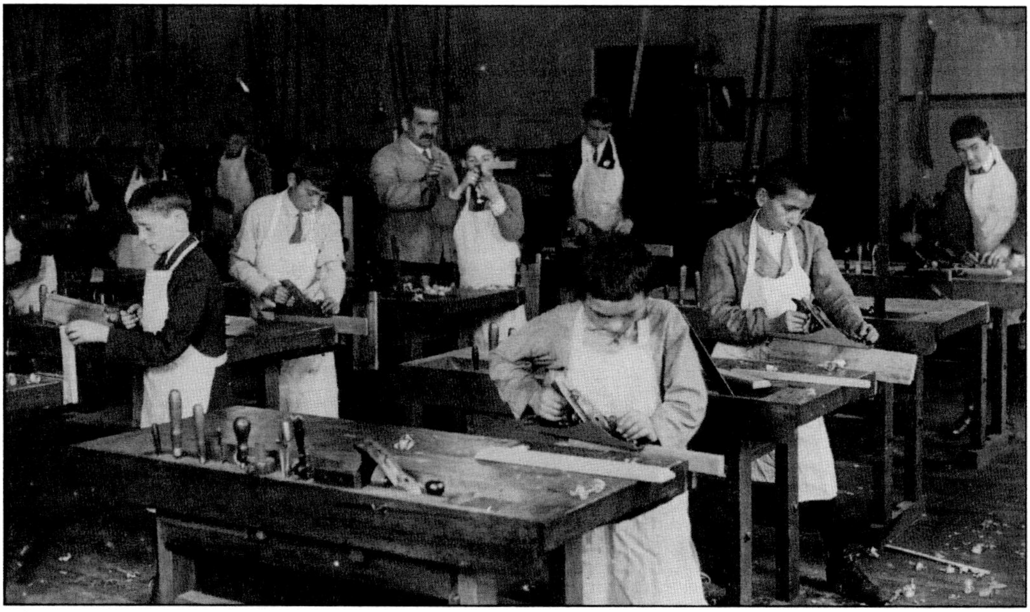

The 1909 picture above shows the well-equipped carpentry room of a Boston trade school. This picture, by Lewis Hine, shows boys training in carpentry. The Boston School Committee was eager to keep children in school, even though many 14 and 15 year olds were opting to leave. In 1907, the Boston School Committee issued 4,856 certificates to children aged 14 or 15 that wished to leave school to start work. The wish of many children to leave school at age 14 convinced the Boston School Committee to offer education in the trades as well as classical studies such as Greek, Latin, and the English language. (Library of Congress photograph.)

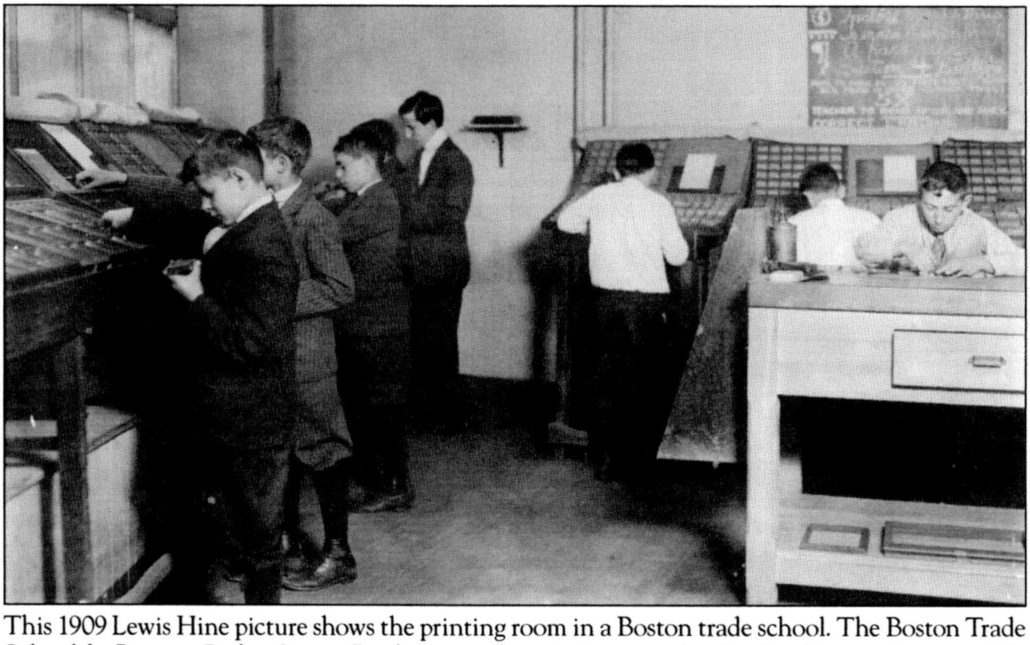

This 1909 Lewis Hine picture shows the printing room in a Boston trade school. The Boston Trade School for Boys on Parker Street, Roxbury, taught printing, woodwork, plumbing, and automobile repair. The Trade School for Girls opened on Massachusetts Avenue and taught dressmaking, millinery, knitting, and cooking.

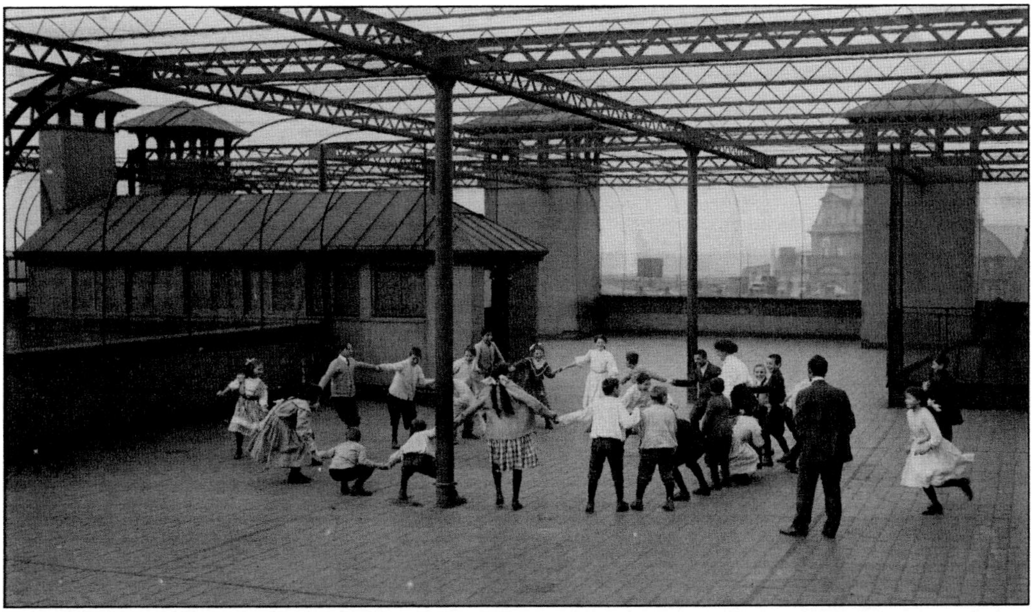

Recently arrived immigrant children are shown playing at a school on Washington Street, Boston, in this 1909 image. Many of the children were soon able to speak and write English, learn American history and customs, and keep up with their native-born peers.

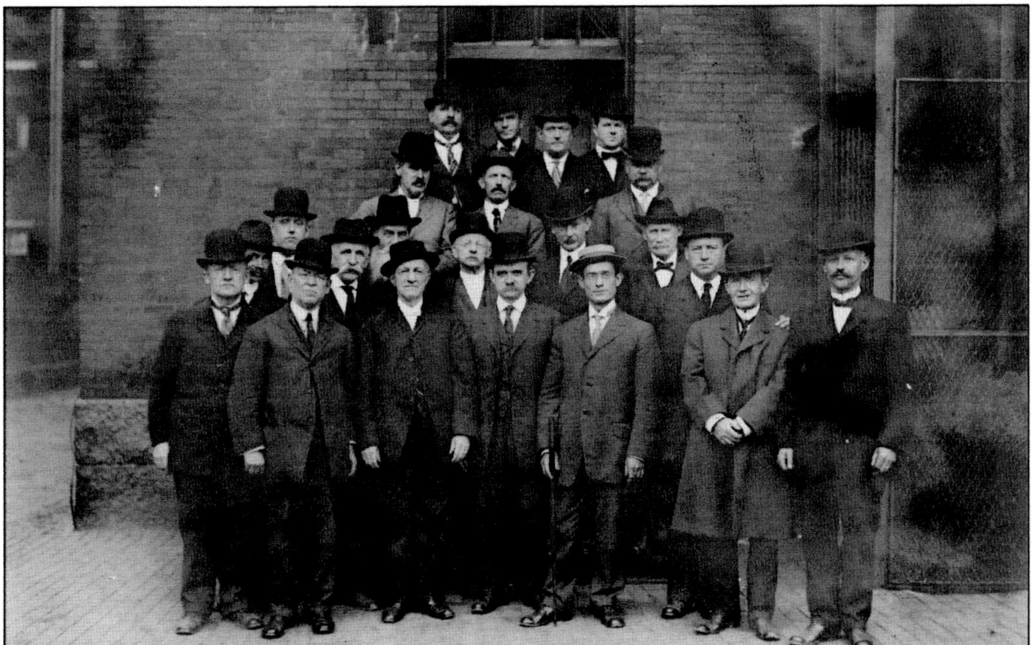

This 1911 Lewis Hine picture shows the truant officers of the Boston school department. They checked on children absent from school and made sure that only boys wearing a badge were out on the streets selling newspapers or shining shoes. Among other duties, these men were authorized to check birth and work certificates for forgery, to ensure that newsboys were off the streets by eight in the morning and were not selling papers during the night hours. The truant officers reported underage newsboys and boys selling without wearing a badge.

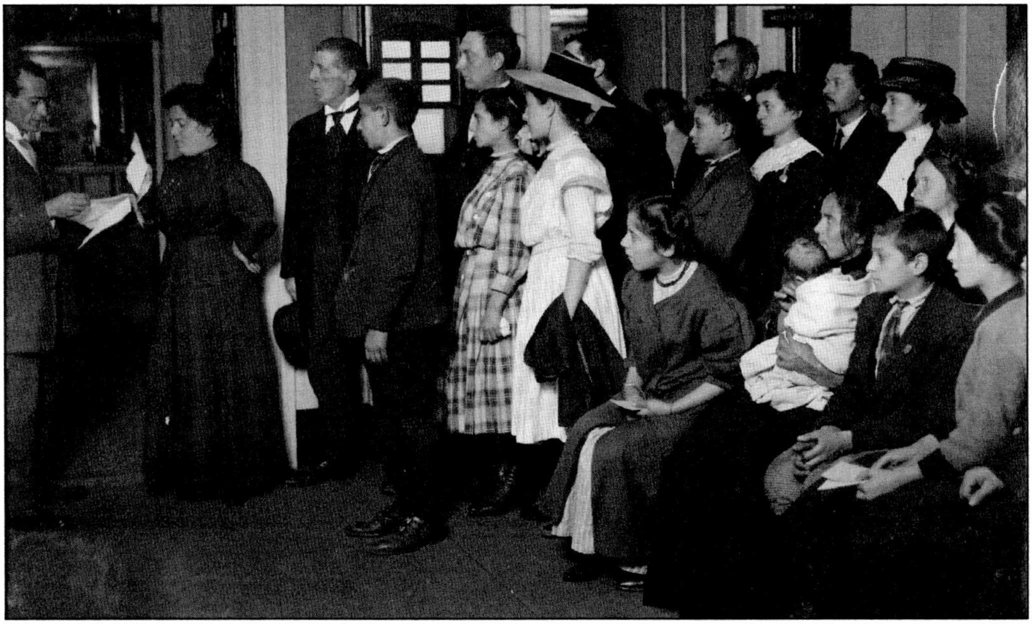

This c. 1911 image, taken by Lewis Hine, is of the offices of the Boston School Committee at 218 Tremont Street. Eager and well-dressed children accompanied by family arrive with their work certificate for final signature by a member of the school committee. During the first decades of the 20th century, about 5,000 children each year applied to leave school early and start working.

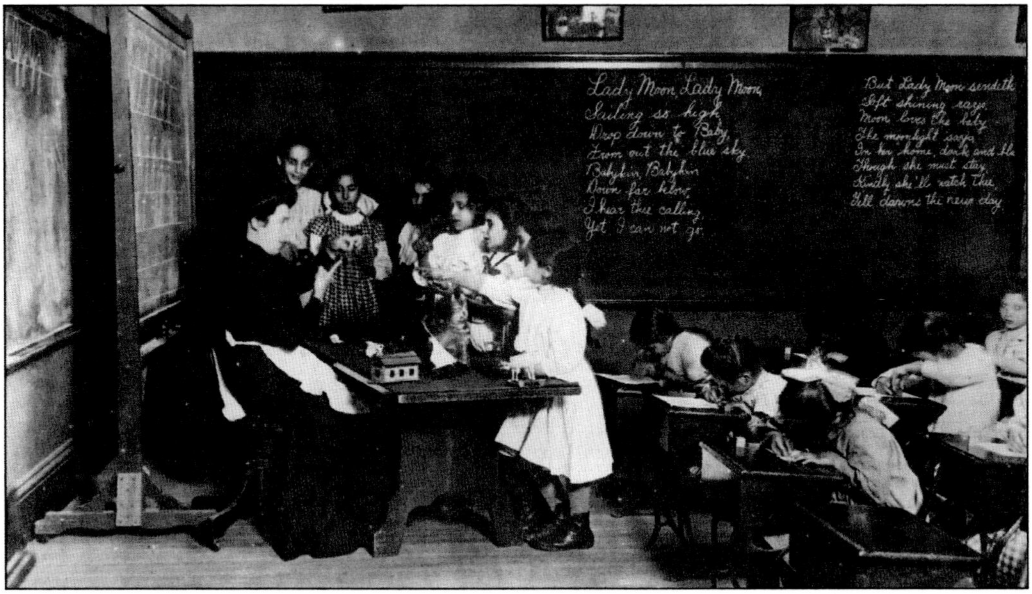

Immigrant children attend the John Hancock School on Hanover Street, North End, in this 1909 image. By the start of the 20th century, the school was packed with 600 girls, mainly immigrants, and many were sent to the Wells School, at the corner of Blossom and McLean Streets, near Massachusetts General Hospital, and to other downtown schools. On the blackboard, the teacher has written an anonymous children's poem: "Lady moon, lady moon,/ sailing so high,/ Drop down to Baby, /From out the blue sky./ Babykin, Babykin,/ Down far below,/ I hear thee calling,/ Yet I can not go."

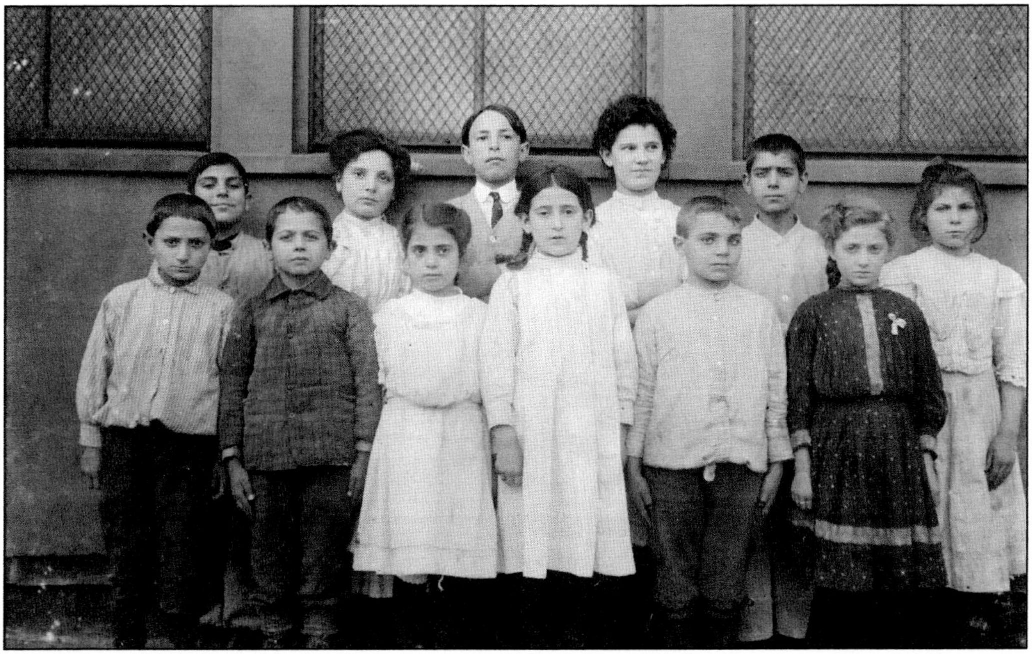

Immigrant children, still dressed in the fashions of their mother country, attend evening classes at a North End school in this c. 1909 image. Boston schools were full, and evening classes were needed to accommodate new immigrants. Within a few years of arrival, children such as these were eager to start work to help support the family.

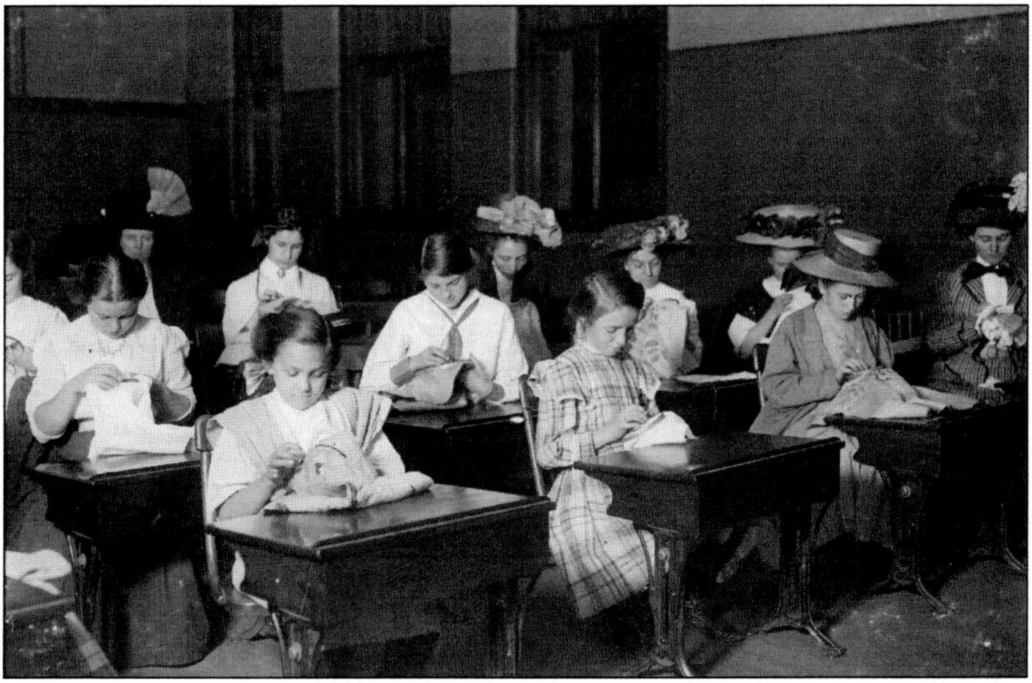

Evening classes in embroidery for girls and women were sponsored by the Boston school department. Embroidery was a common tenement industry, and many an immigrant girl helped her family earn extra money by finishing handkerchiefs and underwear.

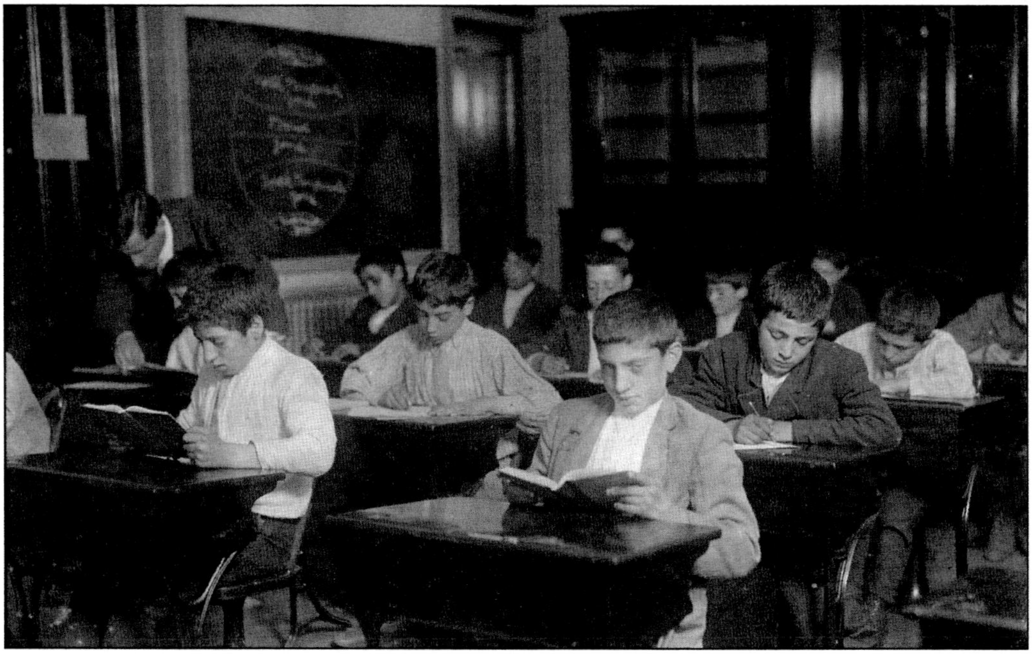

Evening classes to "Americanize" immigrant children were also provided by the Boston school department, as seen in this 1909 photograph. They were called "steamer classes" because the children were admitted shortly after their arrival in America. Dozens of such classes were offered in the Boston neighborhoods to teach English, American history, ideals, traditions, and customs.

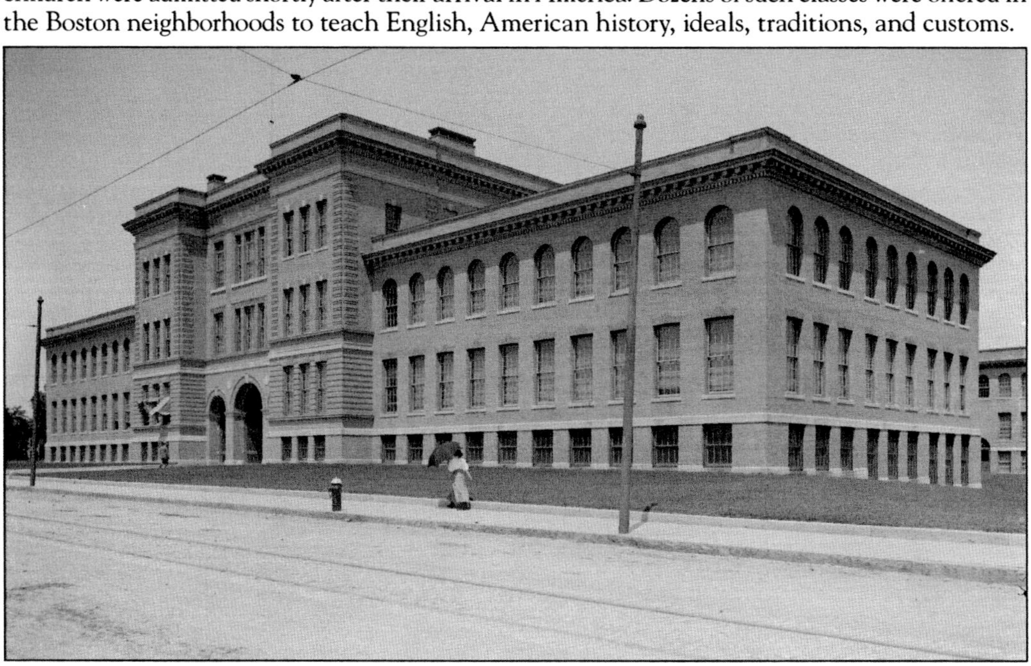

In addition to funding trade schools in Boston and other cities, the Commonwealth of Massachusetts established special schools for its principal industries: textiles and footwear. Textile schools opened in Lowell and New Bedford and shoemaker schools in Brockton and Lynn. The c. 1910 picture shows the Lowell Textile School. In 1972, with the decline of textile manufacturing, the school merged with Lowell State College, later named University of Massachusetts Lowell.

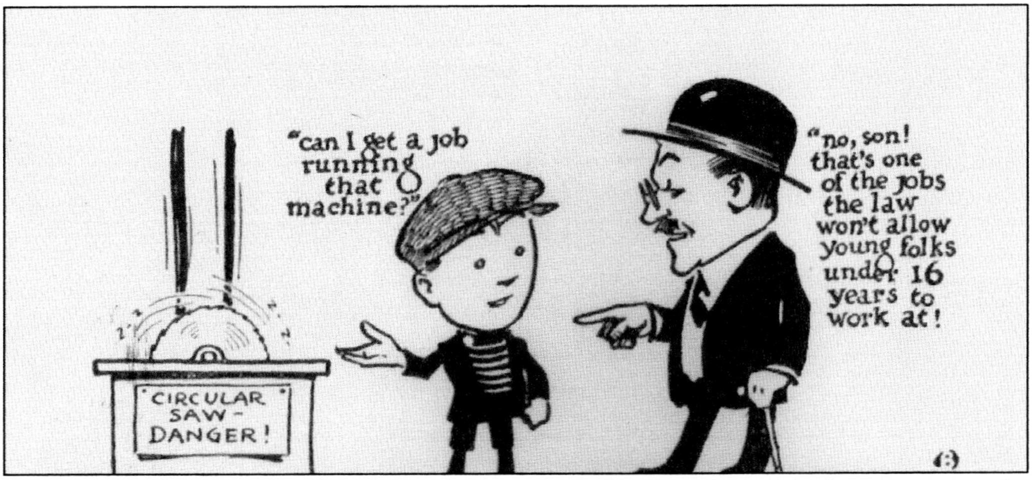

In 1917, the Massachusetts Child Labor Committee (MCLC) explained the laws governing the employment of children. At that time, children under 16 were not permitted to operate dangerous equipment such as circular saws. Present-day Massachusetts laws governing child labor are more stringent. Persons under 18 are prohibited from working on circular saws or operating a forklift. Persons under 16 are prohibited from operating power-driven machinery or rotisseries and from working in factories.

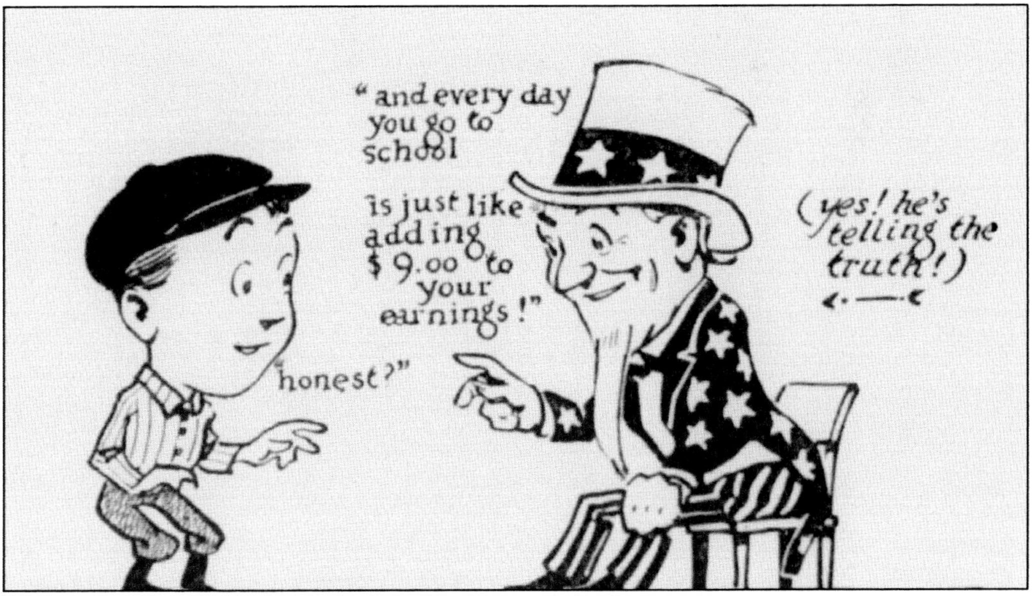

The National Child Labor Committee (NCLC) sought to persuade children and parents that education made better citizens and equipped them for more interesting and better-paying employment. The national organization and its state affiliates sought a national policy to keep children in school until at least age 16 and to ban labor before that age.

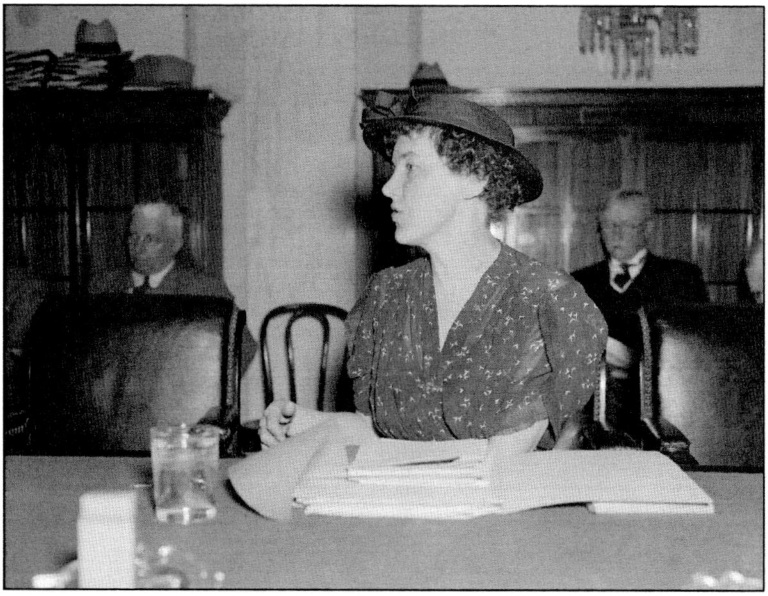

La Rae Brown of Boston, Massachusetts, director of the National League of Women Voters, appeared before the Senate Interstate Commerce Committee to support Sen. Alden W. Barkley's bill to prohibit the interstate shipment of goods made by child labor on May 20, 1937. (Photograph by Harris & Ewing; Library of Congress.)

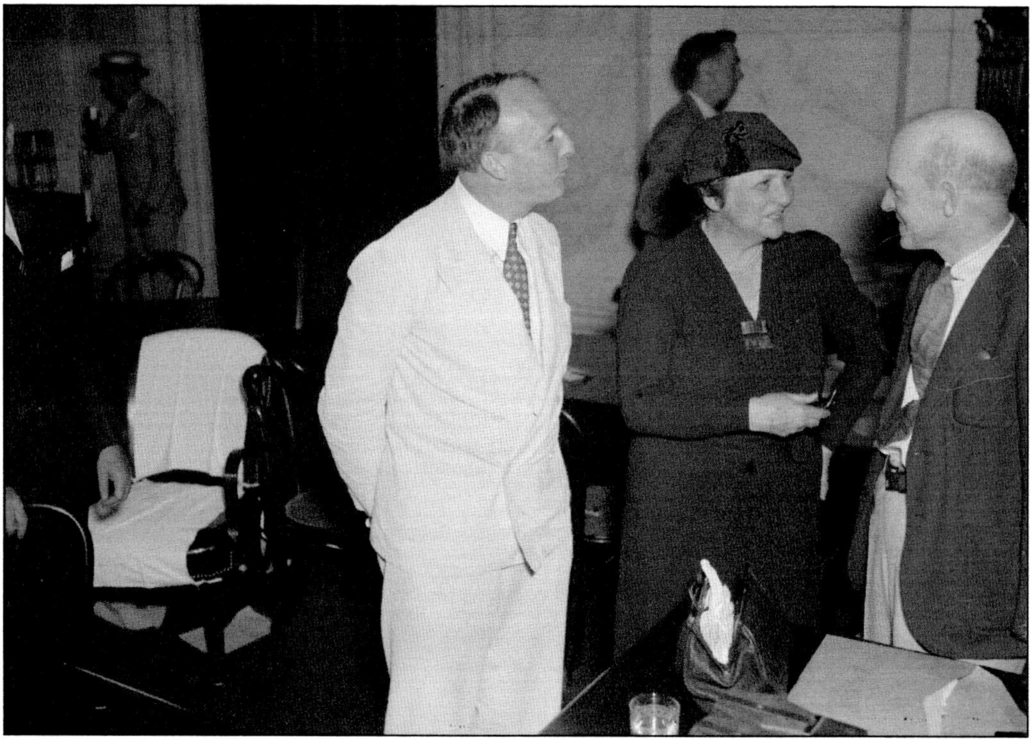

Frances Perkins was born in 1882 on Joy Street on Boston's Beacon Hill. As a student at Mount Holyoke College, she was influenced by Florence Kelley to end child labor and worked for the improvement of the conditions of the workingman and woman. As secretary of labor in the Franklin D. Roosevelt administration, she helped fashion the New Deal legislation. In this picture, she is seen endorsing the Wage and Hour Bill of Sen. Hugo L. Black of Alabama (left) and Rep. William P. Connery Jr. of Massachusetts (right). The objectives of the June 4, 1937, bill were to ban sweatshop conditions and abolish child labor. (Photograph by Harris & Ewing; Library of Congress.)

Three

Street Trades

Boston began to regulate newsboys and bootblacks in 1868. The school department declared in 1908, "No minor under the age of 14 years shall, in any street or public place in the city of Boston, work as a bootblack . . . unless he has a minor's license granted him by the school committee and issued to him by the superintendent of schools." Wearing the badge and carrying a shoeshine box, boys wandered around the streets of Boston, asking men if they wanted their shoes or boots polished. Newsboys in Boston outnumbered bootblacks eight to one. Many were immigrants, some from families with only one parent. The newsboys were not permitted to jump on moving streetcars or to sell without wearing their badge. Newsboys were forbidden to be on the streets before 6:00 a.m. and had to stop working by 8:00 in the morning in order to get to school. They were required to attend school "during some portion of the day [or] attend the newsboys' school at least two hours each day." By 1910, there were 5,000 licensed newsboys in Boston. Two newsboys' schools were established with special hours so the boys could sell the morning and evening editions of the papers.

The Newsboys' Reading Room opened in 1870 at 16 Howard Street, Boston, for the use of "all licensed newsboys without regard to color or sect." Frederick Gray Frothingham bequeathed $30,000, and in 1909, the old Children's Mission was purchased and renovated as the Boston Newsboys Club. Soon, the club had 3,000 newsboy members.

Hersh Baraznik was a Russian immigrant who started selling papers in 1903. A few years later, his fellow newsboys voted him the winner of a scholarship to Suffolk University. Hersh changed his name to Harry E. Burroughs and went on to a successful career in the law. In 1927, he raised $230,000, established the Harry E. Burroughs Newsboys Foundation, and built a new Newsboy's Club. The Burroughs Newsboys Foundation awarded 20 college scholarships each year. The most famous of the Burroughs scholarship newsboys was Theodore Harold White. He graduated from Harvard and went on to a brilliant career as foreign correspondent, winning a Pulitzer Prize in 1962.

Children were also out on the streets selling fruit and vegetables. Dressed in company uniforms, boys delivered telegrams and carried messages back to the office to be relayed elsewhere. Downtown Boston's narrow, cobbled streets made bicycle use difficult, so the messenger boys got around on foot.

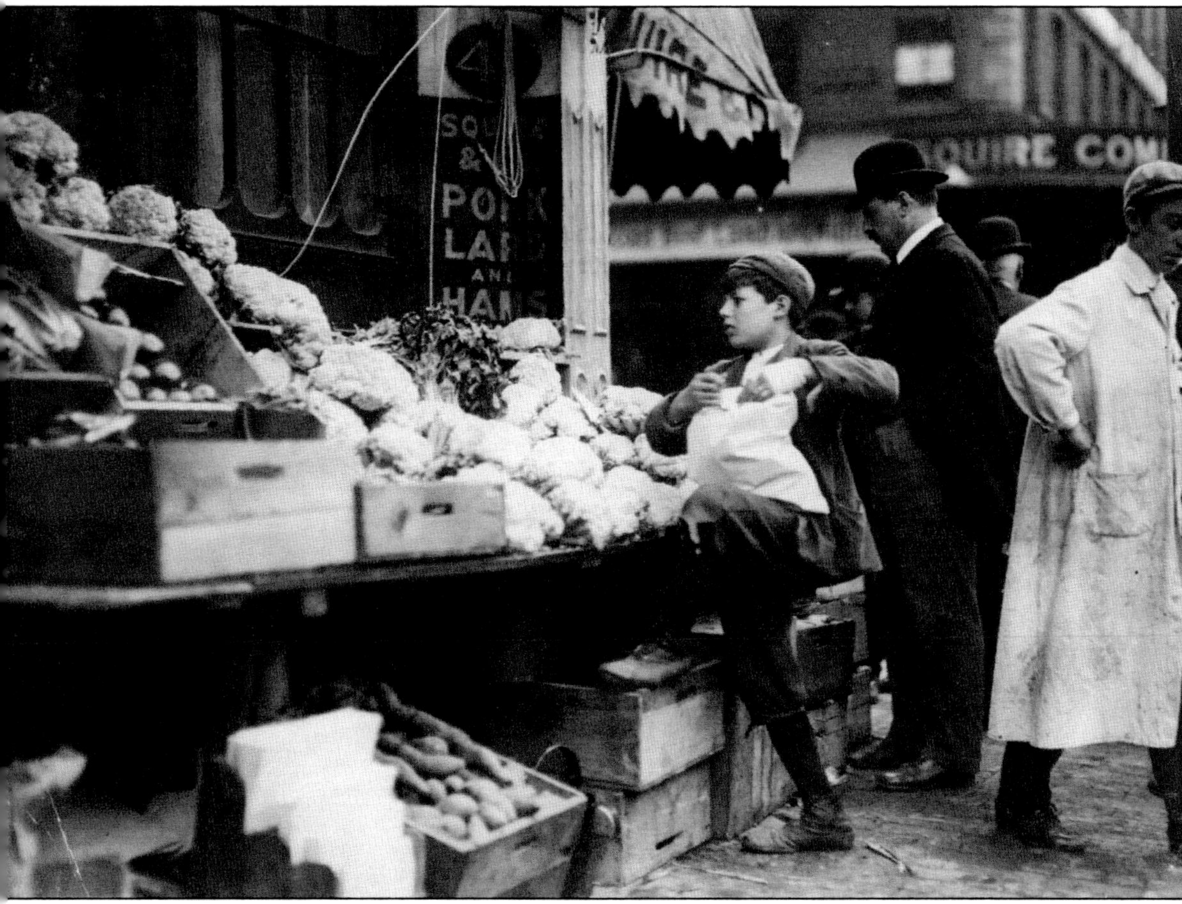

A young vendor with a bandaged hand packs cauliflower at a vegetable stand situated in a small stall at Faneuil Hall Market around the corner from Squire & Co., producer of pork, lard, and hams—a good spot for foot traffic. In 1881, Squire constructed a building that held 30,000 tons of ice cut from local ponds. By 1892, artificial refrigeration was incorporated into a new factory complex that eventually processed 6,000 hogs a day. When this picture was taken in 1915, Squire employed over 1,500 workers, including boys and girls.

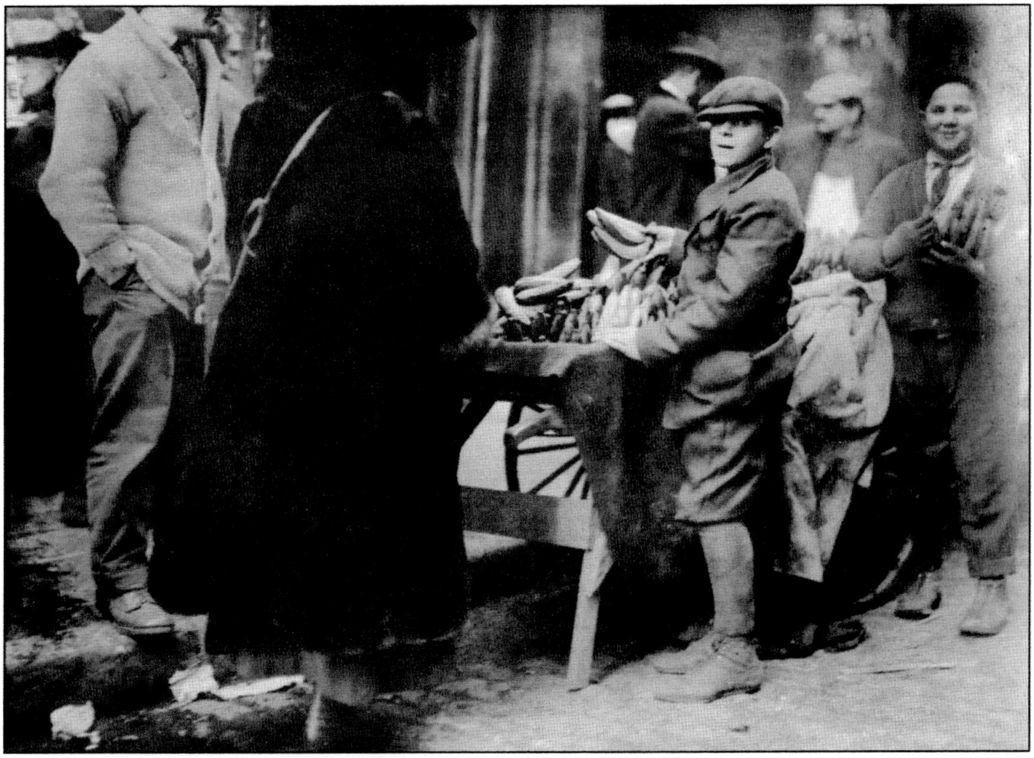

Two boys tend a pushcart in the street market. The fruit of the day is bananas. The Boston Fruit Company began importing bananas, coconuts, oranges, and lemons from the West Indies as early as 1885. Steamships quickly transported the fruit from plantations to Boston's Long Wharf so the boys' wares were fresh and not overripe.

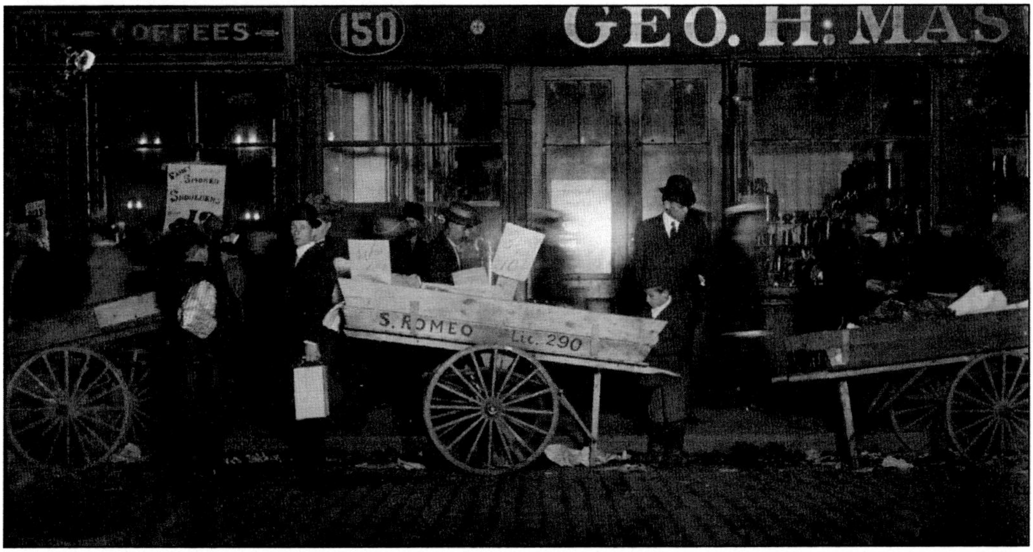

Even in the days before 24/7 grocery stores, the people of Boston could buy fruits and vegetables late into the night. This market is doing a brisk business considering that it is 11:00 p.m. on an October night in 1909. Despite laws forbidding children to work at night, the little boy staffing S. Romero's stand sells tomatoes to his customers.

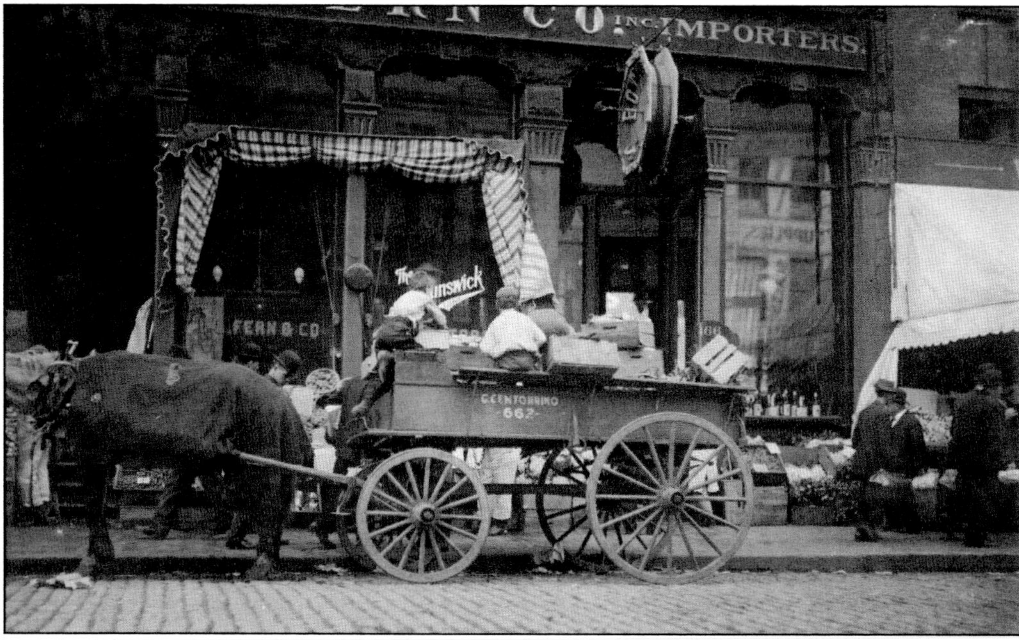

Two little boys are in charge of G. Centorrino's horse and cart, selling vegetables on a cobbled Boston Street and competing with sidewalk stalls in this 1909 image. The number 662 on the cart is the vendor's license number.

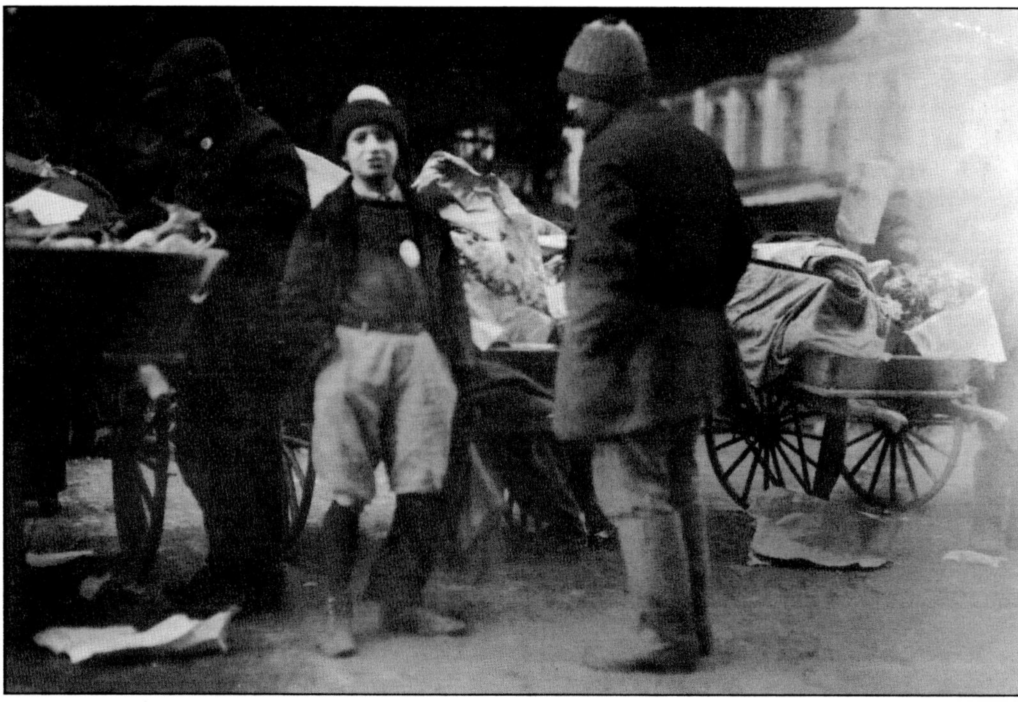

This young fellow stands by his pushcart, at ease and self-assured. Showing his badge to demonstrate his business credentials and wearing his wool hat against the January chill, he chats to a fellow vendor. With the goods in the carts under protective tarps, they are closing up for the day in this 1917 image.

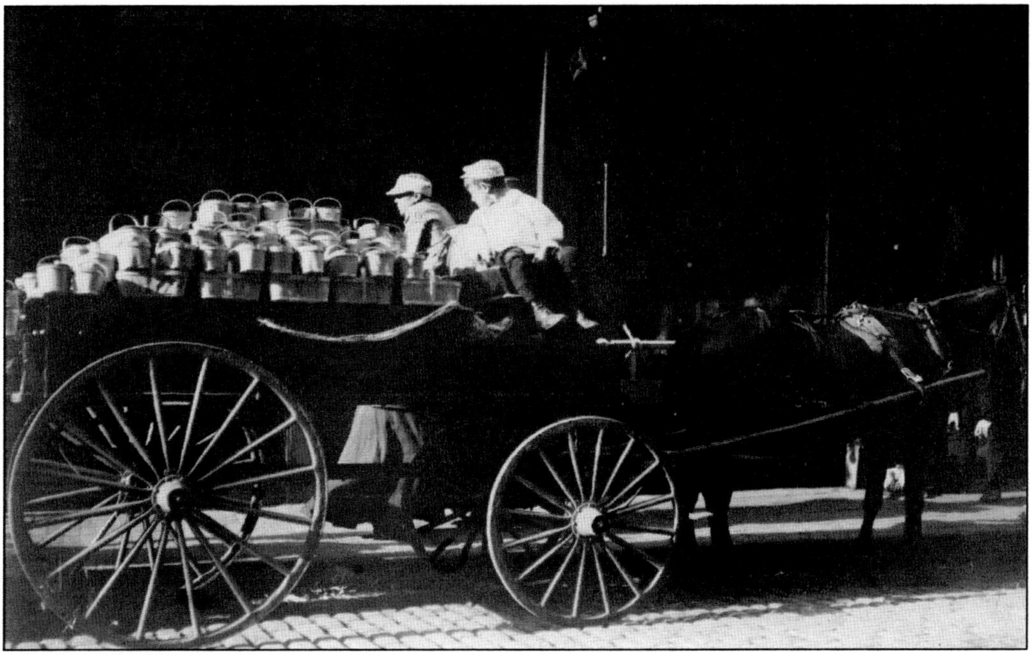

Young vendors tend a tempting display of grapes packed in convenient, ready-to-carry baskets. With perishable wares, it is important to sell before they spoil. In this case, that meant working late into the night on a Saturday in October 1909, staying alert to prevent theft and to encourage sales.

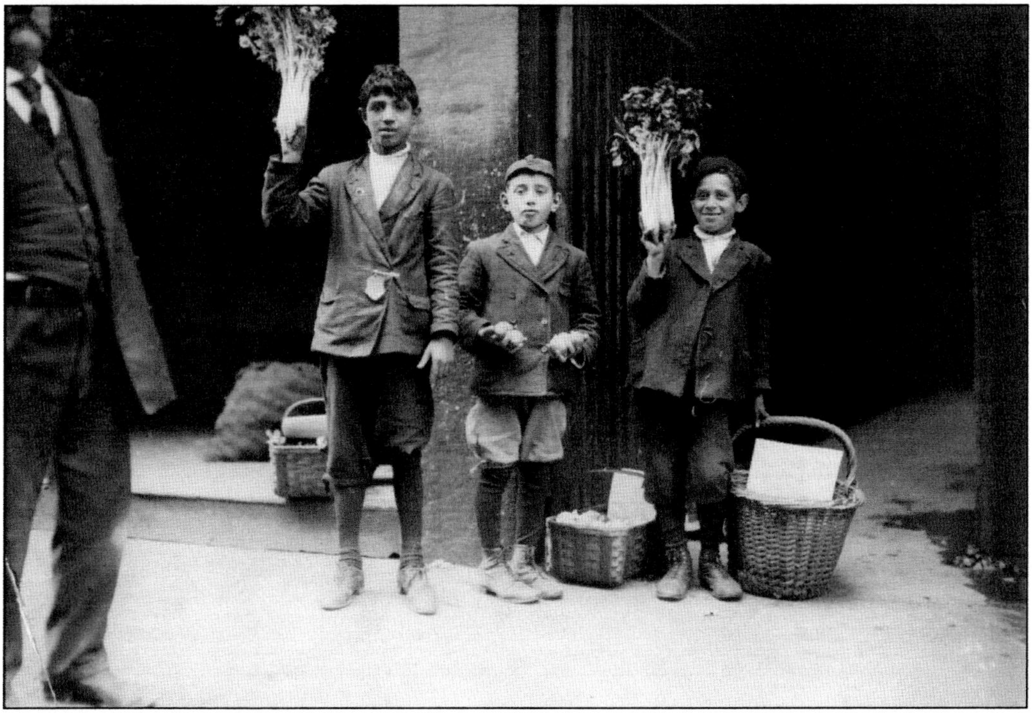

Three young fellows hawk vegetables in this 1909 image, standing in a doorway by their modest baskets of celery and potatoes. The oldest boy has his badge pinned to his jacket, signifying he is a licensed vendor. The smaller boys practice the peddler's trade at his side.

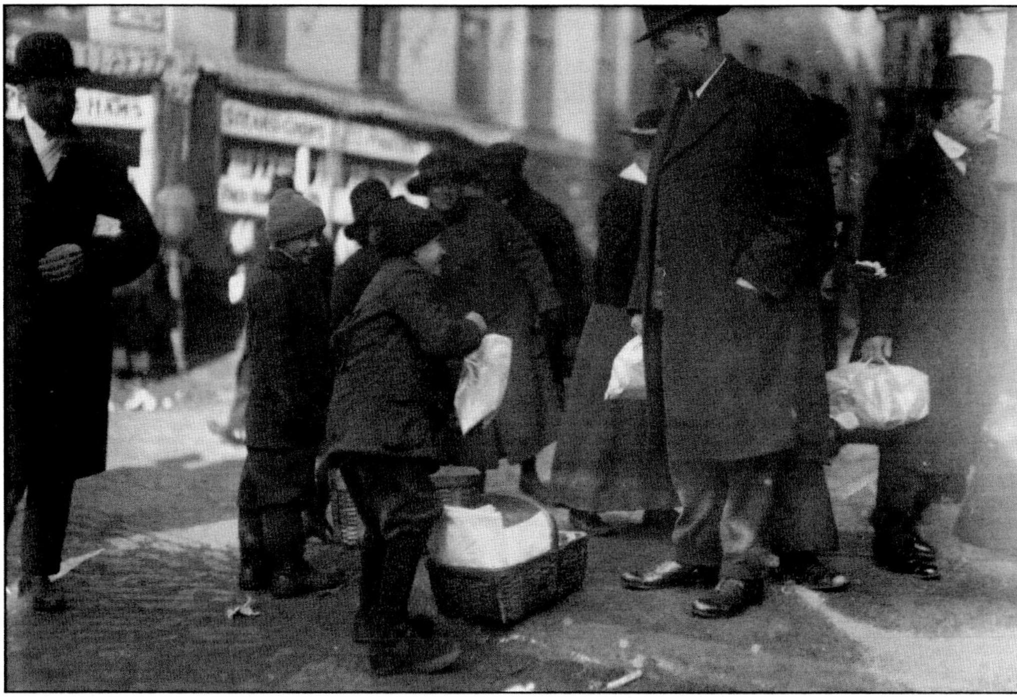

Boys sell lemons at a busy street corner in Boston during the winter of 1917. Children purchased small quantities of fruits and vegetables from the market to resell their goods at a small profit at street corners in the city center.

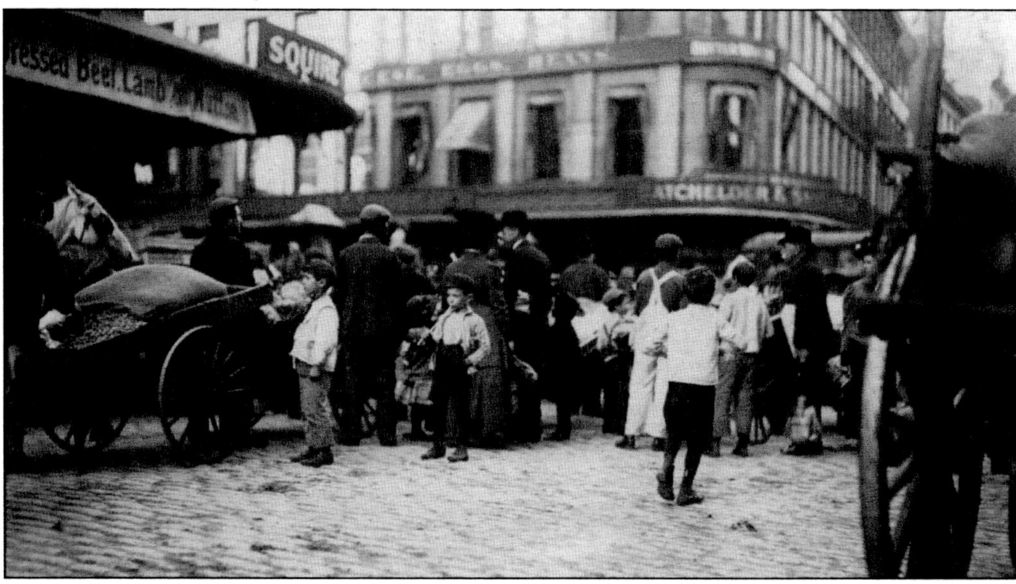

A market corner attracts a crowd; pushcarts and people fill the roadway between Squire ("dressed beef, lamb, and mutton") and Batchelder & Snyder (purveyor of poultry, eggs, cheese, butter, and beans). Children accompany their parents to the market as customers; others work alongside their parents. Other children come to collect discarded produce on the cobblestones or ask for chicken heads and feet at the butcher's back door. Batchelder & Snyder had a store at 47–63 Blackstone Street; that building has been replaced by the Millennium Bostonian Hotel.

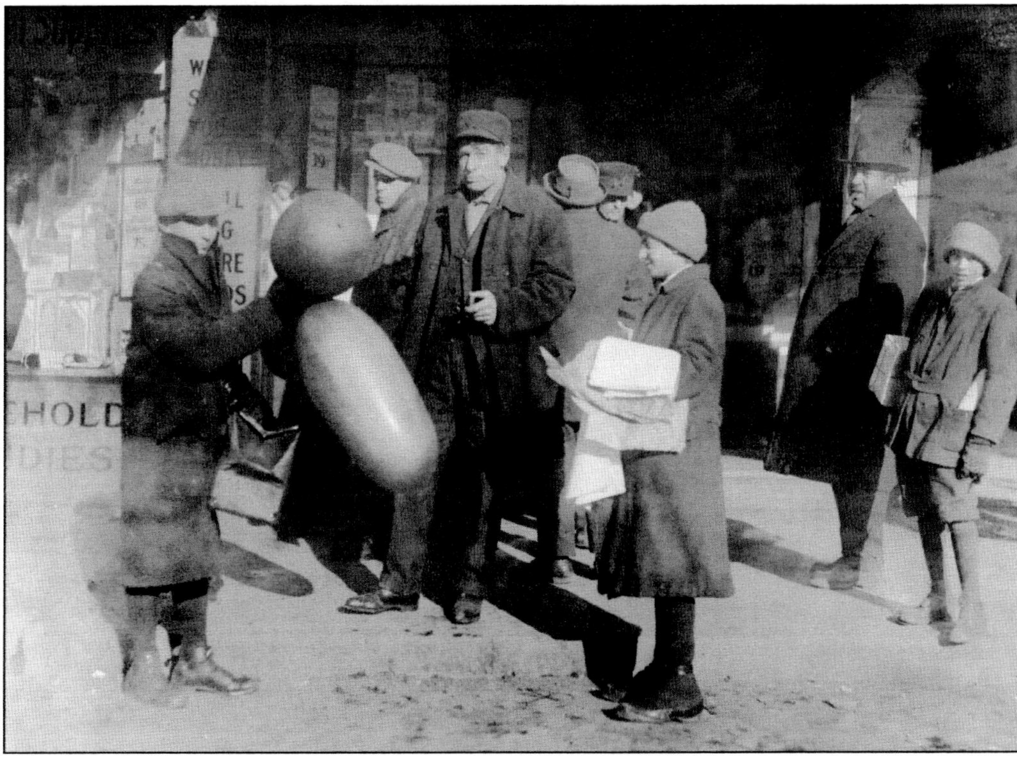

On a cold January 1917 day, boys are out on the streets of Boston, accosting passersby as they offer balloons and handkerchiefs for sale.

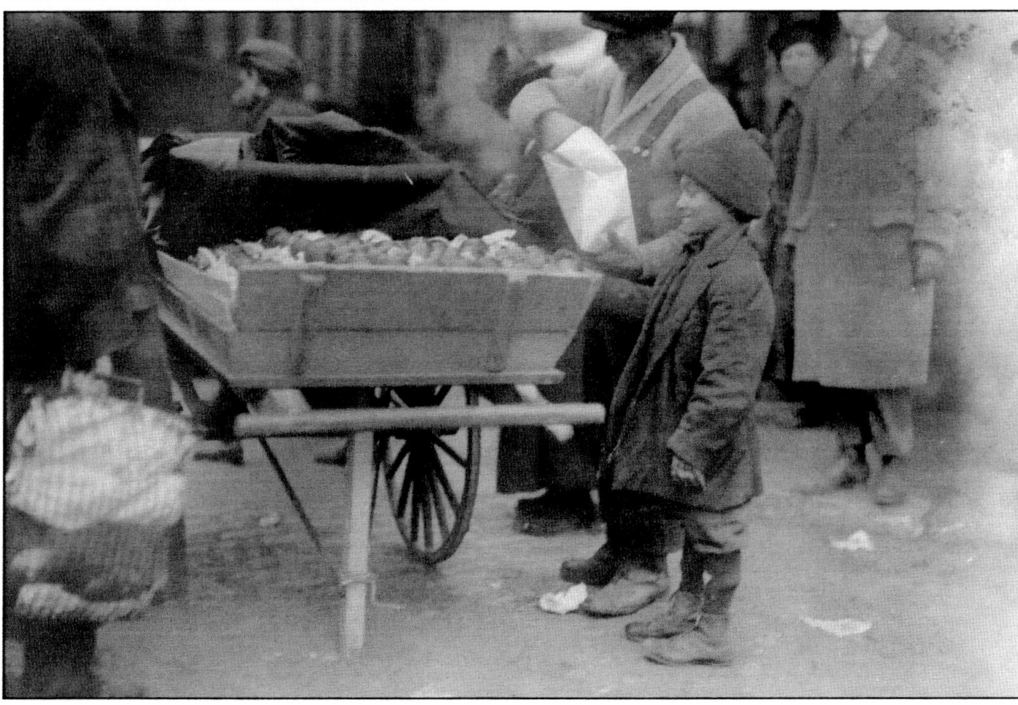

A little boy helps to sell oranges at the market close by Faneuil Hall in this c. 1910 photograph.

Wuxtree! Wuxtree! Reedallabatit!

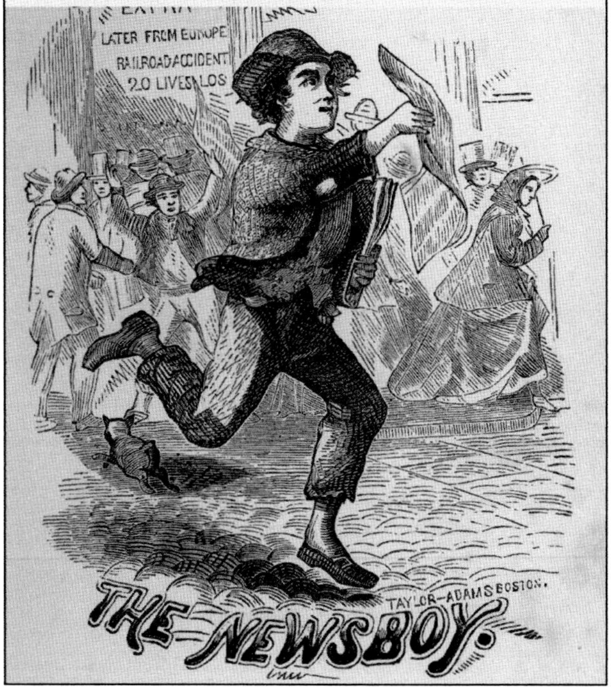

Boston's first newspaper, the *Boston News-Letter*, appeared in 1704. Two years later, the weekly *New England Courant*, owned by James Franklin, brother of Benjamin Franklin, began publication. Newsboys were out on the streets of Boston even before the Civil War. This c. 1870 illustration of a Boston boy calling out in local newsboy dialect, "Wuxtree! Wuxtree! Reedallabatit!" meaning, "Extra, Extra, Read All About It," is from the engravers and lithographers James Taylor and Thomas Adams at 29 Joy's Building, 81 Washington Street, Boston.

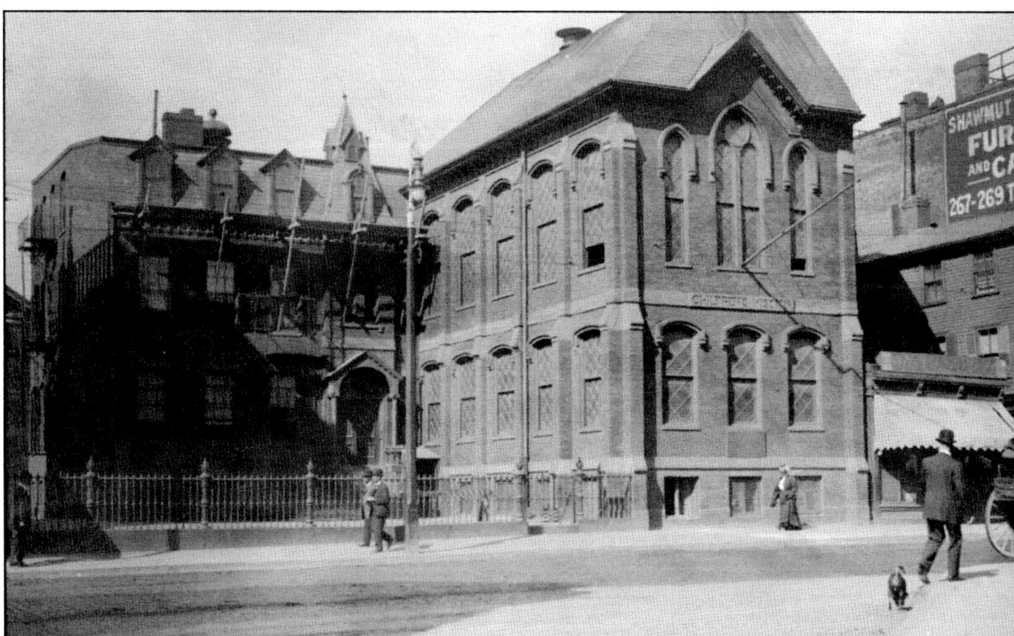

The building at 277 Tremont Street, near the Shubert Theatre, was originally the Children's Mission, a home for neglected and homeless children, built in 1848. In 1909, the Frederick Gray Frothingham bequest of $30,000 was used to convert the building into the Boston Newsboys Club, where the boys could come for food, shelter, and relaxation.

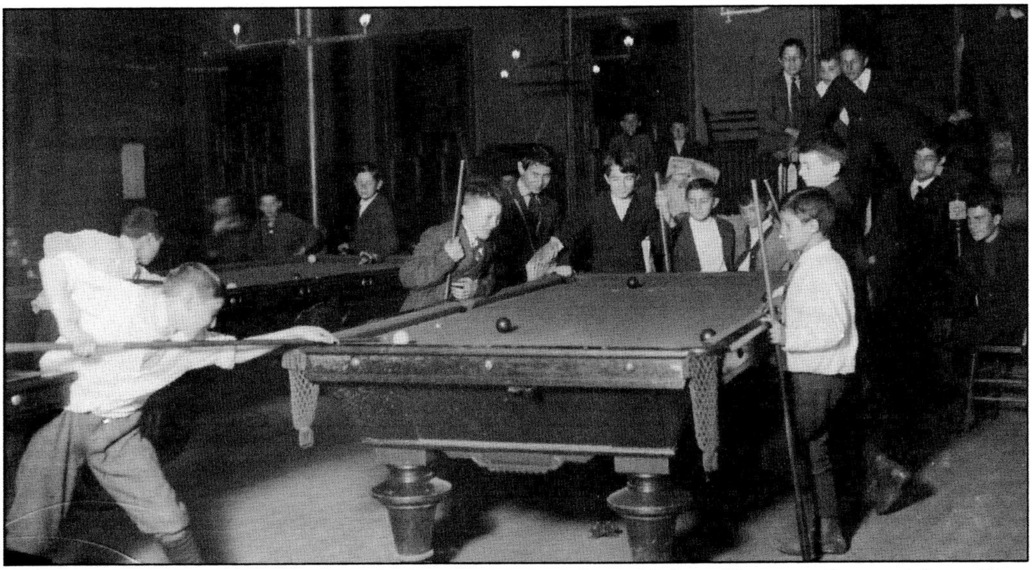

Shown here is the gas-lit poolroom at the Boston Newsboys Club on Tremont Street. After selling newspapers, the boys came to their club to relax over games and play pool. The Newsboys Club was heated against the winter cold and supervised by adult staff. Most of the boys came from poor and crowded tenement homes and welcomed the comforts of their club. Boys frequently got into trouble over licensure and fights over choice street locations for selling newspapers. In 1909, the club became the home of the Newsboys Trial Board, to arbitrate the complaints between boys and to keep these matters out of the juvenile courts. Run by the boys themselves, the board led to a dramatic fall in cases going to the juvenile courts.

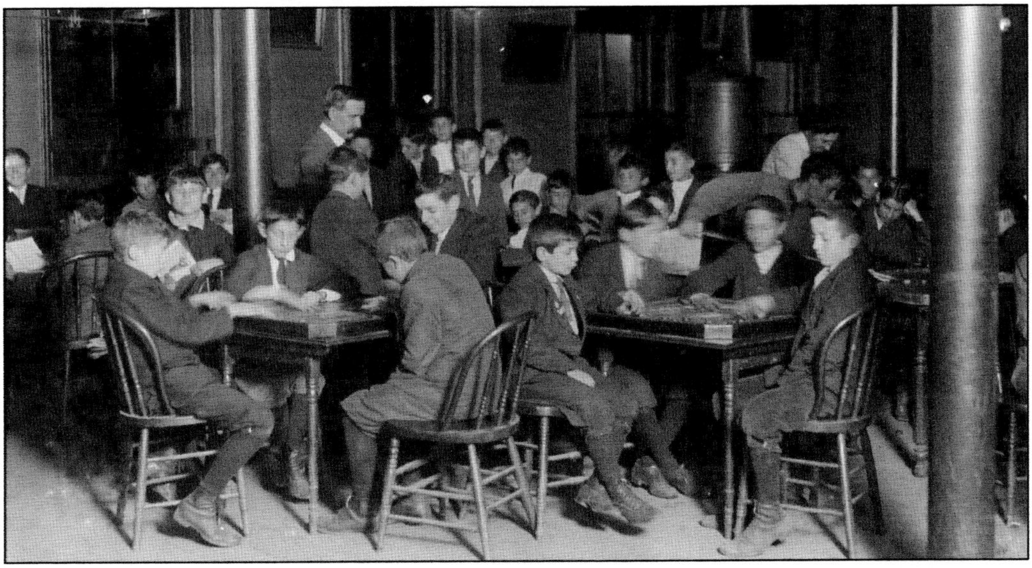

The games room at the Boston Newsboys Club at 277 Tremont Street is seen in this c. 1910 image. Sixteen-year-old Nathan S. Sodekson formed the Newsboys Protective Union to represent the boys against the newspaper owners. The union collected $2,567.16 to establish the Boston Newsboys Scholarship to send one of its members to Harvard College each year. In 1911, Samuel A. Levine won the scholarship. He went on to become a distinguished cardiologist at Boston's Brigham & Women's Hospital.

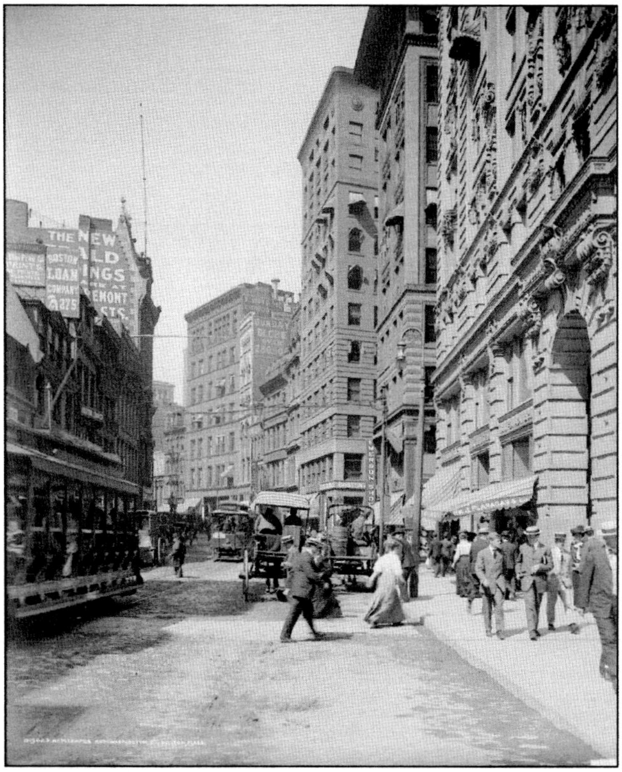

This c. 1905 image shows Boston's Newspaper Row on cobbled Washington Street. In 1900, Boston was a city of 560,937 people who supported the *Boston Globe*, *Herald*, *Journal*, *Post*, *Advertiser*, *Record American*, *Monitor*, and the *Traveler*. Horse carts supplied goods to the stores along the street. In the warm weather, Boston's electrical trolley cars were open; they were replaced by enclosed cars during cold weather.

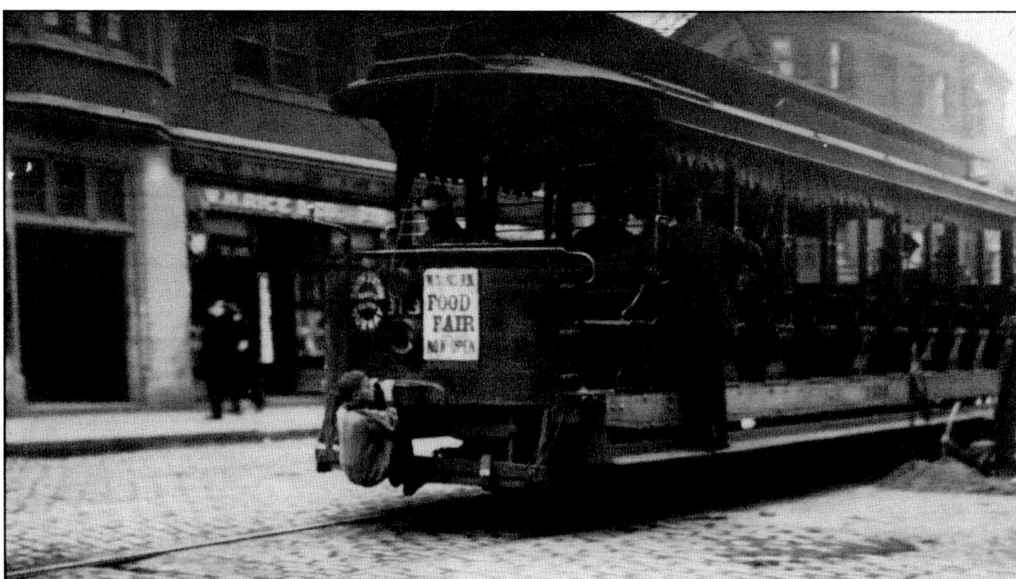

Little boys, out of sight of the conductor, often hitched rides at the back of trolley cars, a dangerous sport. This c. 1910 picture was taken along Washington Street. To keep the violations of license regulations out of the juvenile courts, the school department established a Newsboys Trial Board of three newsboys and two retired judges. From 1911 to 1916, the Newsboys Trial Board heard 2,112 cases. The self-governing Newsboys Trial Board continued in Boston for many years and the concept was implemented in other cities.

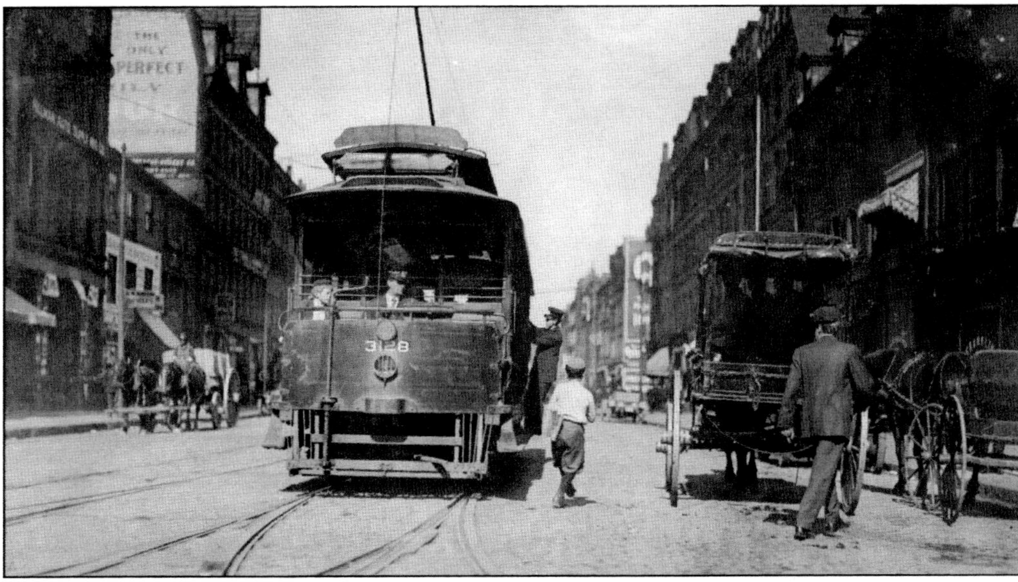

A newsboy is getting ready to leap on a moving trolley car to try to sell his papers before the conductor can catch him in this c. 1910 photograph. This common practice could lead to a citation to appear before the Newsboys Trial Board or even the juvenile courts. A newsboy could also lose his license for jumping on a moving streetcar.

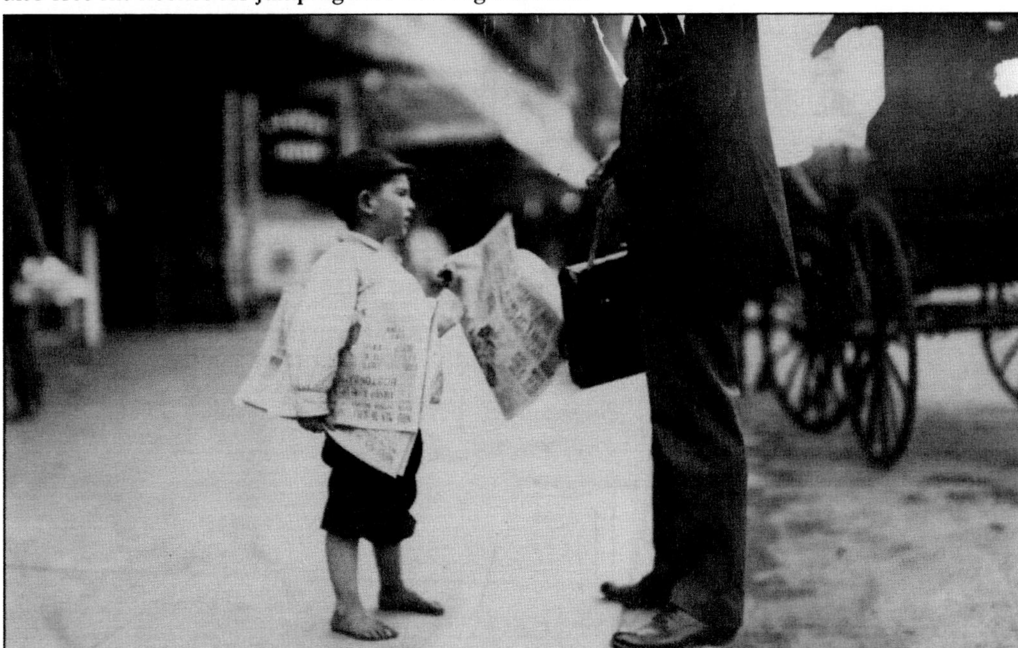

A six-year-old barefoot newsboy sells papers in a Boston suburb in this c. 1910 image. Such behavior was illegal, yet the practice was widespread. Since 1868, Boston and surrounding towns tried to regulate newsboys on the streets early in the morning and late into the night. Boston established two newsboys' schools with classes from 10:00 in the morning until 3:00 in the afternoon. Licenses were issued only to boys older than 12 who attended school "during some portion of the day or attend the newsboys' school at least two hours each day."

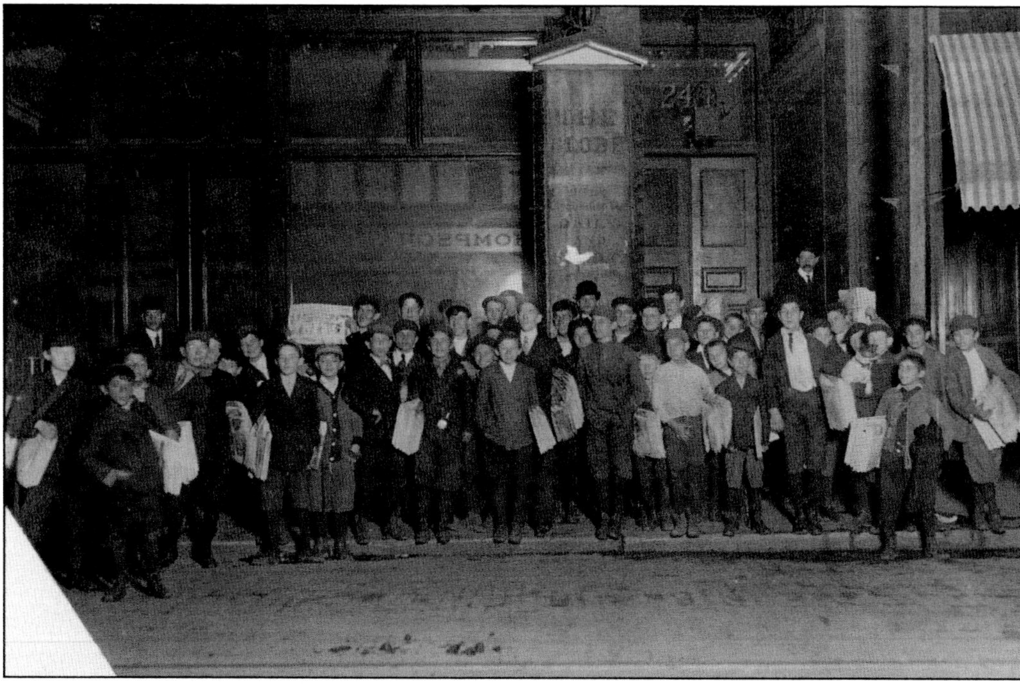

Newsboys are out early in the morning to collect their newspapers and are ready to set out to their chosen street corners to sell the papers. This c. 1910 picture shows boys outside the *Boston Globe* building on Washington Street.

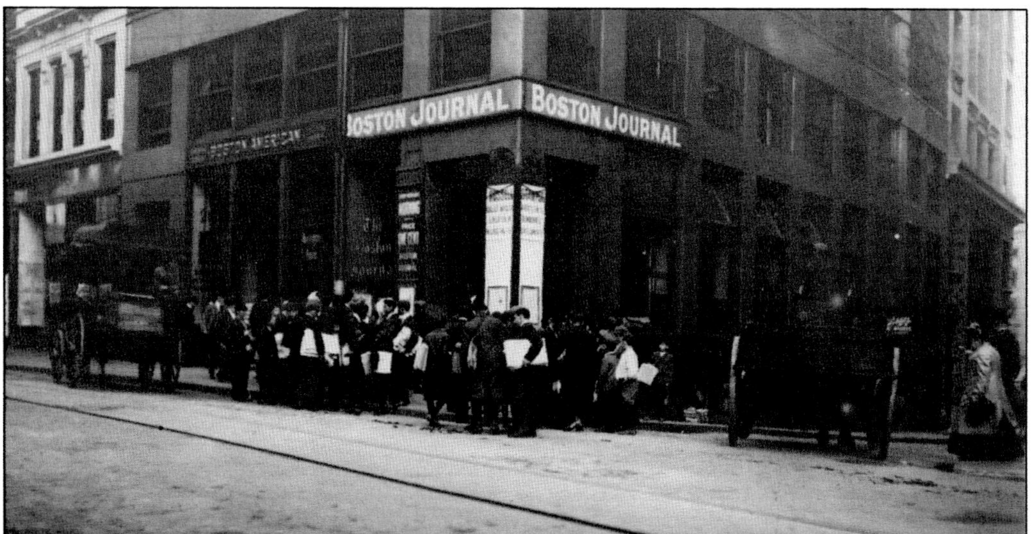

Newsboys gather outside the offices of the *Boston Journal* and *Boston American*. In 1908, the *Boston American*, owned by the William Randolph Hearst chain, raised the price of its newspaper to the newsboys from 1¢ to 2¢ a copy. After the newsboys refused to handle it, the paper hired non-licensed boys. On January 11, a total of 200 newsboys assembled at North Station and attacked the arriving wagons and the new delivery boys. Thousands of newspapers were torn up and scattered in the streets. A policeman who tried to quell the riot was beaten up. After three boys were arrested, hundreds of their fellows followed them to the police station, demanding their release.

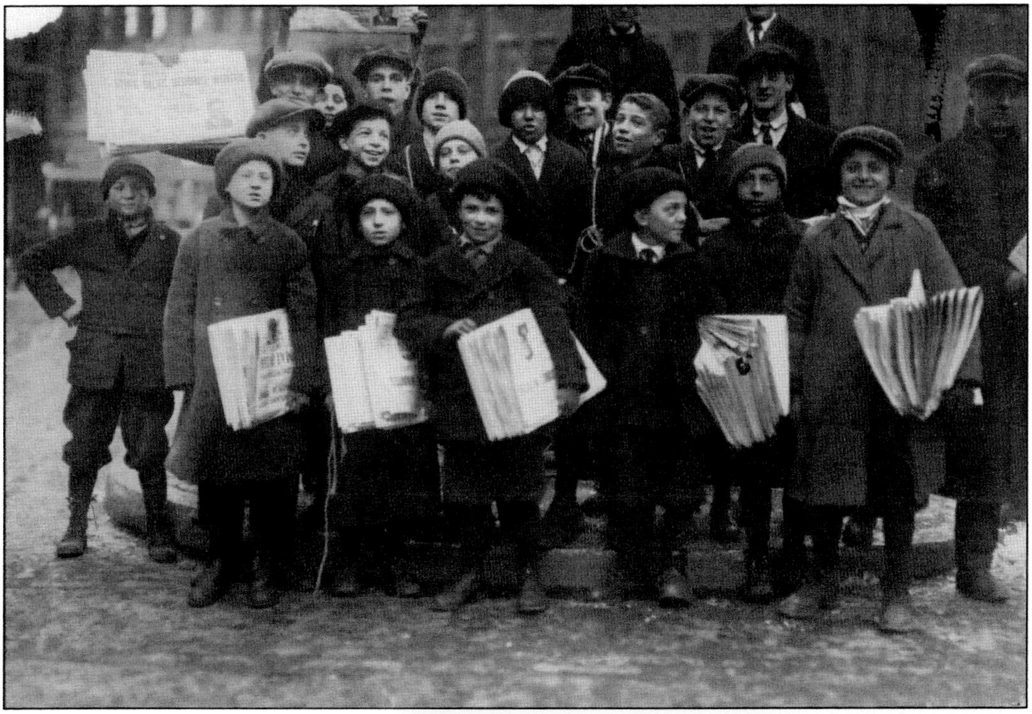

Four of the newsboys in the photograph were 11 years old or younger. The newsboys here are selling the *Boston Globe*, with headlines announcing "Stock Sales Records Wanted" and "Troops Ordered Out of Mexico." In 1916, a total of 5,000 American troops under Brig. Gen. John J. Pershing entered Mexico in pursuit of Francisco "Pancho" Villa. The troops were withdrawn from Mexico in January 1917.

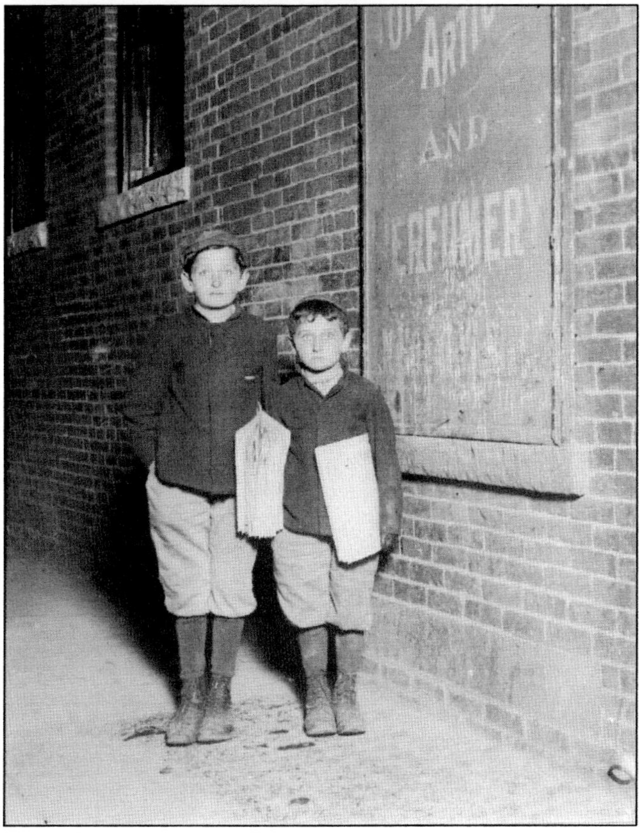

Twelve-year-old Isaac and his seven-year-old brother David sell newspapers at night in a town near Boston around 1910.

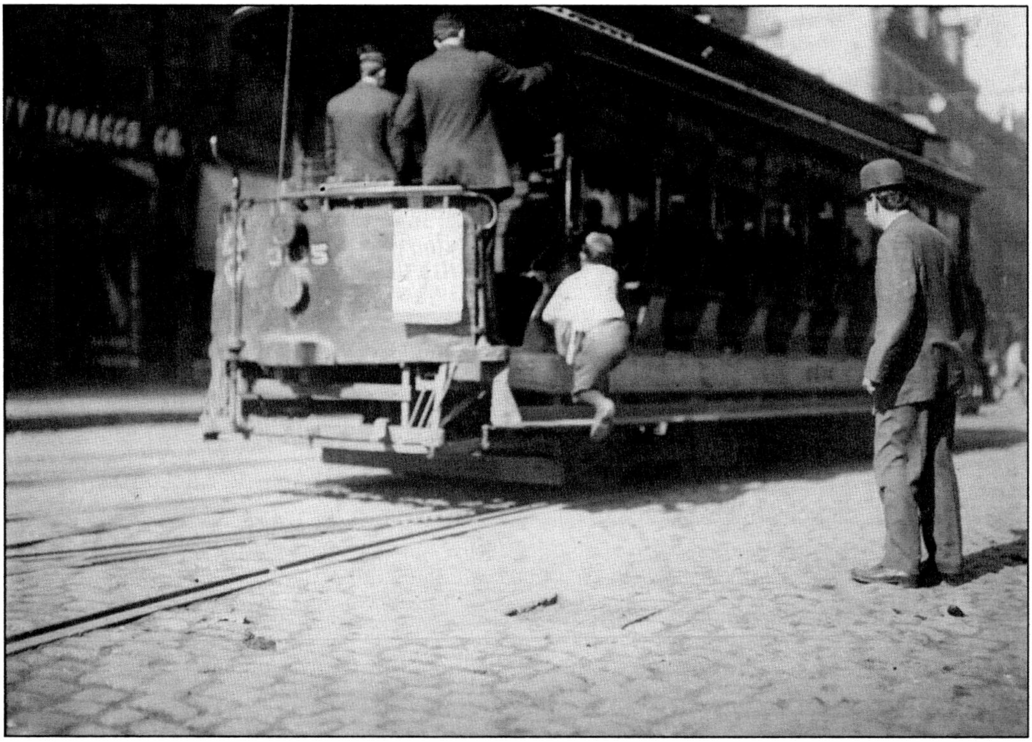

A Boston newsboy jumps on a trolley car along Washington Street, hoping to sell papers to the passengers. An astonished pedestrian looks on, but the conductors have not yet noticed the boy. Such dangerous actions were forbidden by the newsboy code of behavior.

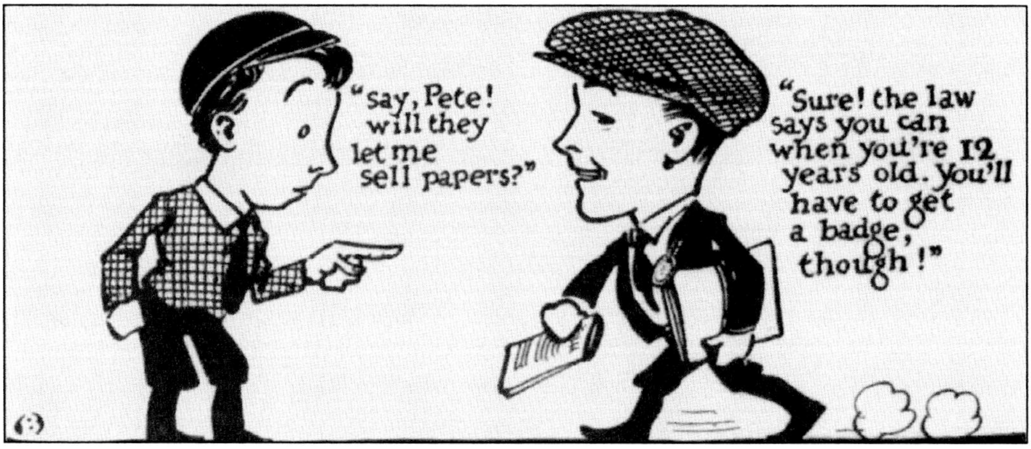

Above, an illustration issued in 1917 by the Massachusetts Child Labor Committee (MCLC) tells children that they need a badge to show they are 12 years or older before they will be permitted to sell newspapers. In 1905 alone, the Boston School Committee issued 2,513 badges to boys wanting to sell newspapers. Boys were forbidden to be out on the streets before 6:00 a.m. and had to stop selling by 8:00 in the morning in order to go to school. Any infraction could lead to the loss of a license.

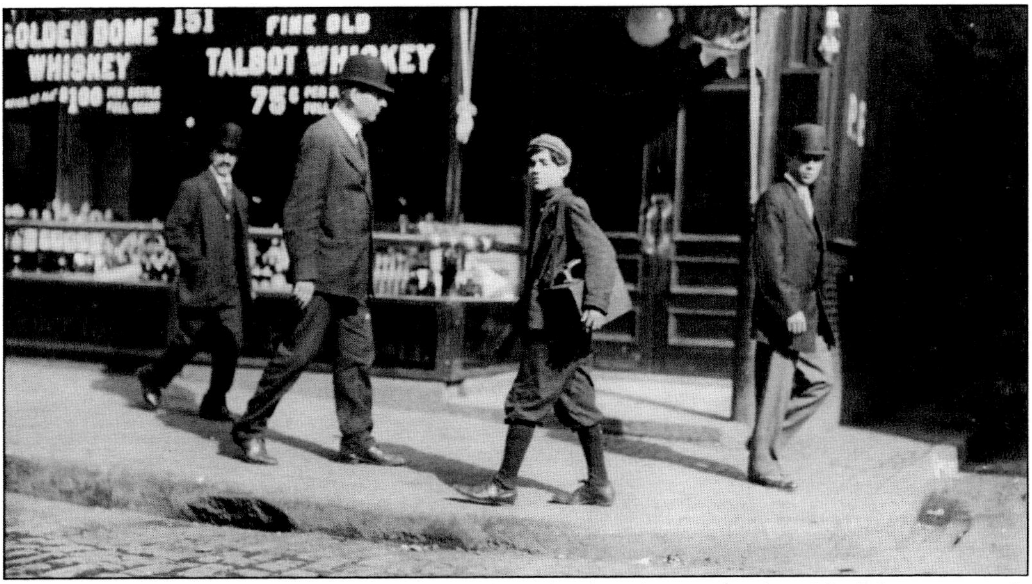

The sidewalks and cobbled streets were rough on leather shoes. This bootblack boy was ready with his portable station to restore the shine to scuffed and dusty footwear. Keeping his own shoes polished was his best advertisement. By 1910, it was becoming less common to see young bootblacks roving around, plying their trade on the streets. Instead, customers began to visit shoeshine parlors, where several boys, mostly new immigrants, worked side-by-side.

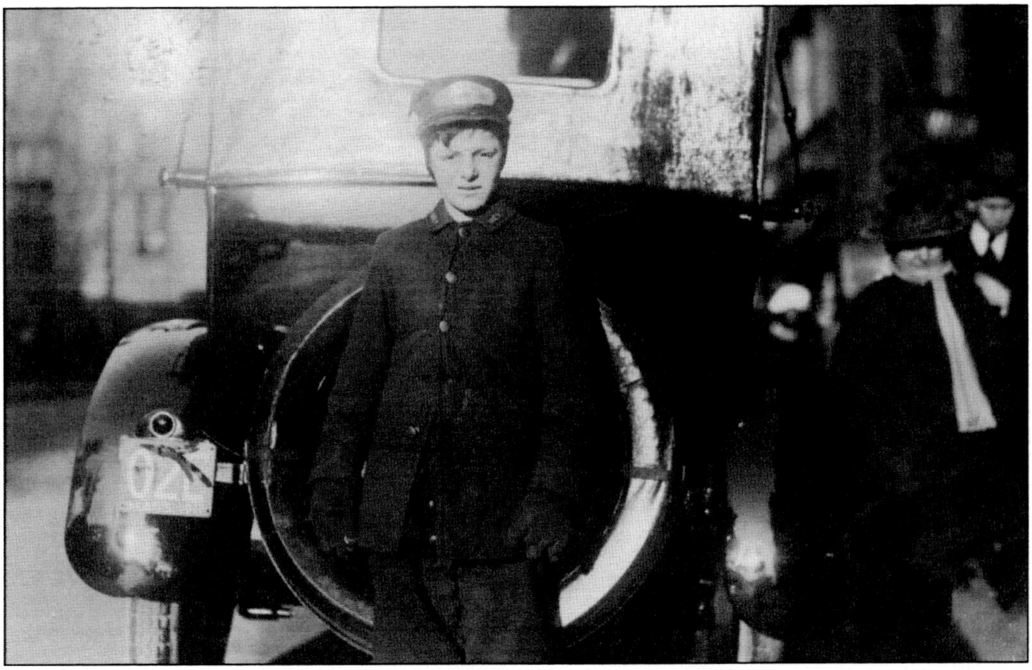

Fourteen-year-old G. Leahy was photographed on January 23, 1917, on Tremont Street, near the Granary Burying Ground. Young master Leahy was close to the headquarters of his employer, Metropolitan Messenger & Mailing Company. Leahy lived across the Charles River at 1249 Cambridge Street, Inman Square, Cambridge, in an apartment in a three-story clapboard building with shops on the first floor.

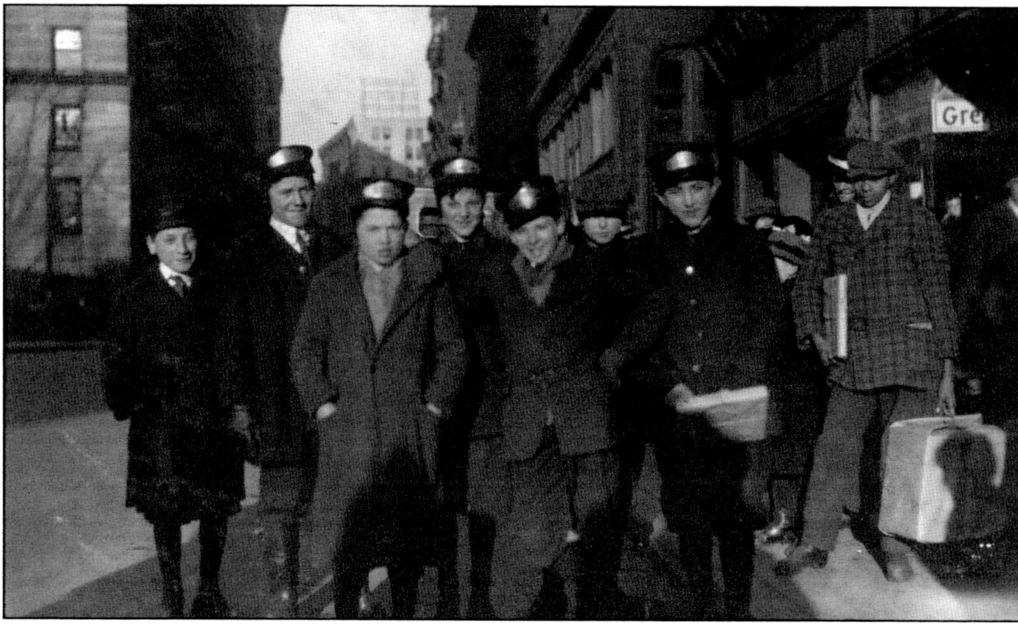

This 1917 picture shows messenger boys of the Metropolitan Messenger & Mailing Company. The Tremont Temple Baptist Church, the first integrated church in the US, is in the background. The smallest boy, Sol Hamber of Everett, is messenger No. 18 of the Special Delivery Messenger Company at 3 Somerset Street. Most of the boys lived in Brighton or Cambridge. The extensive streetcar network made it easy to travel to downtown Boston to work.

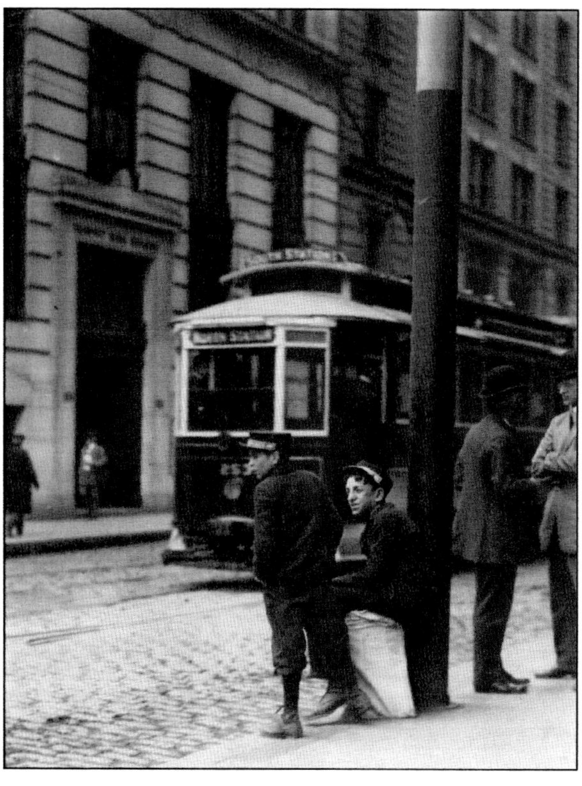

Two Western Union messenger boys, wearing uniforms complete with labeled caps, wait alongside a cobbled street as an electric streetcar goes past around 1909. The Atlantic Avenue Elevated provided service between Boston's North and South Stations. Boston telegram boys usually went on foot rather than by bicycle, due to the often-congested streets and uneven paving. Strikes were frequent; the Messenger Boys Protective Union of Boston, affiliated with the American Federation of Labor (AFL), helped improve the conditions and pay for its members.

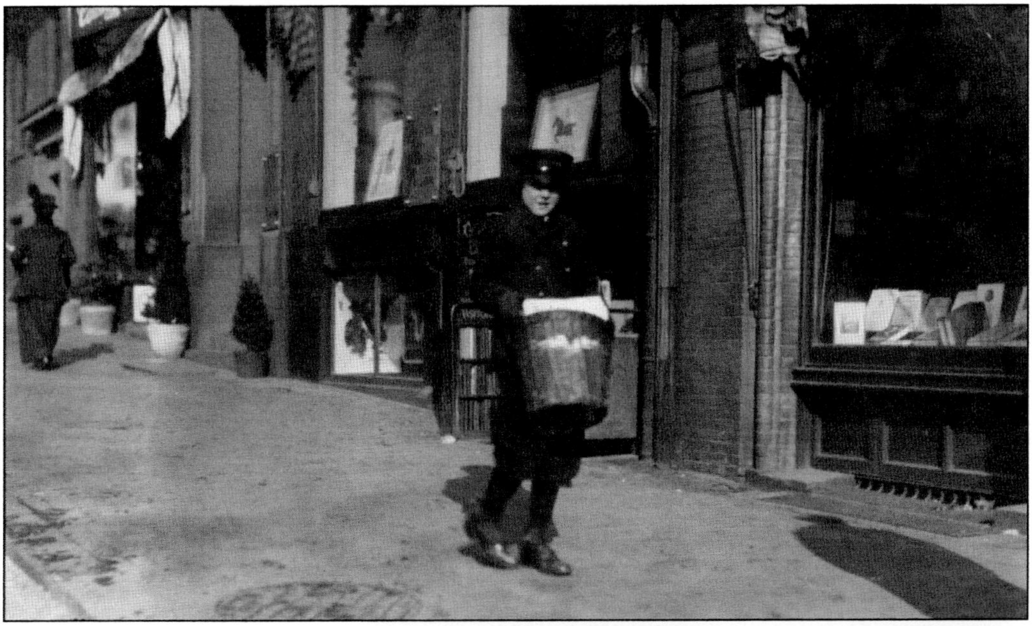

This photograph of 14-year-old G. Leahy, of 1249 Cambridge Street, was taken on Tremont Street, Boston, in 1917. As a messenger boy for Metropolitan Messenger & Mailing Company, at 67 Bromfield Street, he earned $5 in wages, and $2.50 in tips weekly. Leahy was one of some 70 messenger boys working for Metropolitan.

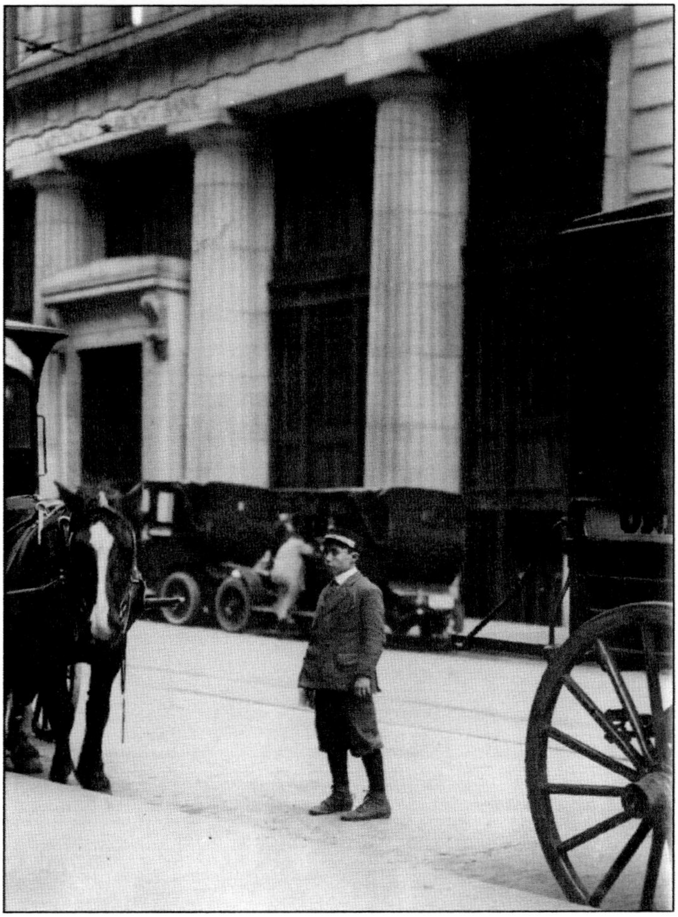

Messenger boy Eugene Fennelly lived at 22 Holmes Street, Allston, off Western Avenue and close to Harvard Stadium. He probably came to work on the streetcar. Eugene is shown here in 1910 crossing Washington Street, close to the banks and newspaper publishing houses.

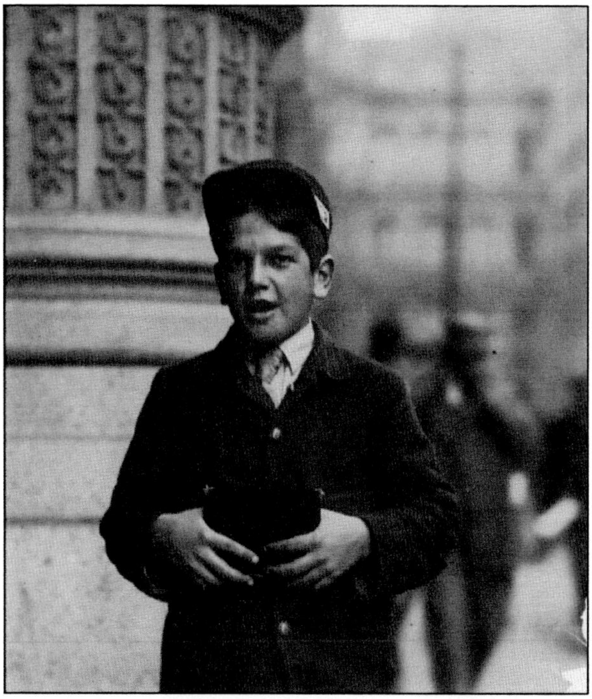

Boys as young as 10 worked as day messengers. Notebook in hand, young Joseph Bicot on Washington Street looks eager to deliver a message. When business was slow, the boys gathered in back rooms, basements, or on street corners and passed the time talking, playing games, or gambling. Boys like Joe learned to shoot craps with their street-wise, worldly colleagues of 14 and 15. Educators and social reformers worried that boys in the messenger service were sent to deliver alcohol and drugs or messages for prostitutes.

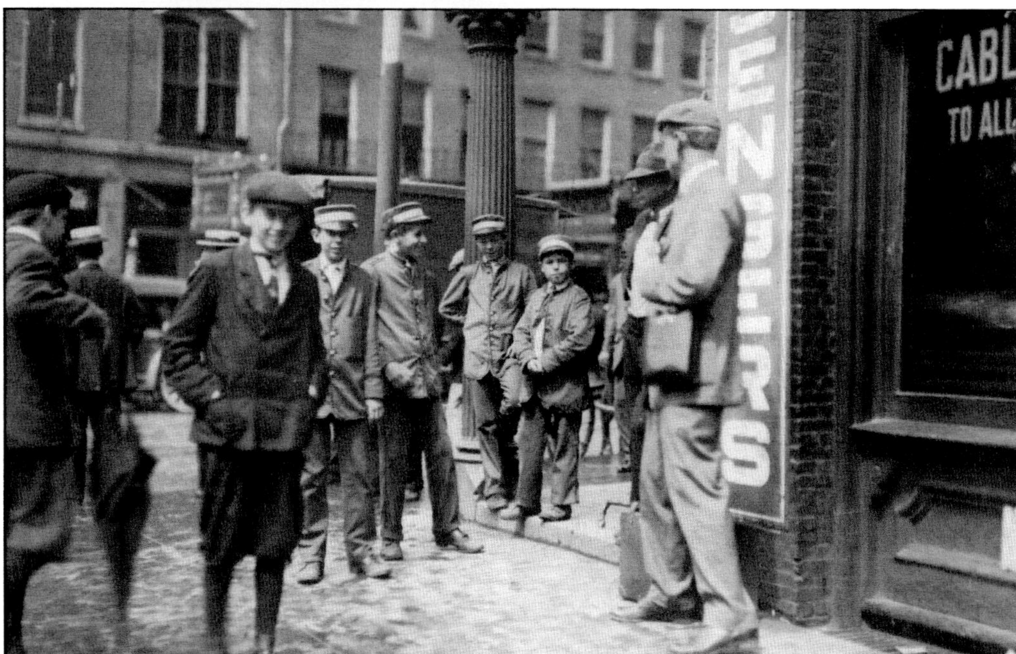

By the 1910s, it was clear that the days of the telegraph messenger boy were numbered. In 1908, the postmaster general announced a policy of no longer hiring young boys as special delivery messengers. That year, the Chicago post offices still had 337 boys on its payroll, Philadelphia had 114, and Boston only 37. This 1911 photograph shows messenger boys in Fall River. These boys were ready to dash off with telegrams from the local cable office. Their uniform jackets had large pouch pockets to secure the tools of the trade: message envelopes, notebook, and pencil.

Ready for another trip into the cold, Abe Singer, 14, sets out to deliver a bouquet and a parcel tied up with string from the Wax Brothers Florists shop on February 2, 1917. Abe's duties included tending the door, cleaning the store, and delivering flowers and parcels.

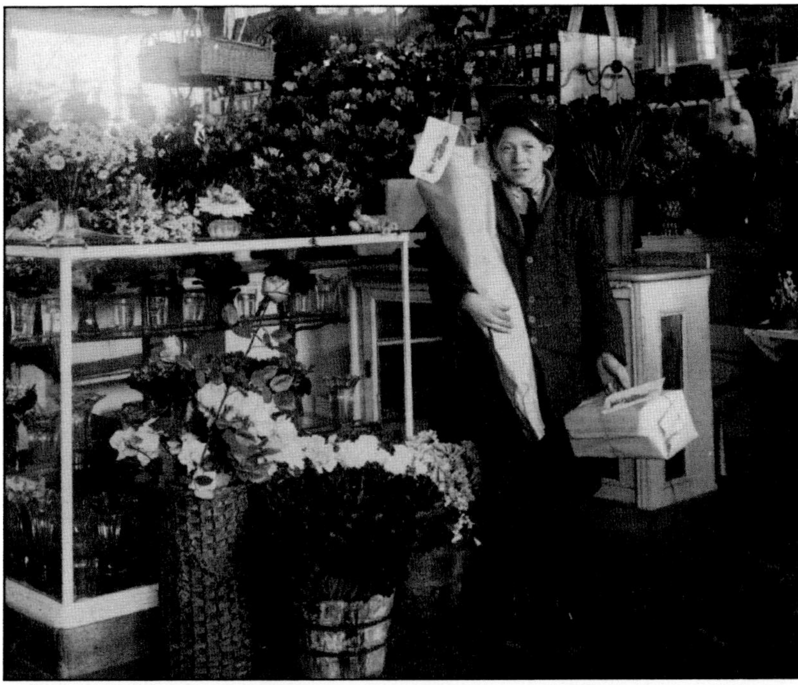

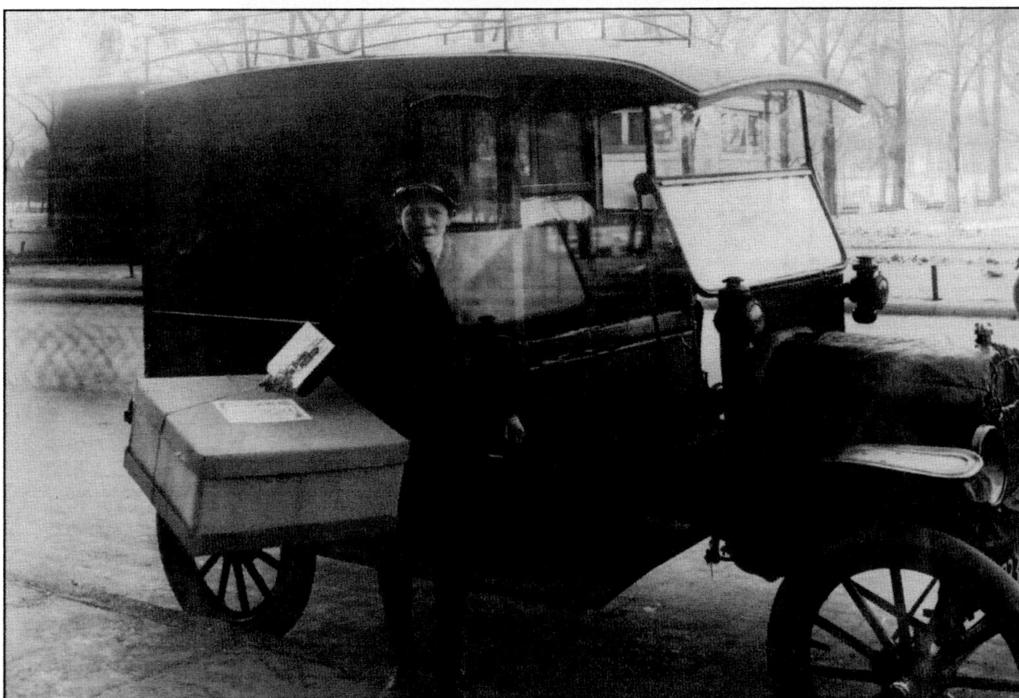

A delivery boy and a delivery truck for Wax Brothers Florists, 143 Tremont Street, Boston, are seen here. Abe Singer prepares for a delivery. Behind him, across Tremont Street, is the Boston Common, with the subway entrance just visible. The hood of the truck is wrapped in an insulating cover: the high temperature that day was 28 degrees Fahrenheit. Driving gloves are tucked under the cushion of the open-air driver's seat.

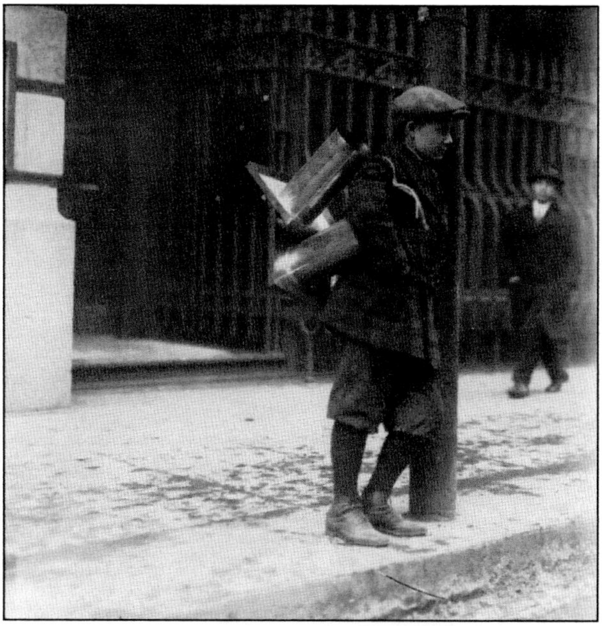

Edward Williams, a 14-year-old messenger for William H. Mitchell & Sons, Co. pauses on his way to deliver ventilation pipes to a work site. The Mitchell plumbing company, at 1 Province Court in downtown Boston, paid Edward $5 a week. Edward lived at 328 East Street, South Boston, an 1873 High Victorian-Gothic structure designed by Boston architect Alexander R. Estey and known as the Monks Building due to its early use as offices of Monks & Co. flour and grain dealers.

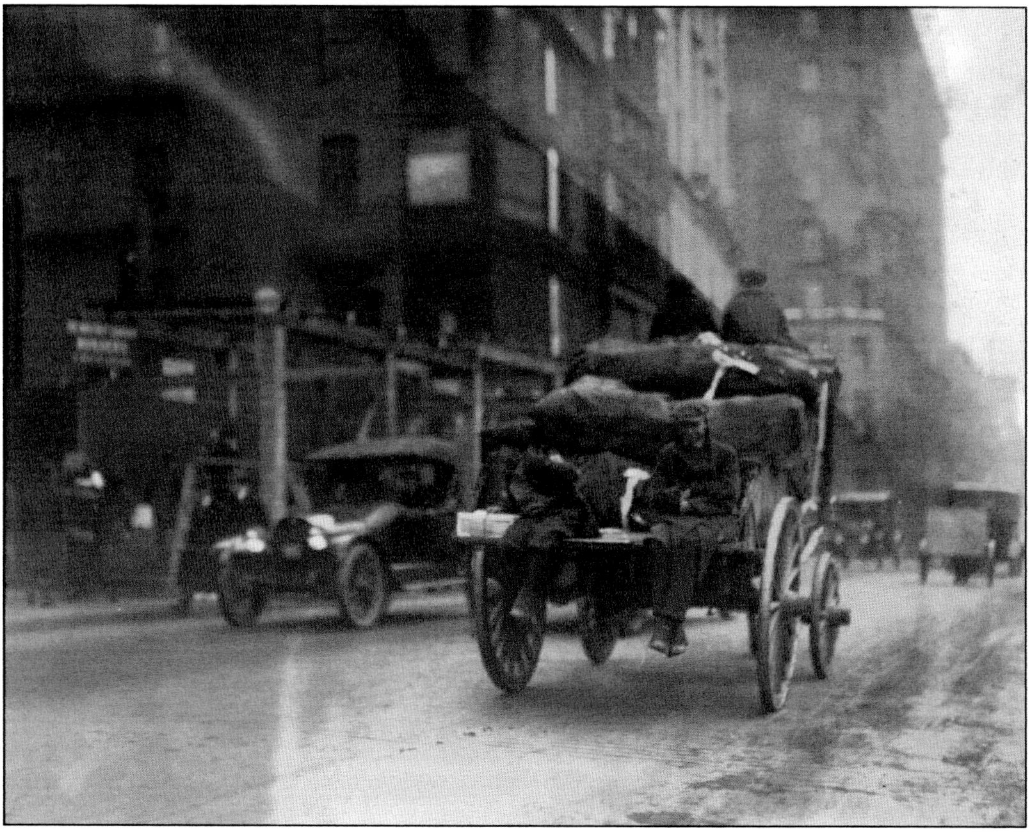

Two hunched delivery boys are grateful to hitch a ride on the back of a wagon on a cold January afternoon in Boston in 1917. One boy rests his hand on the box he is about to deliver. Tremont Street is busy with automobiles, horse carts, and construction.

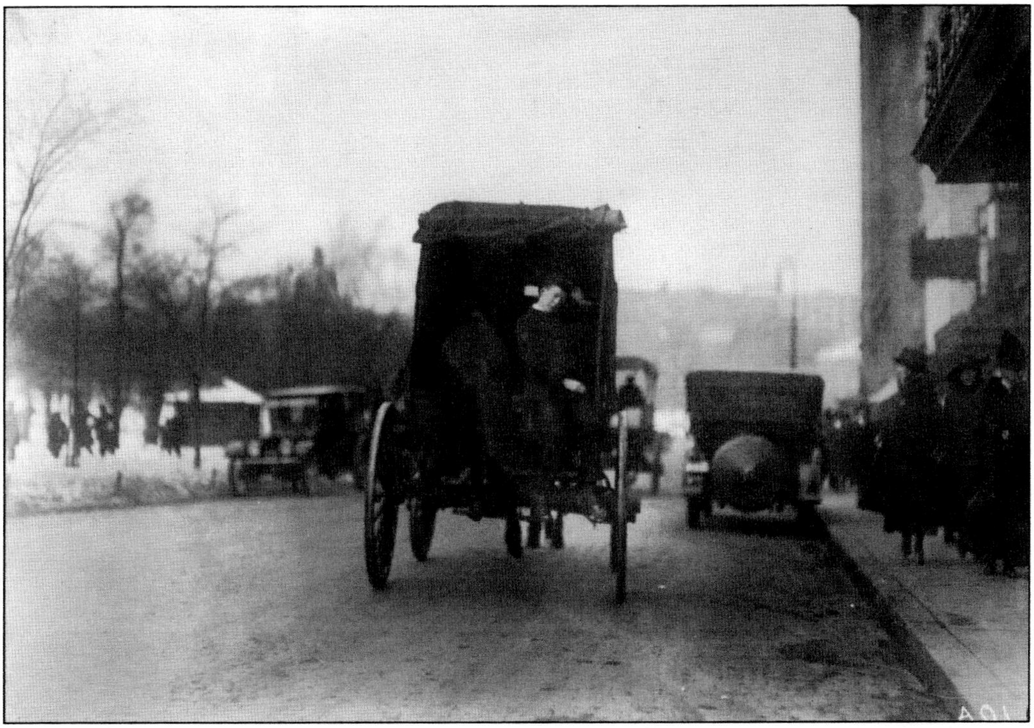

Another delivery van moves along Tremont Street one cold January day, with Boston Common on the left. Delivery boys are huddled in the back of the van. By 1917, automobiles and motorized delivery vans were fast displacing horse-drawn vehicles.

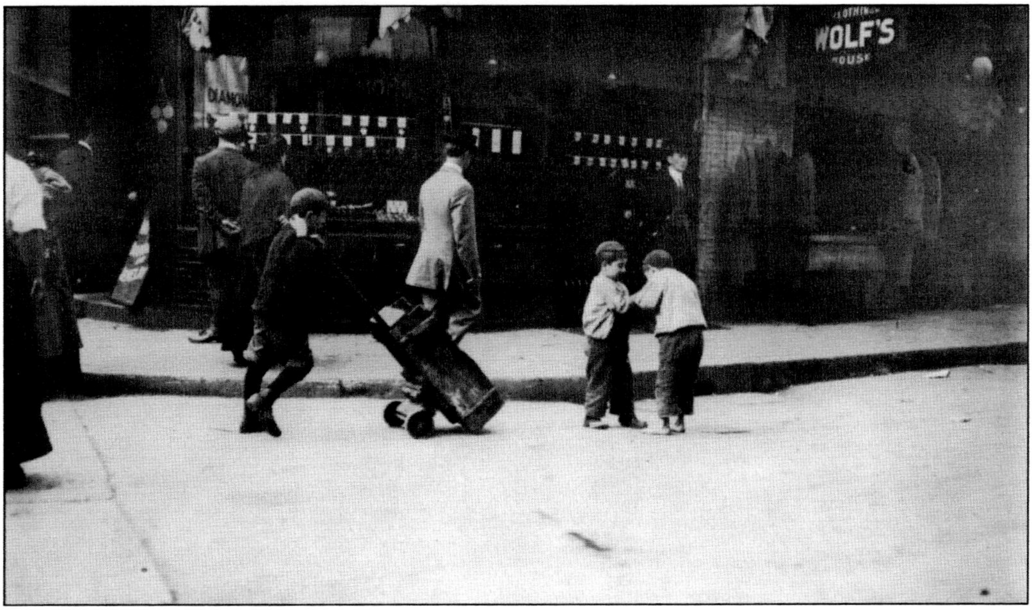

Small street boys share a cigarette. These unsupervised little urchins look no older than six; one is barefoot on this October day in 1909. None of the adults nearby takes any interest in the scene unfolding in front of a pawnbroker's shop. The little fellows will have to make way for a hard-working bigger boy, wheeling a load.

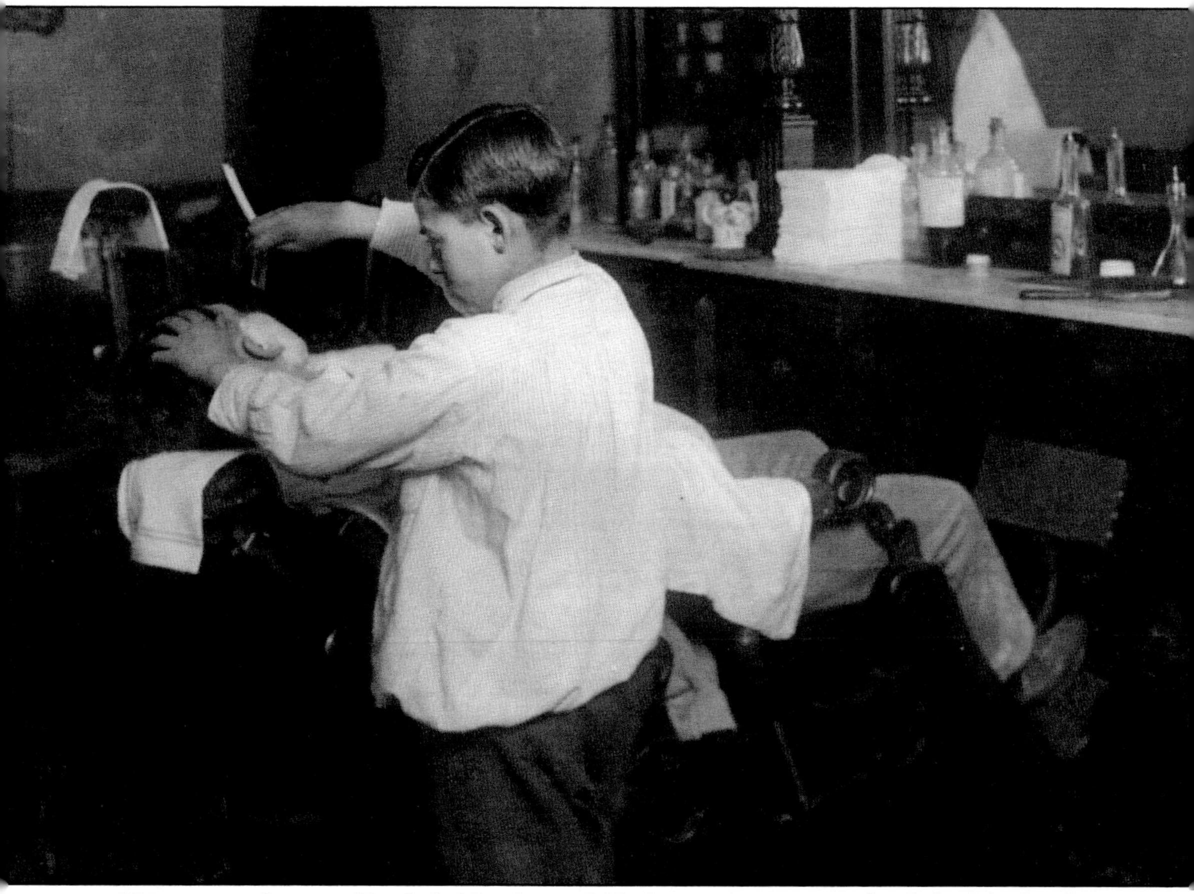

Using a straight razor, Frank de Natale, aged 12, shaves a customer at his father's barbershop on Hanover Street in Boston's North End. Frank attended school in the mornings and worked as a barber in the afternoons and on Saturdays. The date is February 1, 1917. Less than two years later, a 50-foot-high tank exploded on Commercial Street, five blocks away, propelling 2.3 million gallons of molasses in a destructive flood that knocked down buildings, killed 21 people, and injured 150. The de Natale barbershop, a safe distance away, survived. Today, a coin-operated laundry occupies the commercial space.

Four

Tenement Work

Before the Civil War, Massachusetts was the leading textile producing state of the nation. After the war, Boston emerged as the nation's leading center for ready-made clothing, but the Fire of 1872 severely disrupted the clothing industry.

Because of mass immigration, the townhouses of Boston's South End, West End, and North End were subdivided into crowded rental tenements in conditions hardly fit for human habitation. Middlemen found it cheaper to bypass the factories and sent work to immigrant families willing to work at home for starvation wages. By the 1880s, the tenement sweatshop system was as pervasive in Boston as it was in New York, Chicago, and Philadelphia.

In 1895, Rufus R. Wade, the chief of the Massachusetts district police, wrote:

> No more serious problem has developed in recent years . . . than that relating to the manufacture of clothing in tenement-houses. The sweatshop system has made rapid strides in Boston and some of the other cities of the commonwealth. The people who toil twelve to fourteen hours in the sweat shops for less than the means of comfortable subsistence, and, in addition, are compelled to employ the labor of their children to avoid starvation. . . . Little children have been found crouching upon piles of garments in various stages of manufacture. Their slight strength enlisted in some parts of the work, shut out from the air and sunlight, and in an atmosphere foul with unmentionable forms of filth.

In 1898, Massachusetts law forbade children younger than 14 years from working in factories, driving many children to work at home. By 1901, wages for tenement work in Massachusetts were higher than in New York. As a result, this industry rapidly moved away from Boston to the less regulated New York.

In its annual report published January 1, 1913, the Massachusetts Child Labor Committee (MCLC) reported on child labor in the tenements: "The children work long hours and often late at night, by lamplight. Small children of five, seven, and nine years of age work in a bending position. . . . This is bad for the eyes, causing mental strain, interferes with the child's schooling." The report stated that the children suffer from the work, with cut fingers, bent backs, and the lack of playtime. "These children, meagerly paid, [are] engaged in a variety of jobs including finishing men's clothing, adjusting buttons to garters, crocheting bed slippers, making chain bags, finishing suspenders and sewing buttons on shoes."

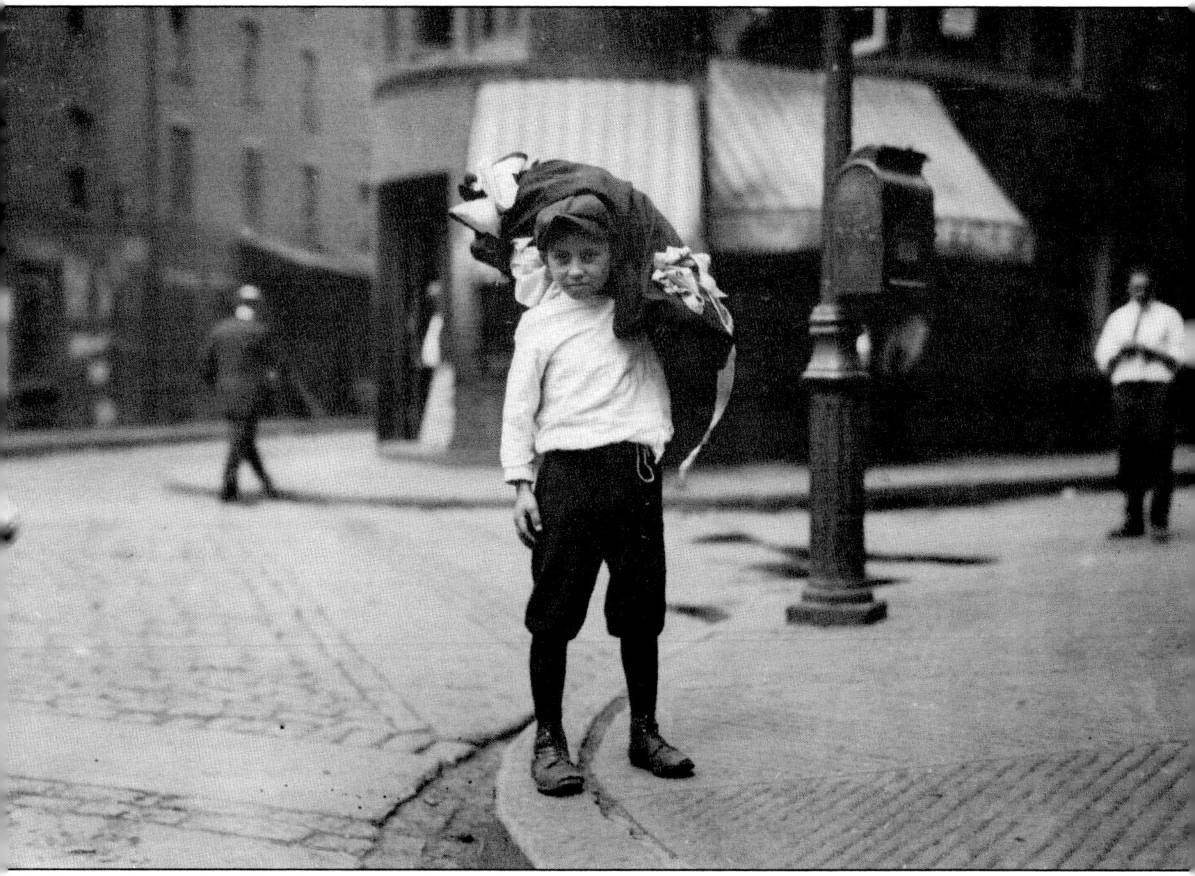

Twelve-year-old Vito Romano delivers items of clothing finished overnight at his home at 76 Charter Street, North End, Boston.

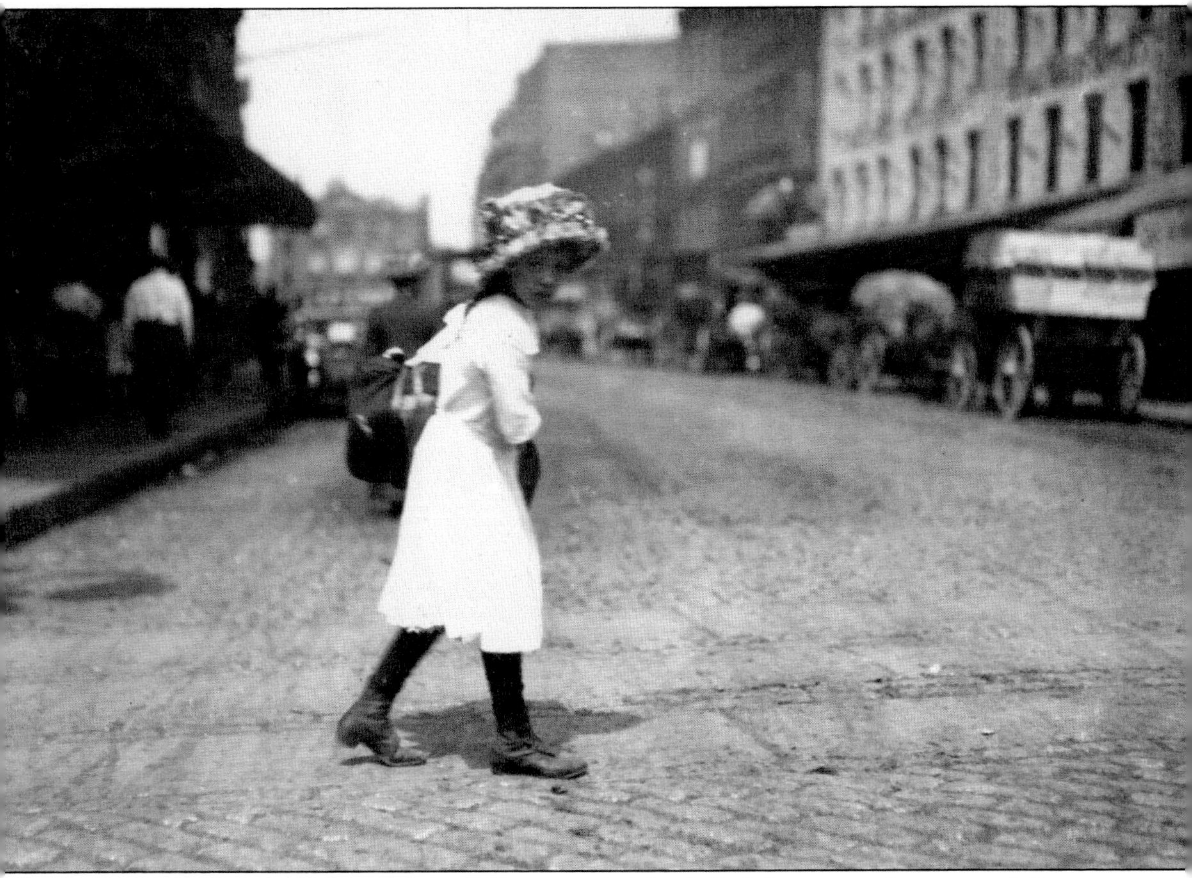

A nine-year-old girl is crossing Hanover Street, in the North End, Boston, on her way to deliver clothing. With her family, she finished eight pairs of paints a day at 8¢ a pair, a total of 64¢ for a day's work.

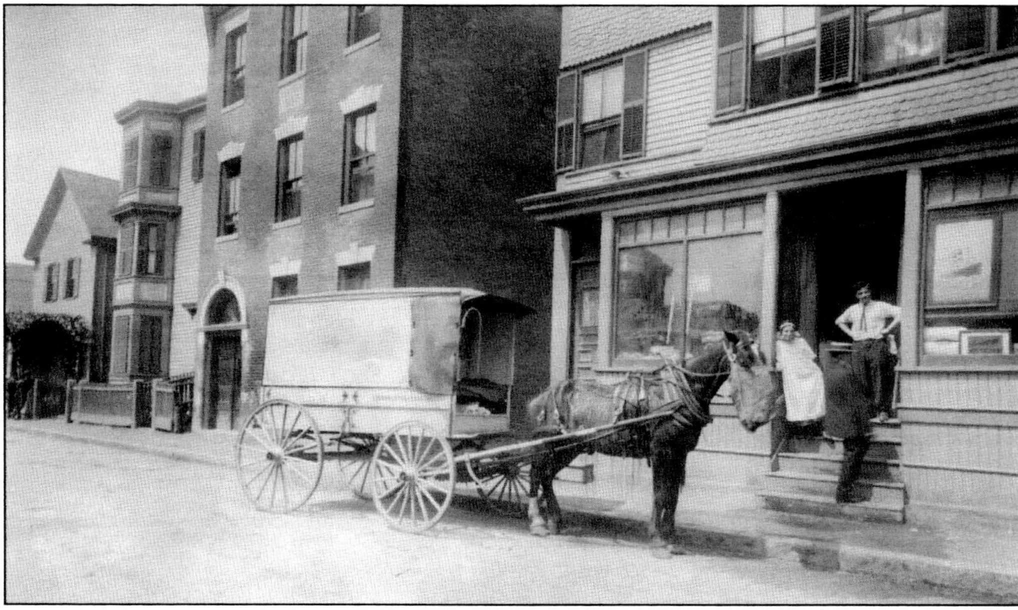

This 1912 image shows a middleman's horse-drawn wagon in use to deliver cloth to Somerville tenement homes for sewing and embroidery. Many tenement children worked with their parents. In 1913, Massachusetts law made work at home illegal for these young children. Experts claim that the monotonous work in the sweatshop saps the child's strength and alertness of mind, leaving him apathetic and lacking in vigor.

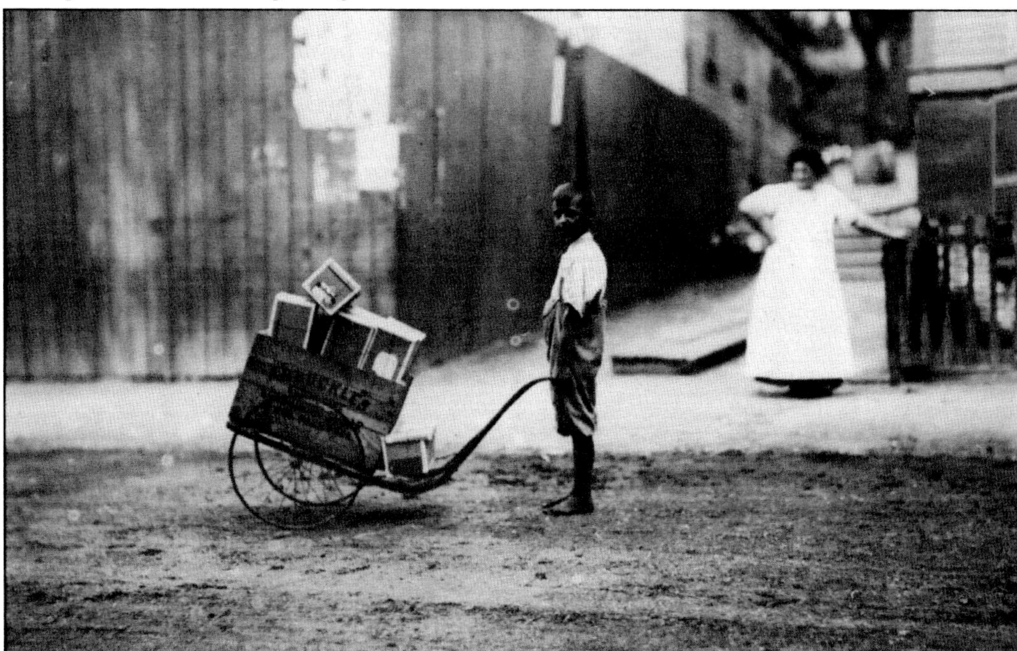

A boy is using an Arbuckle wooden crate and two-wheeled cart to carry tags for finishing to his home in Roxbury. John and Charles Arbuckle of Pittsburgh, Pennsylvania, packed roasted coffee or sugar into one-pound packages and shipped them—100 at a time—in wooden crates such as the one shown in this picture.

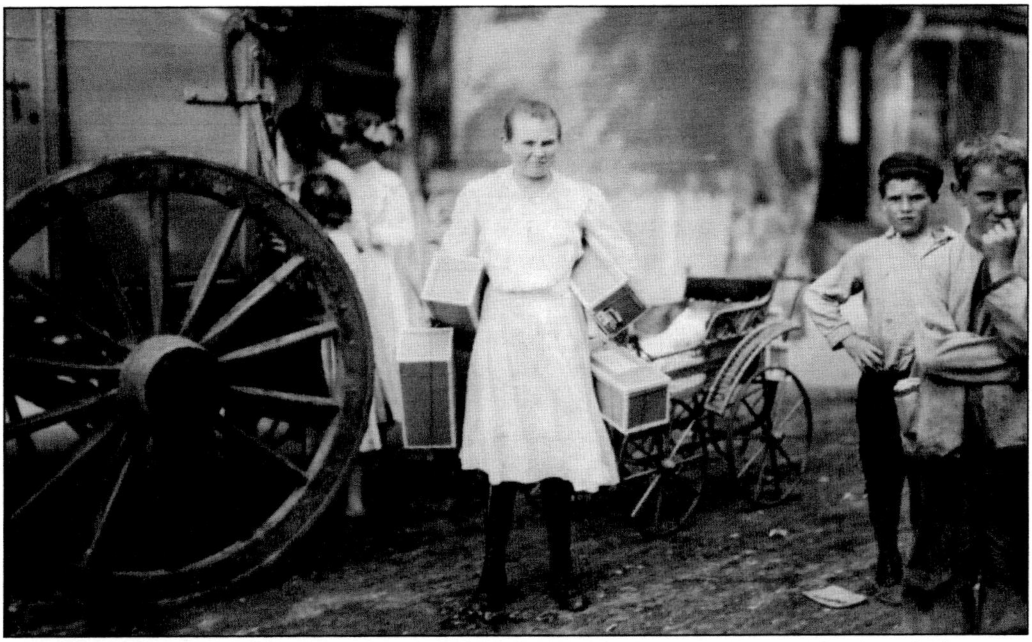

In 1880, the Dennison Manufacturing Company built a factory at the corner of Vale and Thornton Streets in Roxbury. The company contracted with people in the houses surrounding the factory to do piecework. This 1912 picture shows a girl carrying home a load of tags from Dennison's for tying and packing.

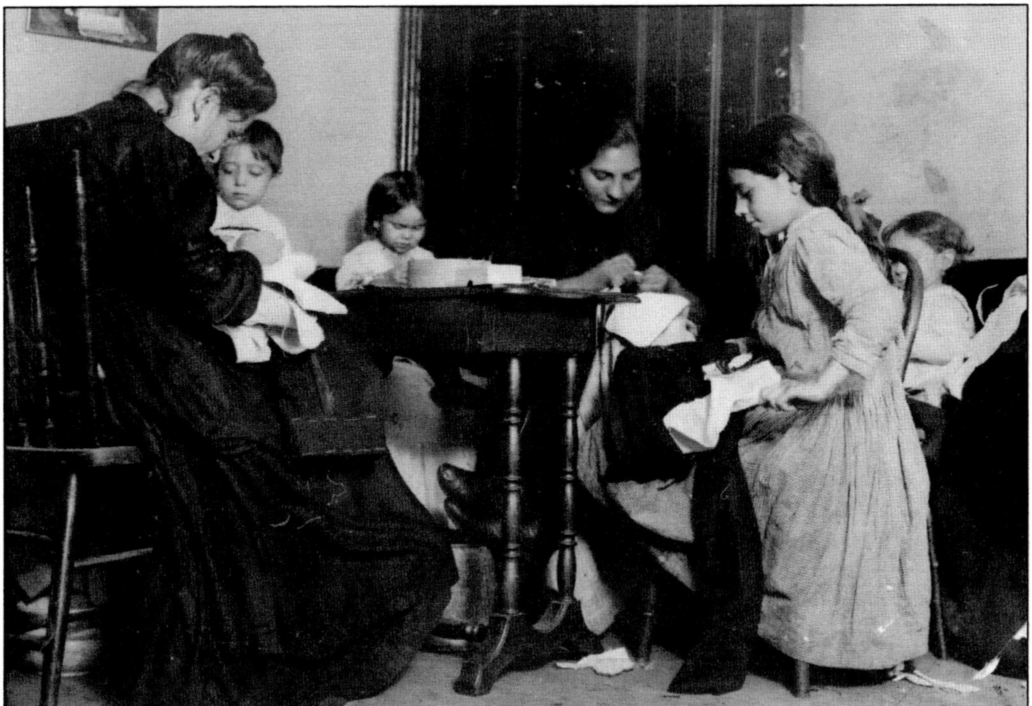

Thirteen-year-old Catina Termine, at right, sits with her mother and siblings around the table at 10 Hanover Street doing piecework for a clothing company. Smaller children watch and try to help.

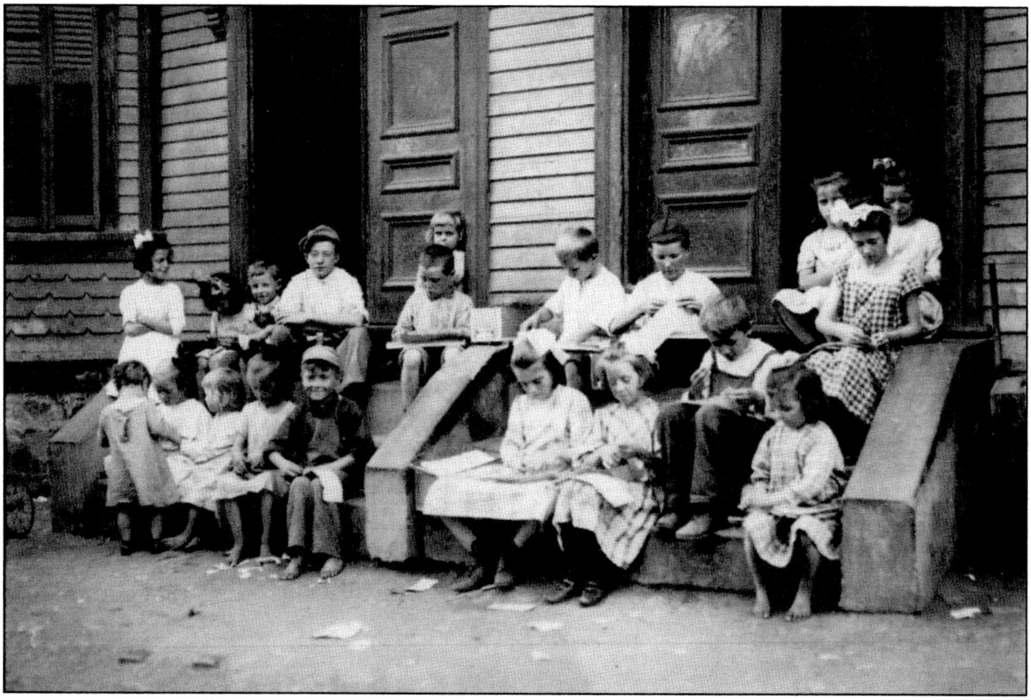

A Mrs. McCarthy lived at 88 Marcella Street, Roxbury, a few blocks away from the Dennison Manufacturing Company at the corner of Vale and Thornton Streets. As a subcontractor, she mobilized local children to tie pieces of string to the Dennison tags.

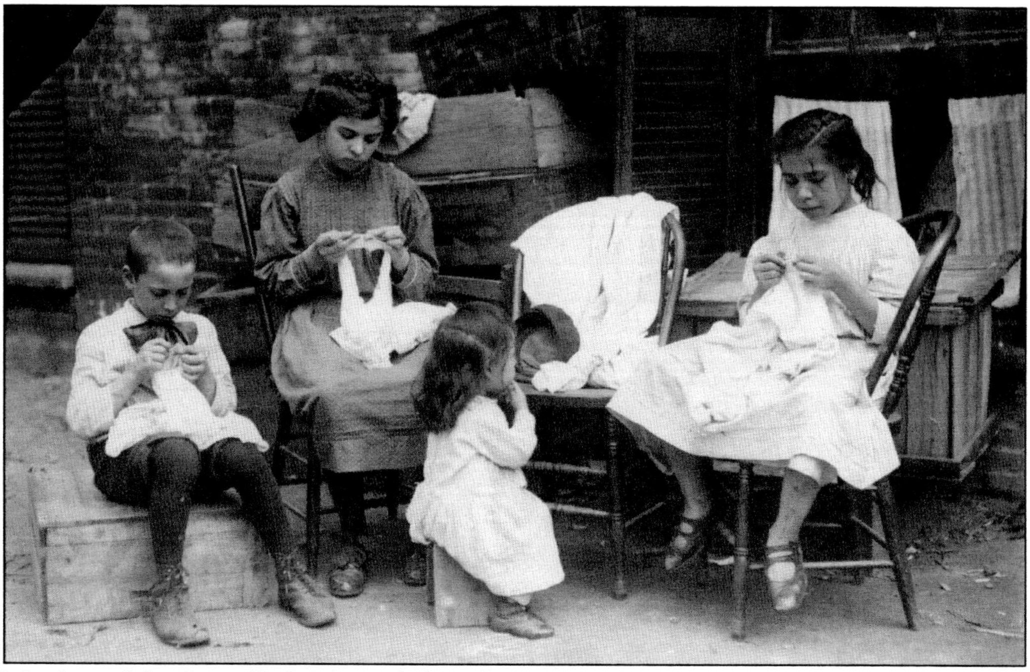

Members of the Catarella family, including the son, are doing crochet work in the backyard of their home in Somerville in 1909. Joe Catarella, age 9; his cousin Mary Lazzaro, age 13; and his sister Lena, age 10, crochet as the younger sister watches attentively.

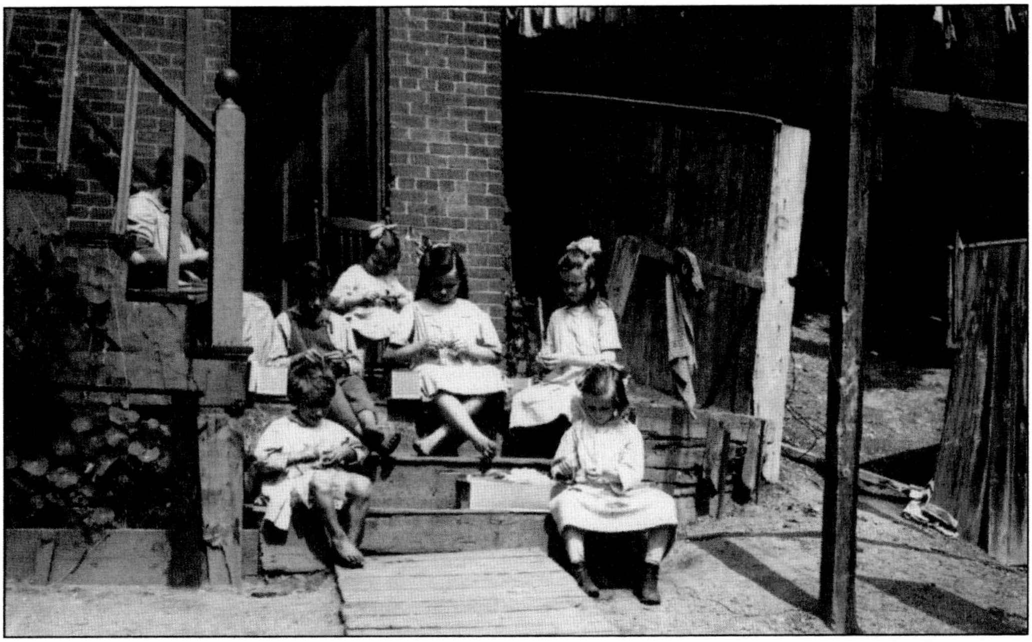

A Mrs. Donovan and her family at 295 Highland Street, Roxbury, are tying tags for Dennison Manufacturing Company in this 1912 image. Her children, aged 12, 11, 9, 7, and twins of 4 years, helped with the work, often until late at night. The family made $30 a month on average. Dennison's ran a factory in Boston, as well as a larger one in Framingham, and operated retail stores in Boston, New York, Philadelphia, and Chicago.

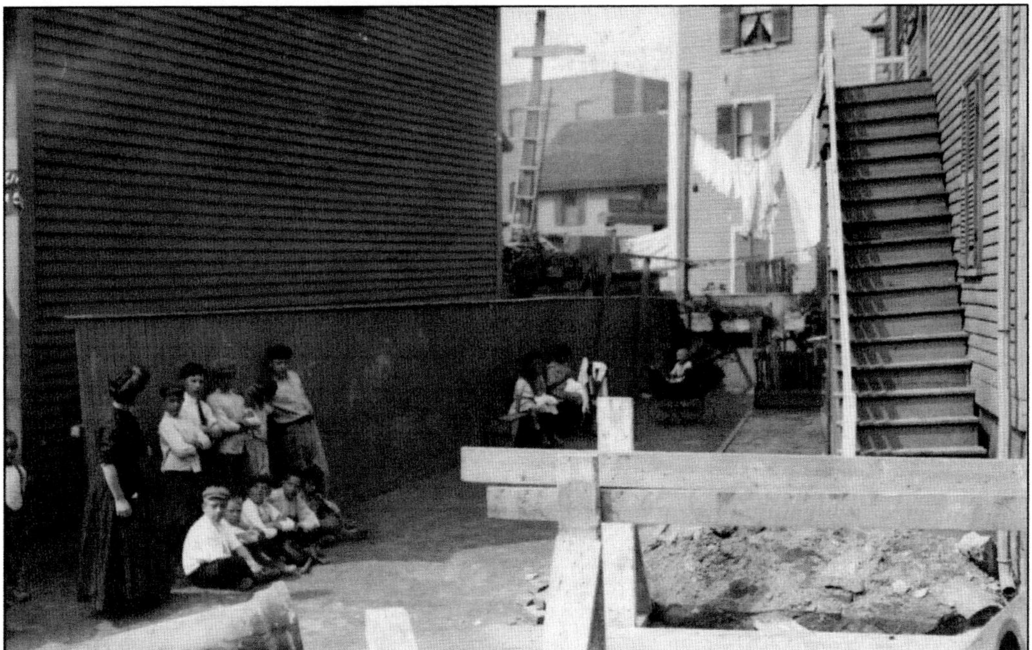

In this 1912 photograph, boys and girls are seen taking a break from work at 52 Medford Street, Somerville.

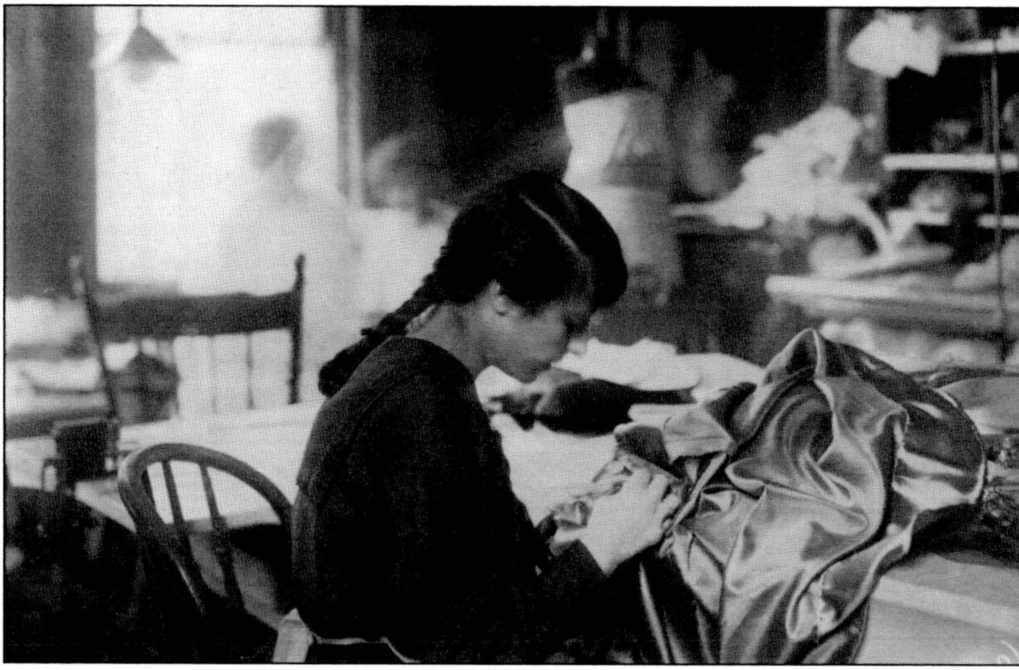

Angelina Guinzali, age 15, works at Madame Ball, a dressmaker at 603 Boylston Street, Boston, in 1917. The Boston city directory for 1910 listed 696 dressmakers working out of their homes. A third, including Madame Ball, are custom dressmakers that hire junior staff. The large department stores sell ready-to-wear clothing.

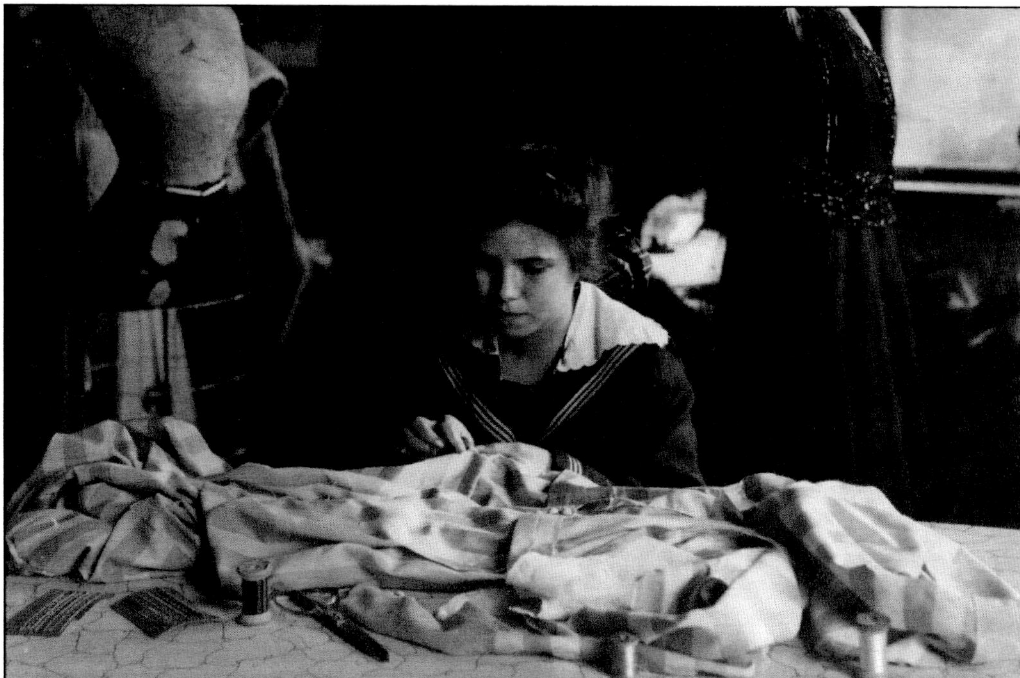

Helen Anderson, age 16, works for Madame Robinson's Gowns, another custom dressmaker, located in the Pierce Building at Copley Square in 1917.

In 1828, Jennie Collins was born in Amoskeag, New Hampshire. As a girl, she worked in the textile mills of Lowell and Lawrence. She moved to Boston and became an advocate for working girls and women, campaigning for the eight-hour workday and votes for women.

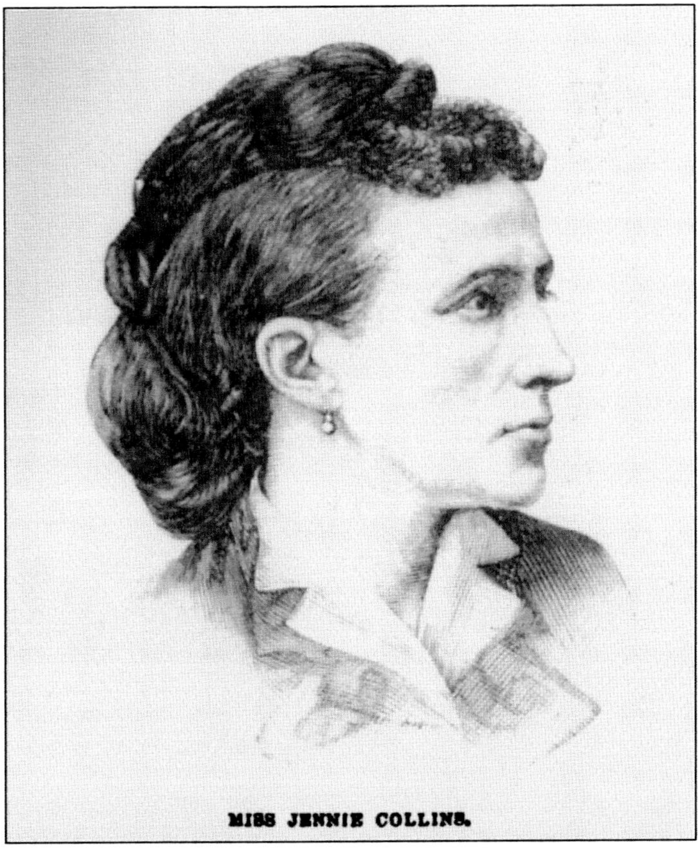

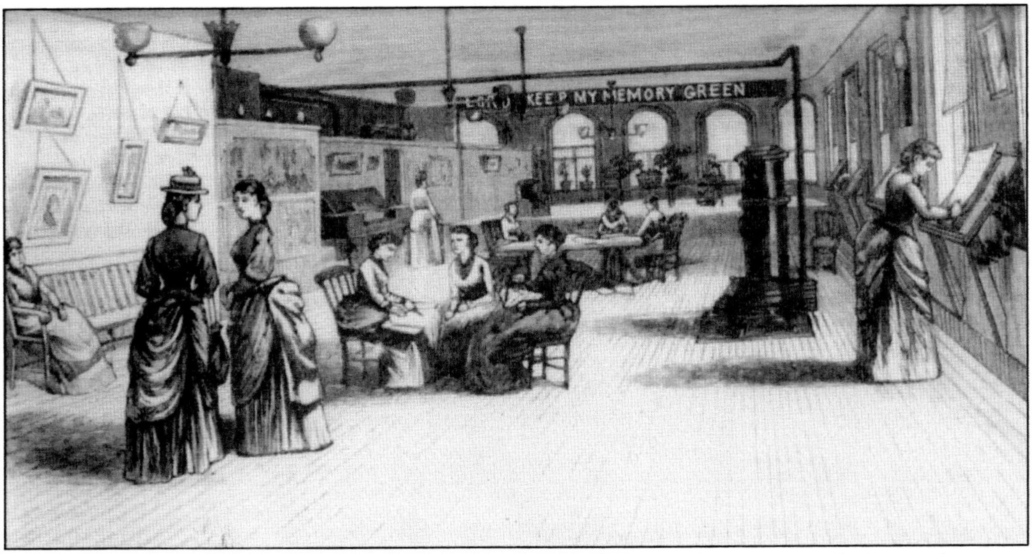

In 1870, Jennie Collins opened Boffin's Bower on Washington Street, named after a character in Charles Dickens's *Our Mutual Friend*. With its reading room, piano, and cafeteria, Boffin's Bower became a meeting place for out-of-town girls and women working in the clothing factories. Following the Fire of 1872 that destroyed several of the clothing factories, out of work girls found food and shelter at Boffin's Bower.

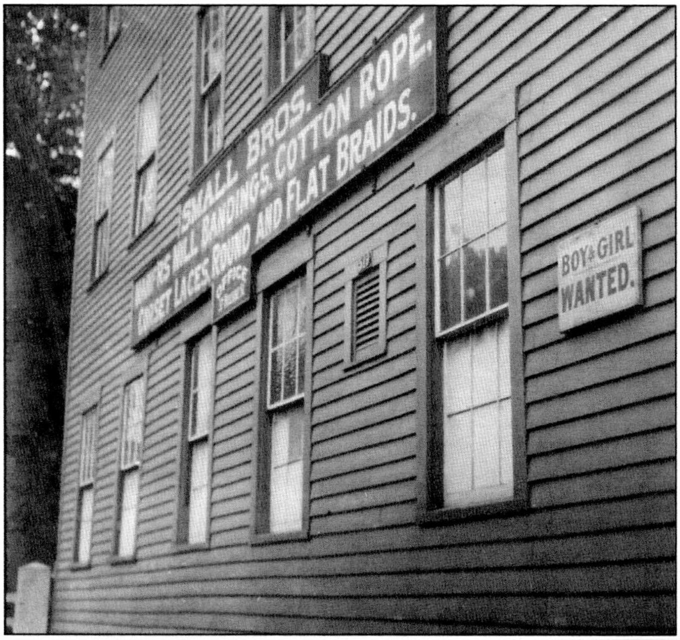

Located at Fall River, Small Brothers were makers of cotton rope and other cotton products. The sign seen in this c. 1910 photograph shows that the company sought to hire boys and girls. Rope making began in Boston in 1641 for use on ships, fishing nets, and rope bridges. The trade expanded to other towns, including Plymouth and Fall River.

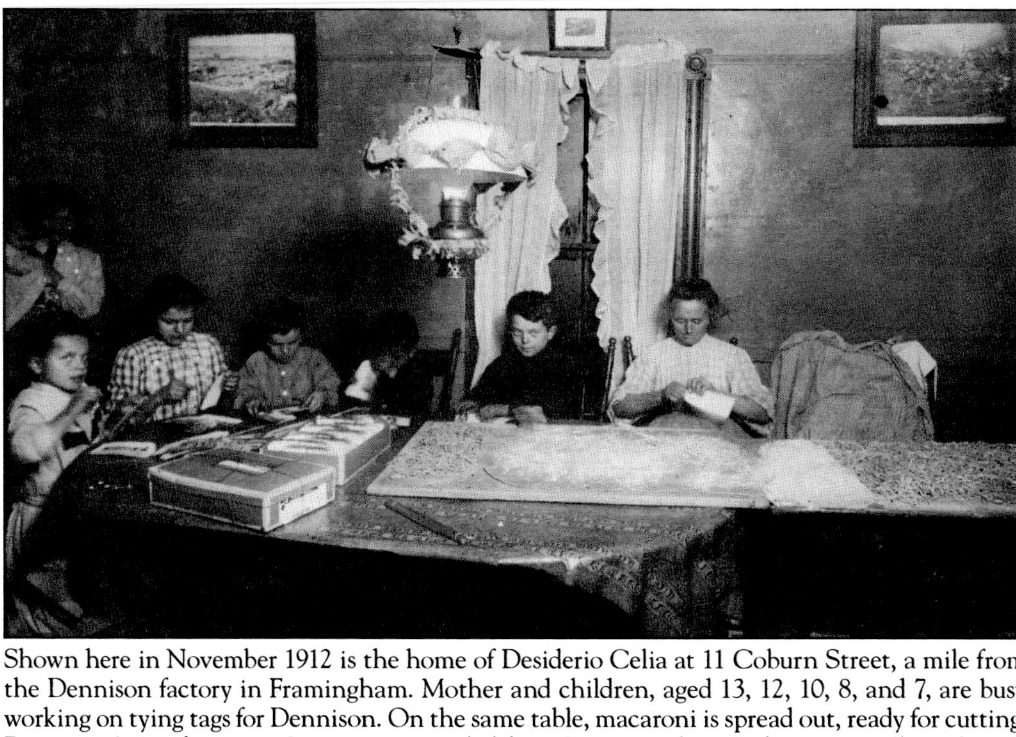

Shown here in November 1912 is the home of Desiderio Celia at 11 Coburn Street, a mile from the Dennison factory in Framingham. Mother and children, aged 13, 12, 10, 8, and 7, are busy working on tying tags for Dennison. On the same table, macaroni is spread out, ready for cutting. Dennison Manufacturing Company expanded from Boston and opened its Framingham factory in 1897. Known as the "Tag Makers," the company sold Handy Boxes "containing a collection of articles which are in constant use in the home," such as shipping tags, key tags, marking tags, rubber bands, paper clips, and gummed labels, at a cost per box of $2. Dennison's in Framingham followed its Boston factory practice of sending out work to homes close by the factory. Dennison was the largest employer in Framingham.

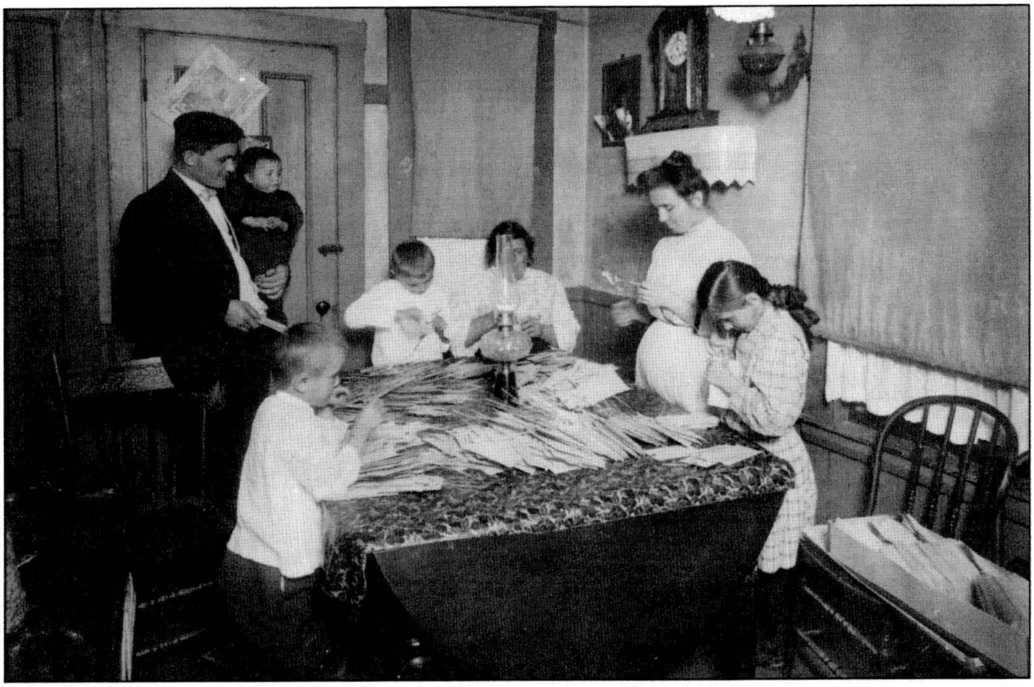

The home of Rufini Morini and his family, at 6 Coburn Street, Framingham, is seen in this November 1912 photograph. Mrs. Morini and another mother are busy working on tags for Dennison with three children, aged 10, 8, and 6. Each family earns about $10 a month from the tags.

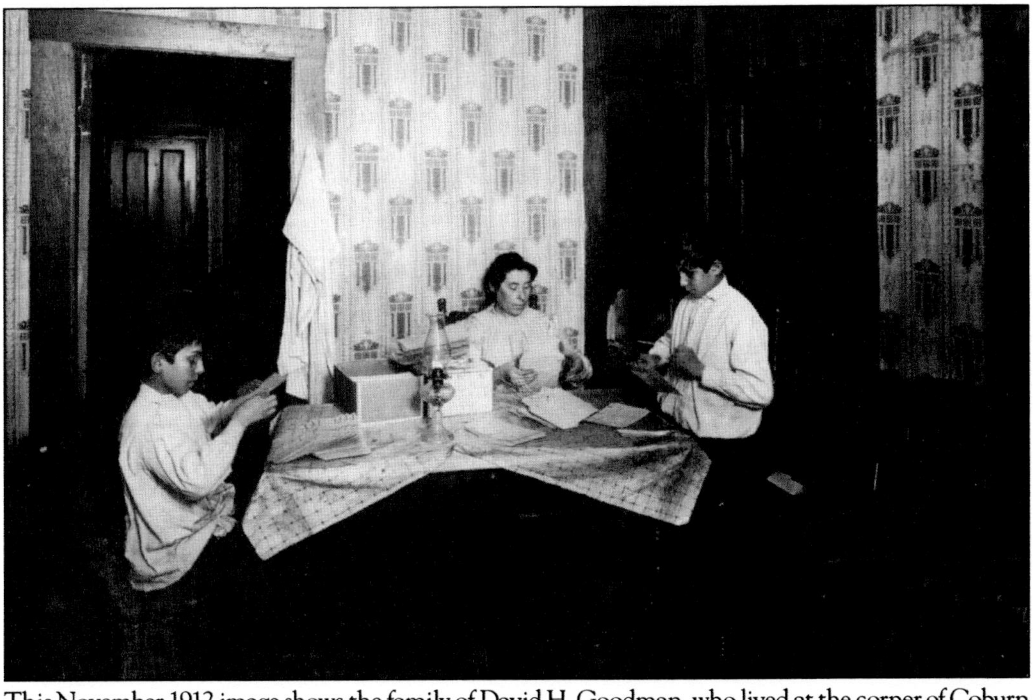

This November 1912 image shows the family of David H. Goodman, who lived at the corner of Coburn and Mellen Streets in Framingham. Mother and children, aged 14 and 10, are busy working on tags for Dennison. David is an umbrella mender. The family income is between $25 and $35 a month.

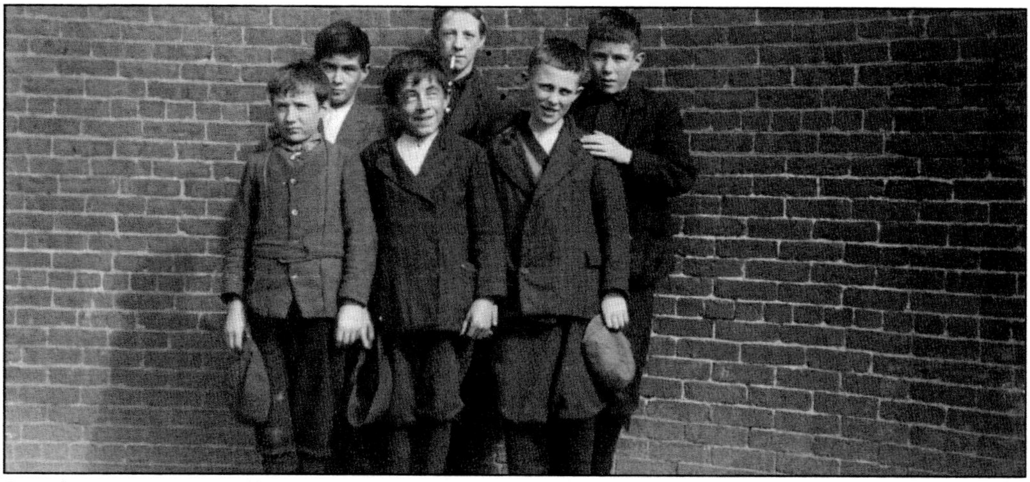

Seen here are a group of boys employed at the Dennison Manufacturing Company in Framingham in October 1911. From left to right are (first row) Robert Magee, Edward Foster, and John Neary; (second row) Cornelius Hurley, John Risheck, and Michael Keefe.

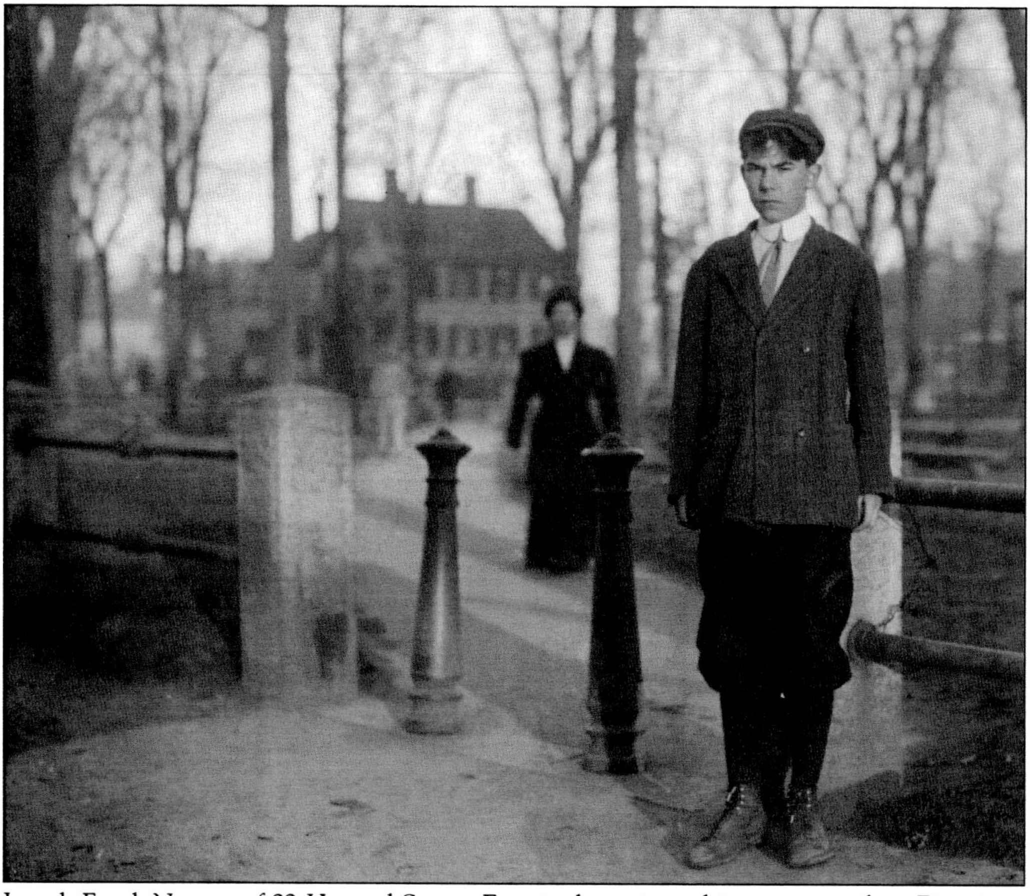

Joseph Frank Nugent of 22 Howard Street, Framingham, is on his way to work at Dennison Manufacturing Company in October 1911. Employed in Department 8A, Joseph makes paper boxes.

Five

SCAVENGERS

The Massachusetts Child Labor Committee (MCLC) reported in 1915 on child scavengers, saying, "More than 500 children in Boston alone" were engaged in scavenging or stealing. A child seen roaming around the markets "with a sack slung over his shoulder" was likely a scavenger. Such a child "searched for fruit, vegetables, pieces of meat, fish heads, almost anything which can be eaten or can be made into soup. Some of the material is discarded refuse, which they have the right to take [but] much of the material is obtained by petty larceny, which hurts their morals. . . . These children go also into ash barrels and pick up even worse rubbish than in the market. . . . Frequently children pick from refuse barrels material, which they can eat on the spot."

Children at demolition sites scampered over piles of rubble and scaffolding, collecting wood or coal to take home or sell. In 1914, Dr. Joel E. Goldthwait, chief of the orthopedic department at Massachusetts General Hospital, reported that the children were "permanently injured by the constant strain involved in carrying loads for long distances."

Children collected coal from the factory yards, dumps, wharves, and barrels. Children "even jump on passing coal trains in order to steal coal." Children as young as five years old daily rummaged through the city refuse dumps, collecting rags, cans, glass containers, pieces of wood, or discarded clothing. The MCLC report of 1915 described child scavenging in Boston:

> They pick with bare toes sticking out of their shoes, on the coldest winter days. Their hands shake so they barely hold their bags. The ashes crack the skin. Barrels and boxes are obtained from the market, and from the downtown stores, sometimes the boys are given the barrels, frequently they "crook" or steal them. The boys sell the boxes and barrels to small stores and dealers for five, ten or fifteen cents. Many children are compelled to bring wood home every evening, under penalty of being beaten. This leads them to steal wood. Coal is gathered at dumps, ash barrels, wharves, yards of large factories, and railroad yards. It frequently involves trespassing and the work in rail yards is very dangerous. The children even jump on passing coal trains, in order to steal coal. . . . Work at dumps is dangerous to the health, self-respect, and morals of children.

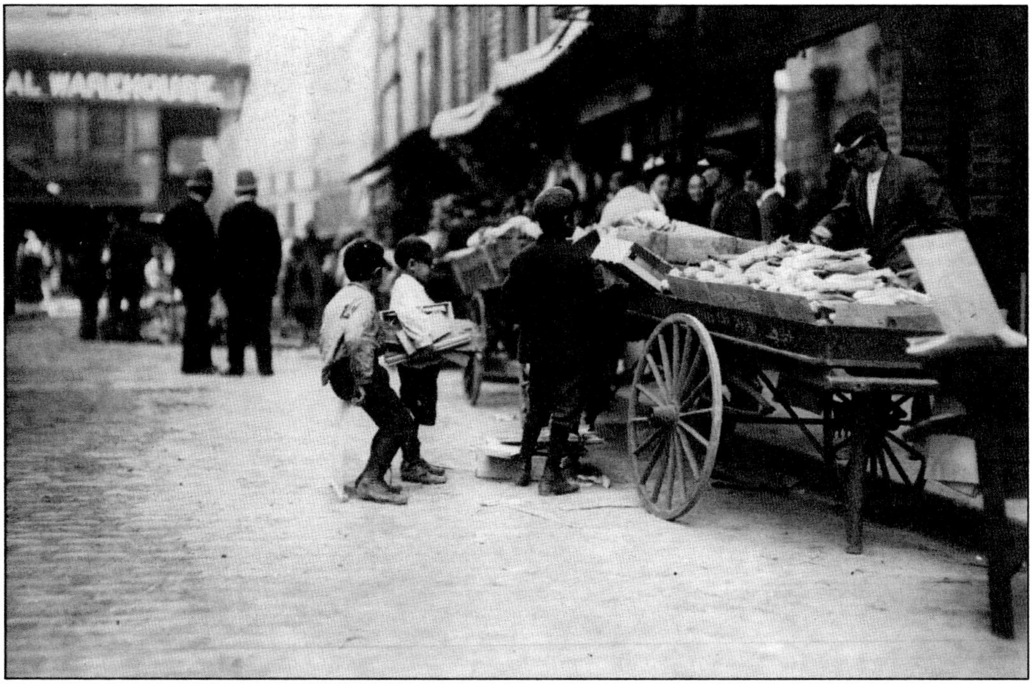

The boys here are collecting wooden crates for firewood from a pushcart dealer at a Boston street market in 1909. Two policemen stand nearby. According to the Massachusetts Child Labor Committee (MCLC), "more than 500 children in Boston alone" were engaged in scavenging or stealing.

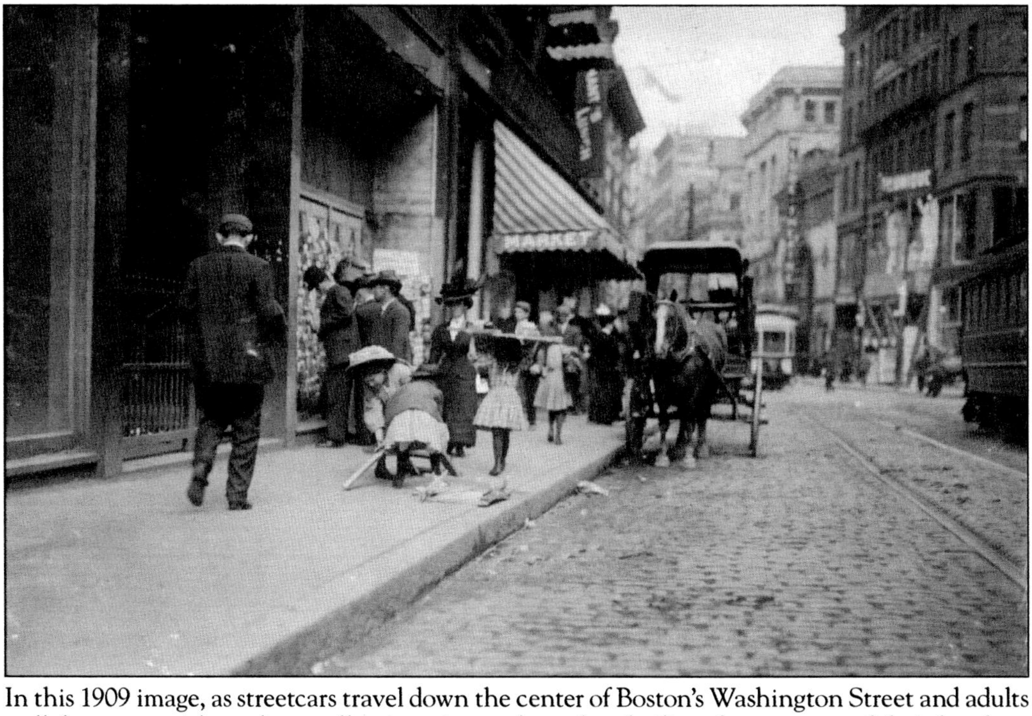

In this 1909 image, as streetcars travel down the center of Boston's Washington Street and adults walk by, young girls are busy collecting pieces of wood and piling them on top of their heads to carry home.

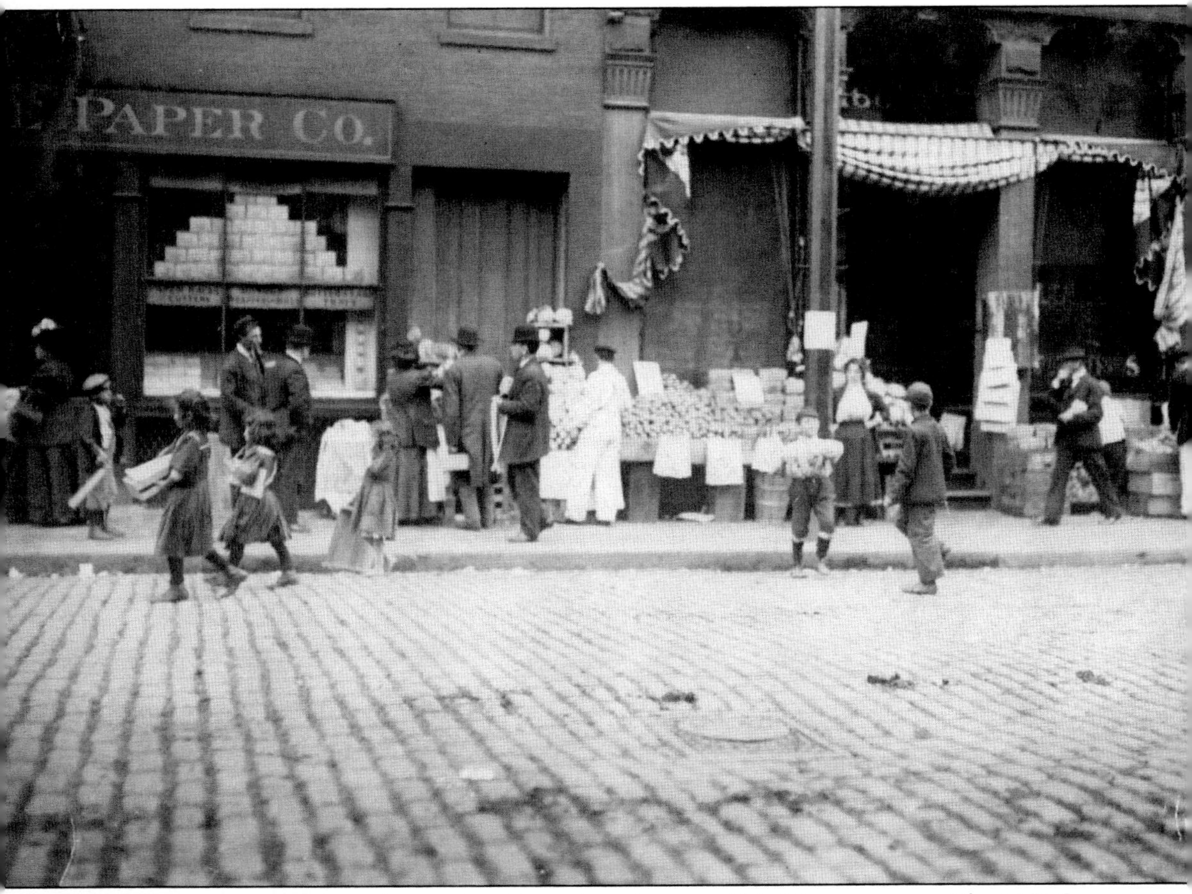

Girls are seen scavenging wood at a sidewalk market along a cobbled Boston street. The MCLC reported in 1915 that a child seen roaming around the markets "with a sack slung over his shoulder" was a likely scavenger searching "for fruit, vegetables, pieces of meat, fish heads, almost anything that can be eaten or can be made into soup."

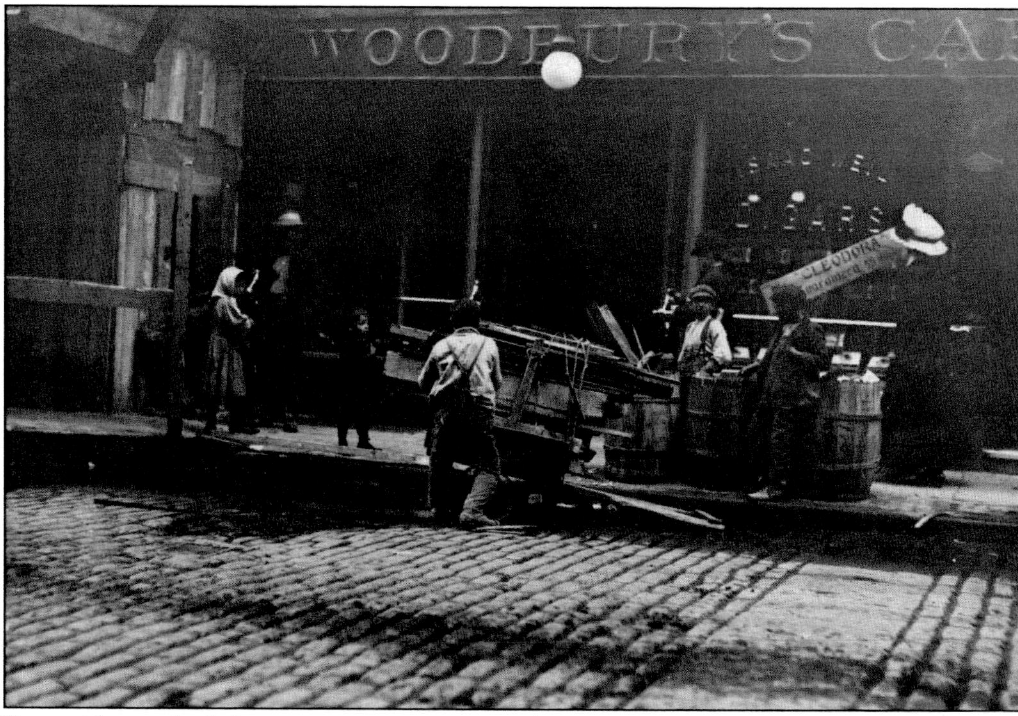

Boys with a makeshift cart are scavenging wood at a construction site. Some of the wood is discarded but "much of the material is obtained by petty larceny, which hurts their morals."

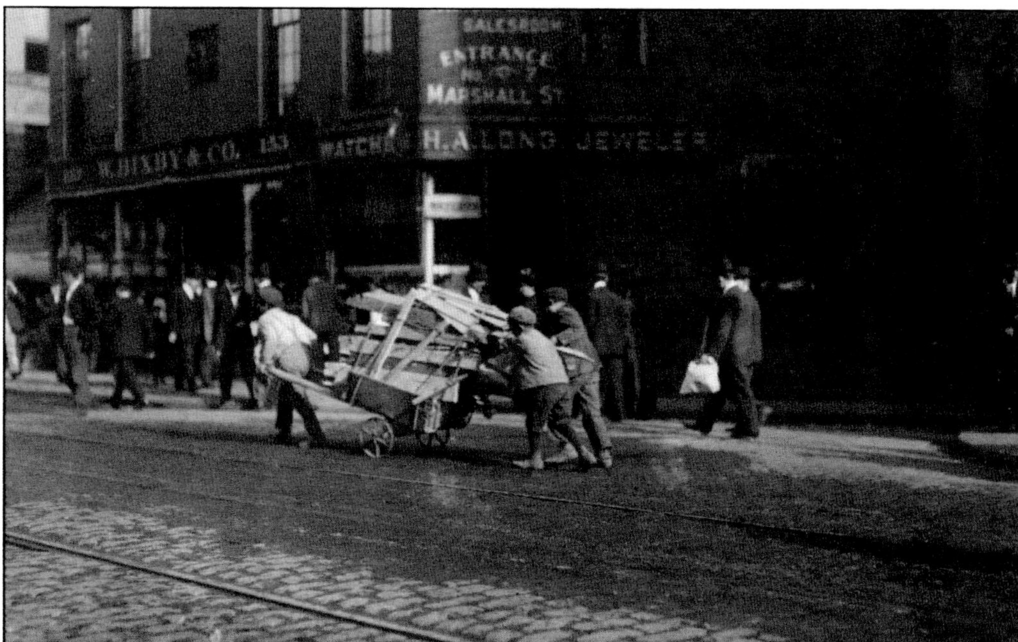

With one pulling and two pushing the wood-laden cart, the boys are headed down Washington Street along the streetcar tracks. People walking along seem hardly to notice. The boys will sell the wood or take it home for firewood.

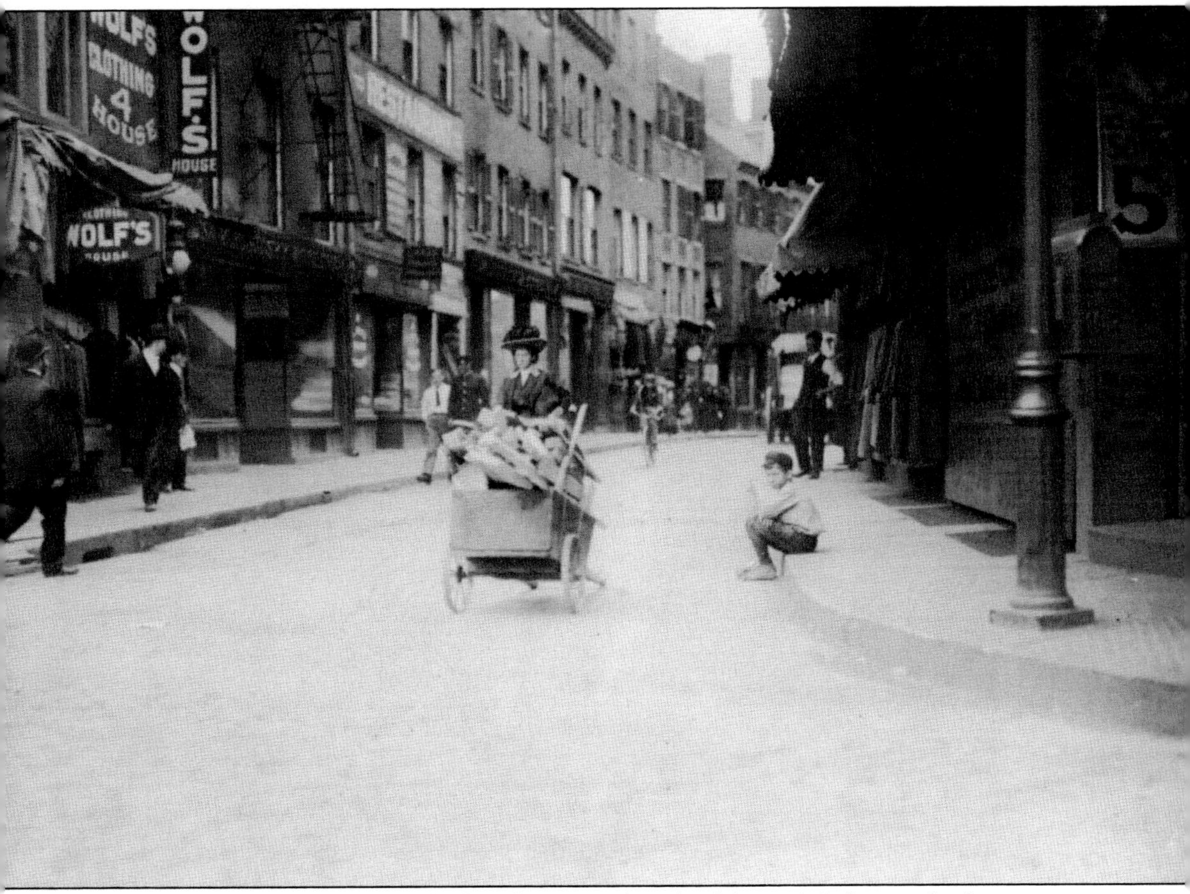

A little boy is sitting on a North End sidewalk, resting from his labors while leaving his heavy cart in the middle of the street. He has collected pieces of wood along the way. Scavenging without permission could land a child in the Boston Juvenile Court. In 1906, Harvey Humphreys Baker (1869–1915) was appointed chief judge of the Boston Juvenile Court. A progressive, he opposed placing children in jails alongside adult offenders. He adopted a clinical approach, believing that the child in trouble needed help rather than punishment.

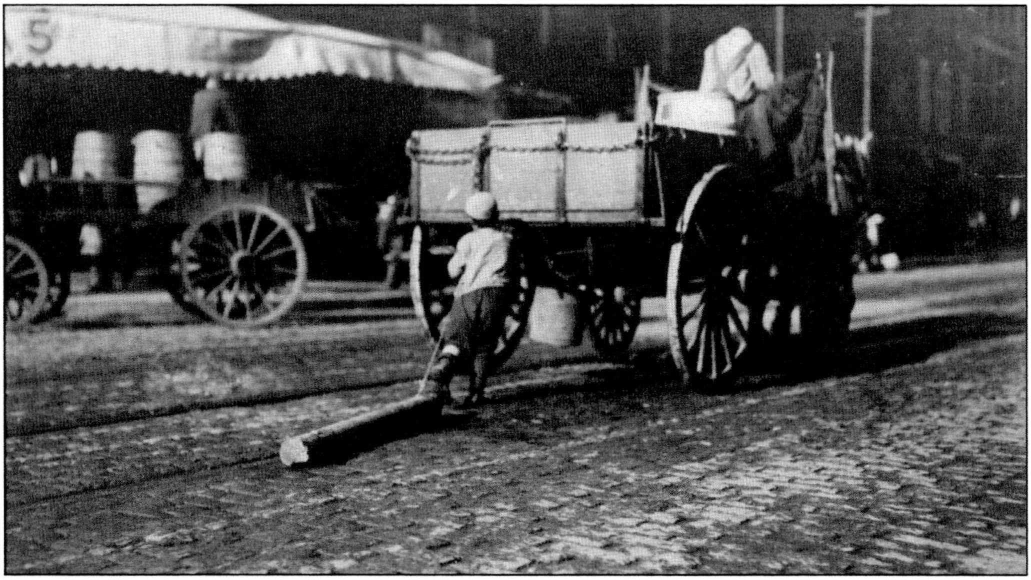

This 1909 image shows another Washington Street scene. The small boy has acquired a log of wood too heavy for him to carry. He is busy tying the log to the back of a horse-drawn cart traveling in the direction of his home.

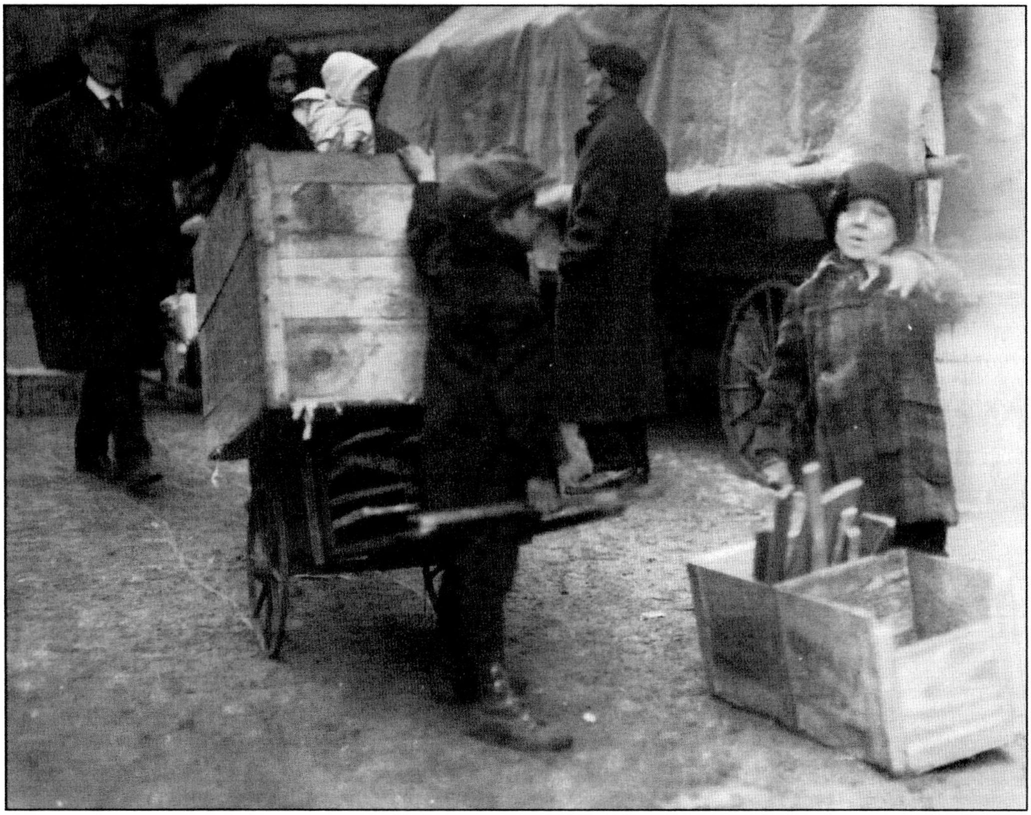

Two small boys carry to the market-scavenged wood in a hand-pulled cart. Dressed for the January 1917 cold, the boys set up to sell firewood.

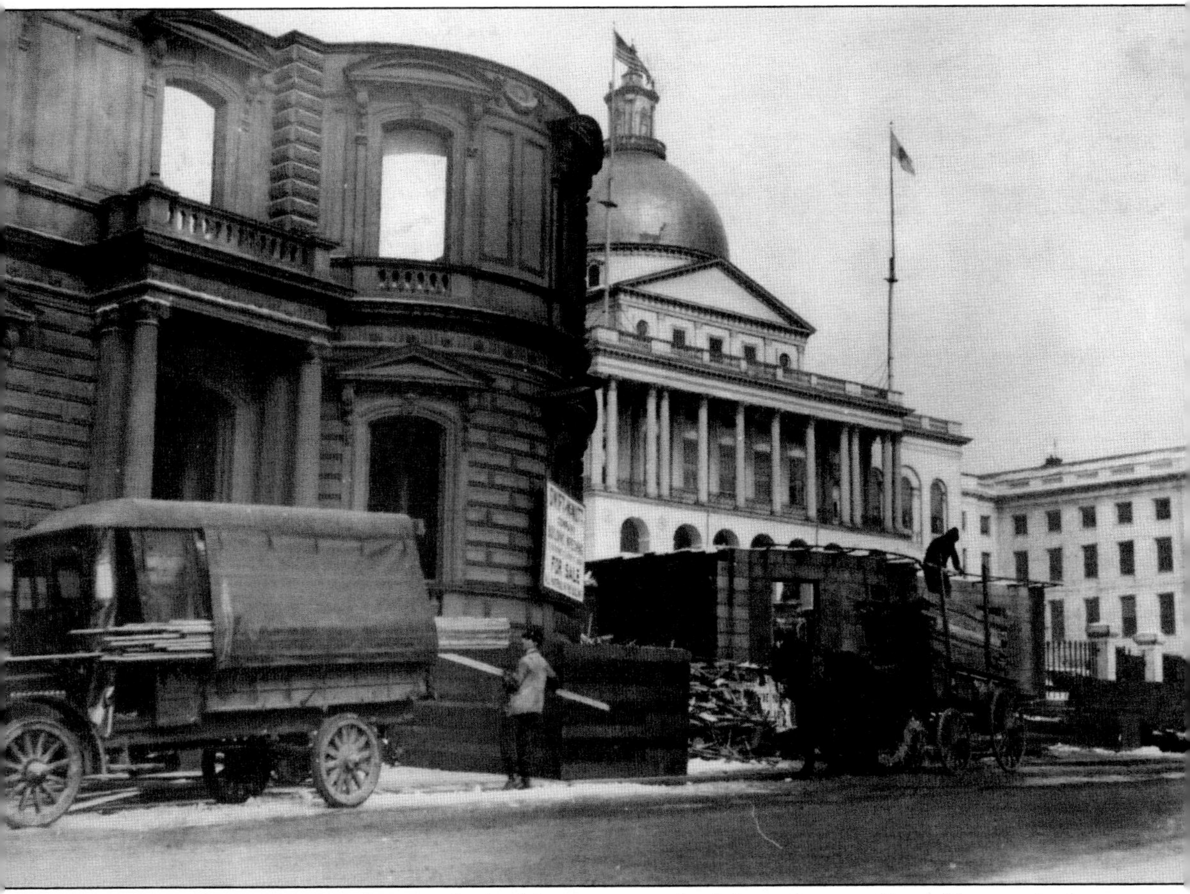

This picture shows the demolition of a building next to the Massachusetts State House, sited on Beacon Hill facing Boston Common, in 1917. Boys are busy loading the wood on a cart and truck. Charles Bulfinch was the architect of the state house; the dome was originally copper, later gilded with gold leaf.

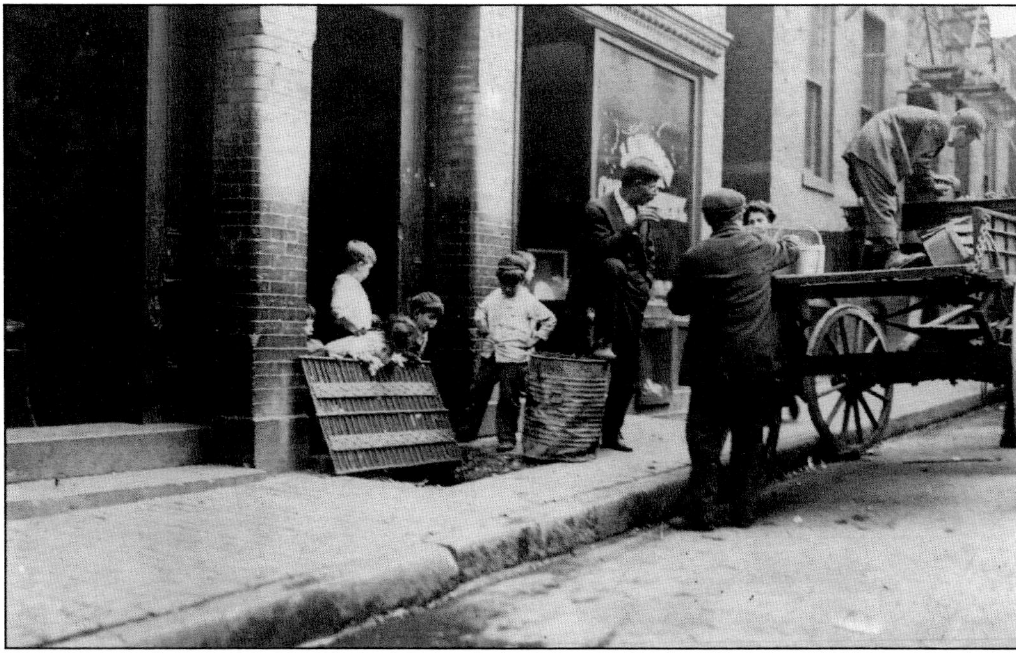

Children stand dangerously close to a metal grate used to cover an opening in the sidewalk. A man stands nearby with one foot on the trash can while other men are busy with the street vendor. With both parents working and large families, children often roamed together without adult protection.

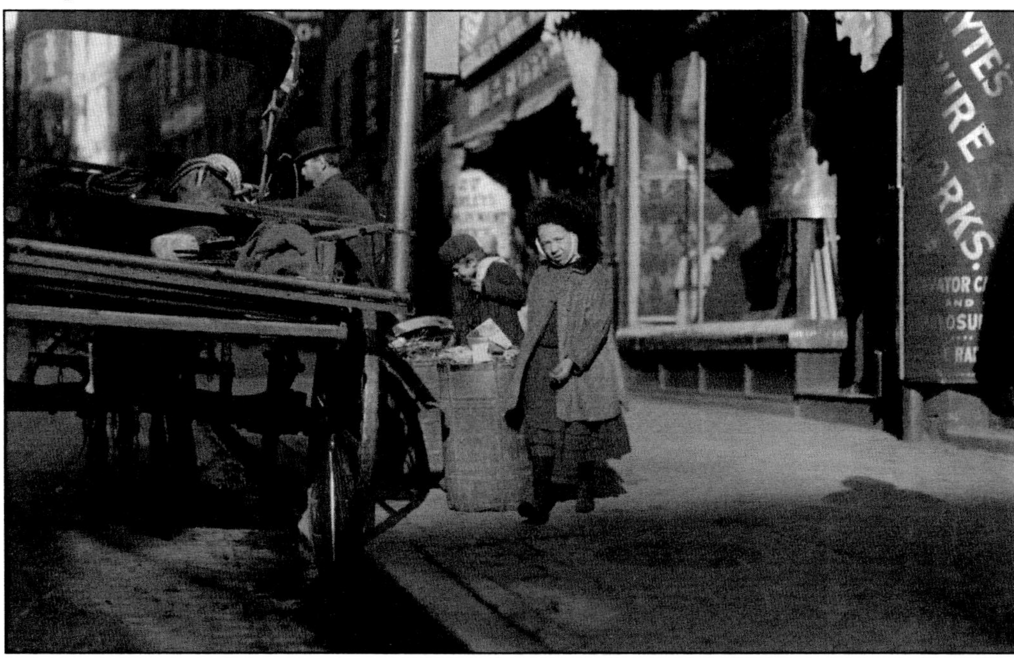

Children check the contents of trash cans on Washington Street in this 1910 image. The MCLC report of 1915 states, "These children go also into ash barrels and pick even worse rubbish than in the market. Frequently children pick from refuse barrels material, which they can eat on the spot."

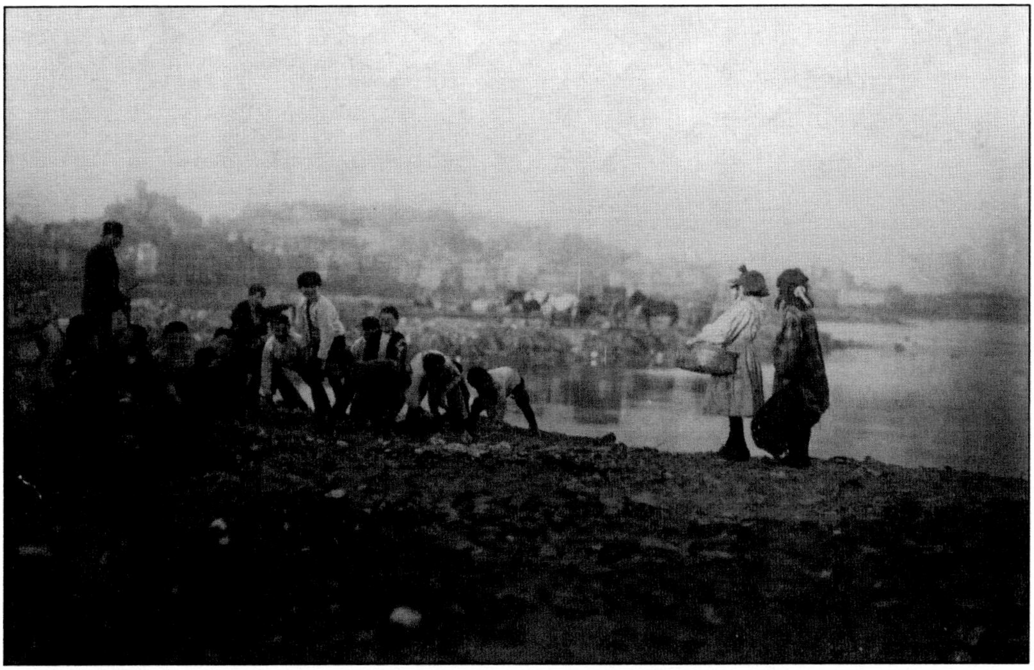

For decades, Boston dumped its trash and sewage on the swampy Columbia Point facing Boston's harbor beyond South Boston, at the edge of the city limits. Young children regularly scavenged the trash for saleable items. This c. 1910 Lewis Hine picture shows a dozen children rifling the trash for rags, cans, glass containers, pieces of wood, or discarded clothing. In the background are horse carts bringing new trash to the dump.

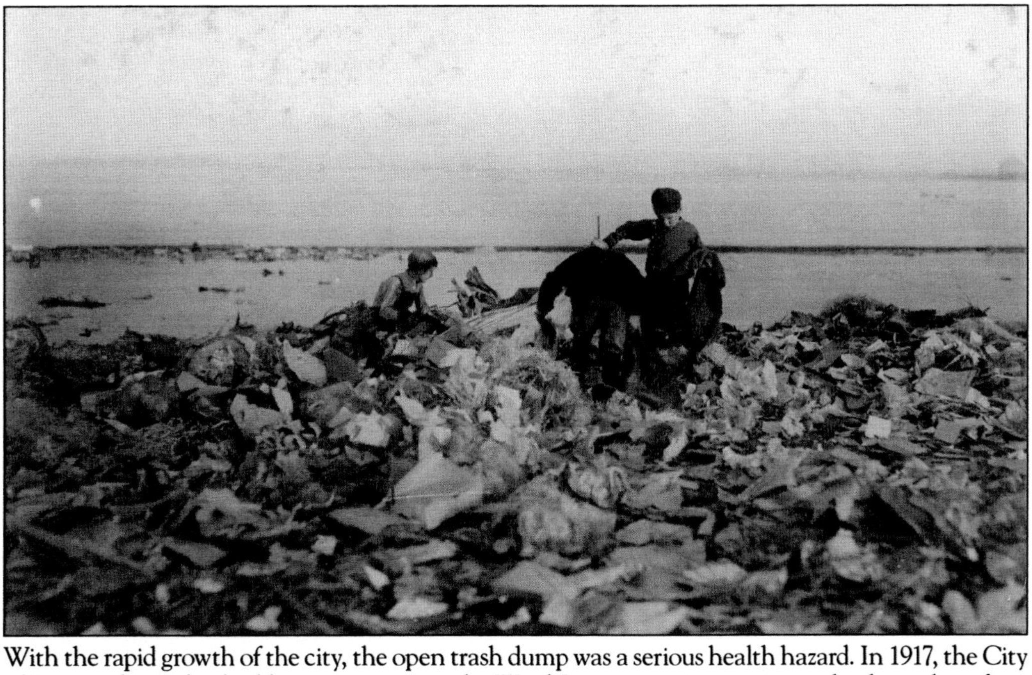

With the rapid growth of the city, the open trash dump was a serious health hazard. In 1917, the City of Boston planned to build an incinerator at the Ward Street receiving station and to burn the refuse. This picture shows three boys standing on the mounds of trash dumped at the ocean's edge.

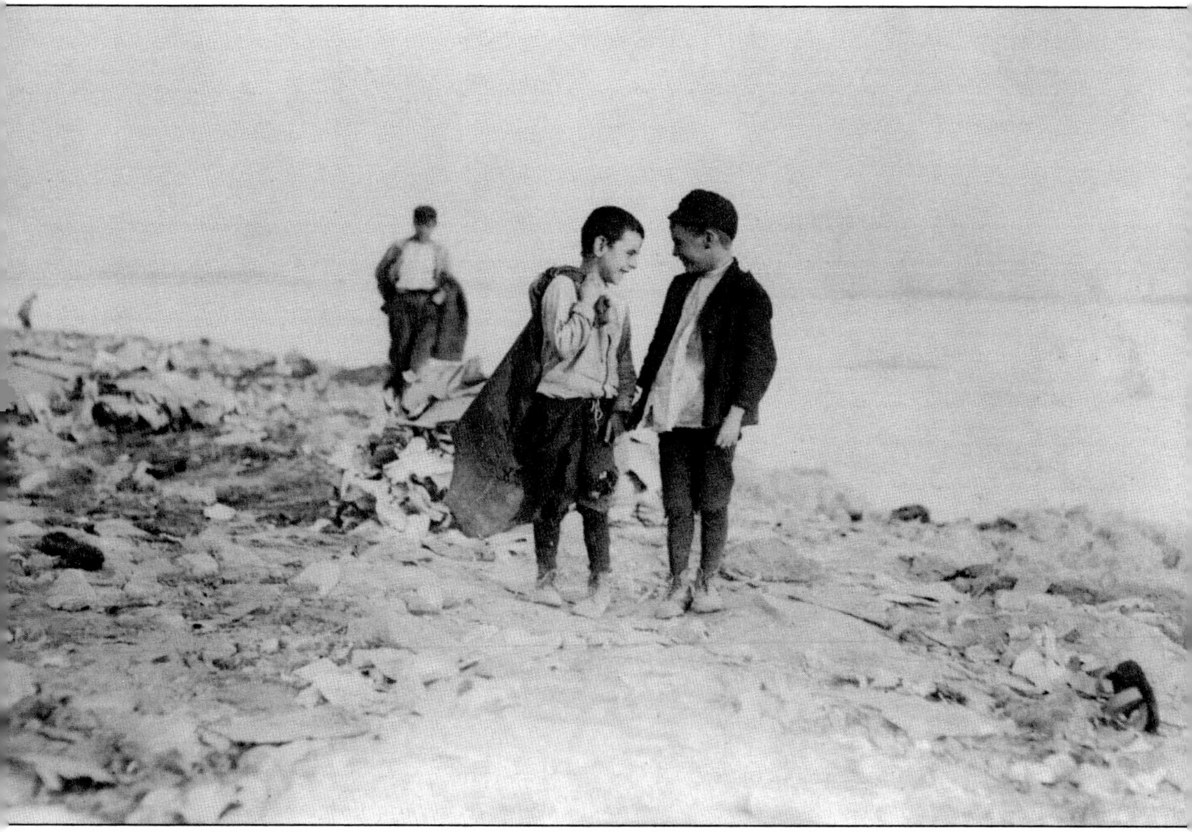

Two small boys share a joke as they stand among the trash at Columbia Point in 1909. The area was reclaimed and is now the Kennedy Memorial Library; the University of Massachusetts Boston stands on top of the former city dump.

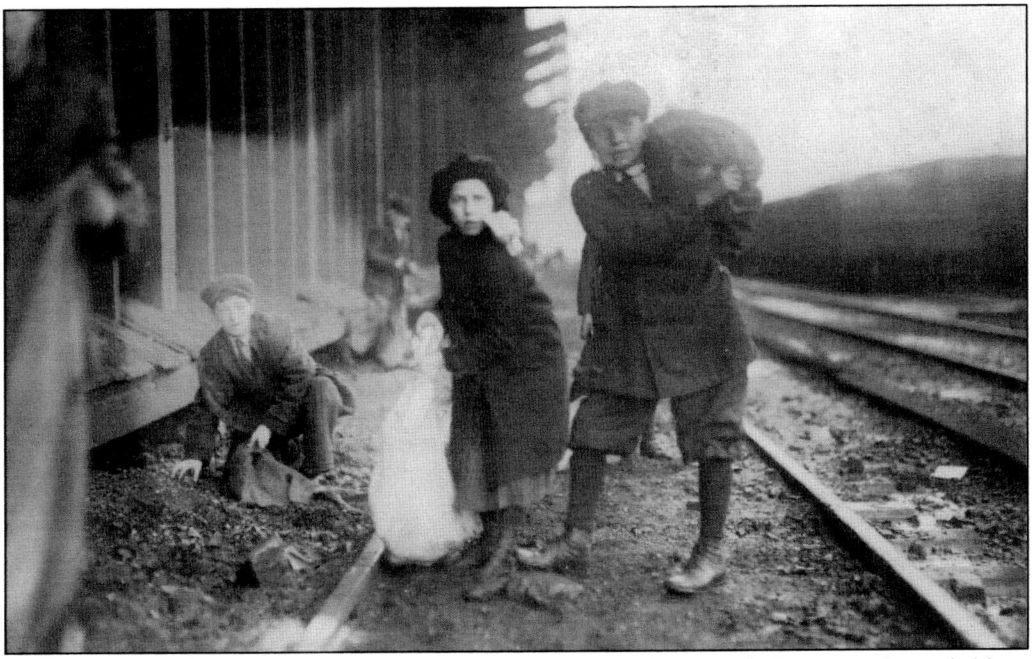

A regular place for pilfering was the freight train terminal at South Boston, where children collected lumps of coal that had fallen to the ground. This activity involved trespassing and picking while trains were moving. This 1917 picture shows anxious children with sacks standing on the rail tracks.

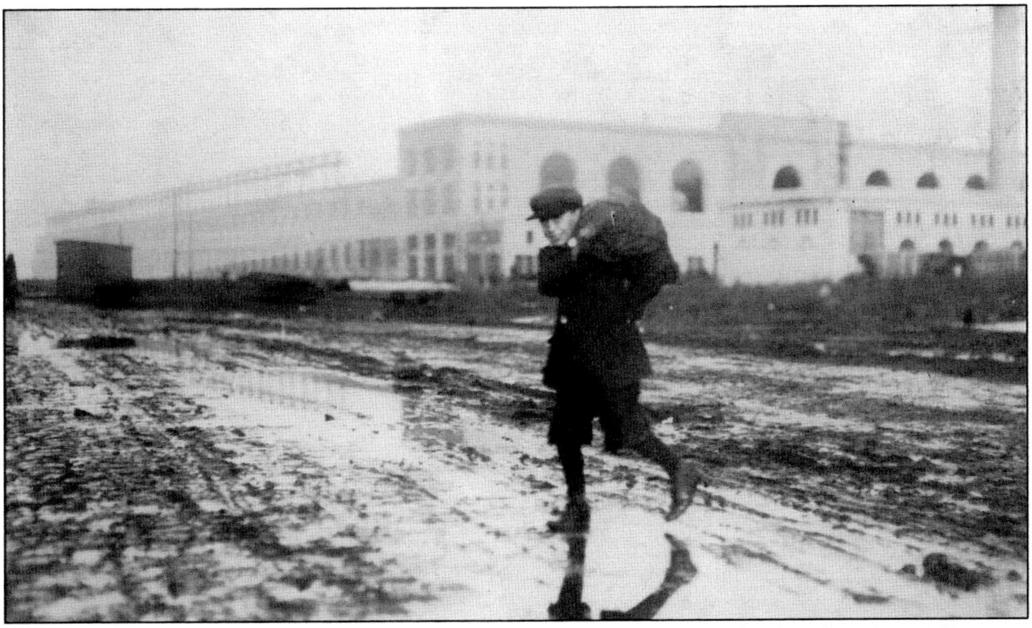

A boy is walking through the mud and carrying home a heavy, full sack of coal in this 1917 image. This photograph shows the immense Commonwealth Pier, completed in 1913 and used for freight and passengers of the White Star and Hamburg-America shipping lines. During World War I, it was used as a military receiving station. The building is now part of Boston's Seaport District, home to finance, high tech, law, and life science companies.

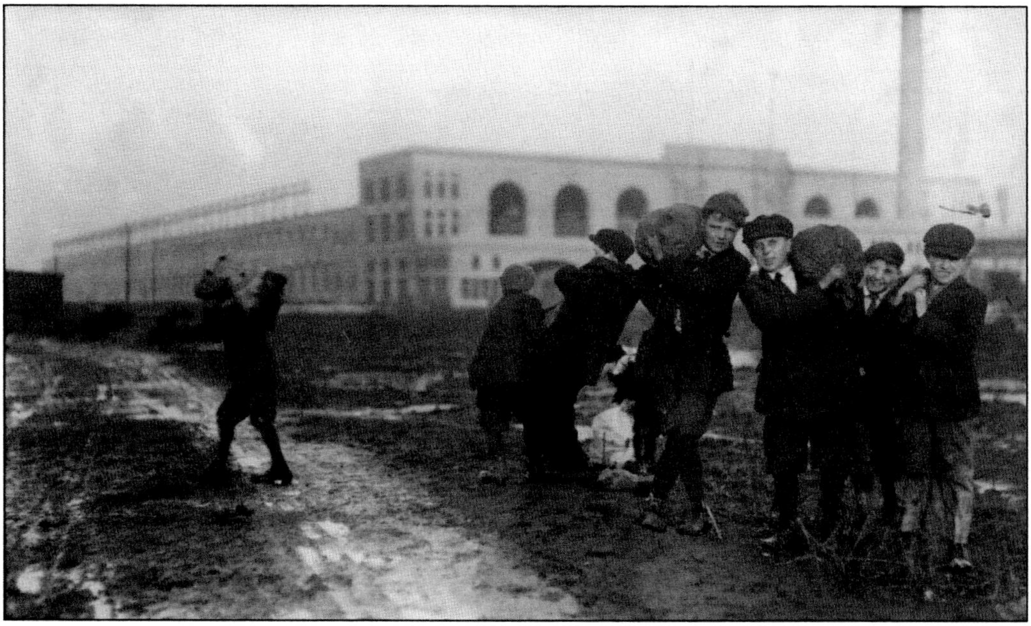

Another Lewis Hine picture from 1917 shows a group of boys, their bags filled with lumps of coal, posing for the camera. Commonwealth Pier is shown in the background. In 1914, Dr. Joel E. Goldthwait, chief of orthopedics at the Massachusetts General Hospital, published a paper titled, "Effects on Children of Carrying Burdens." Goldthwait claimed that children were "permanently injured by the constant strain involved in carrying loads for long distances."

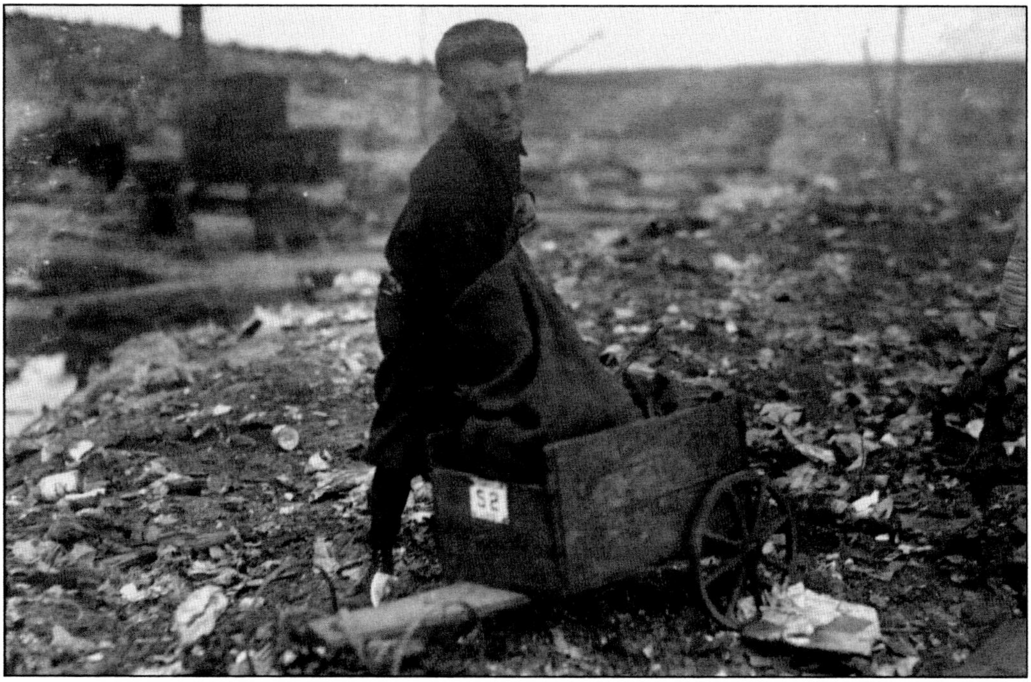

Scavenging from the trash in city dumps was widespread. This 1917 picture shows 11-year-old Charlie Stubbs of 141 Plain Street rummaging through the trash in the Fall River dump. Like the cities of Lowell and Lawrence, Fall River was a major textile center.

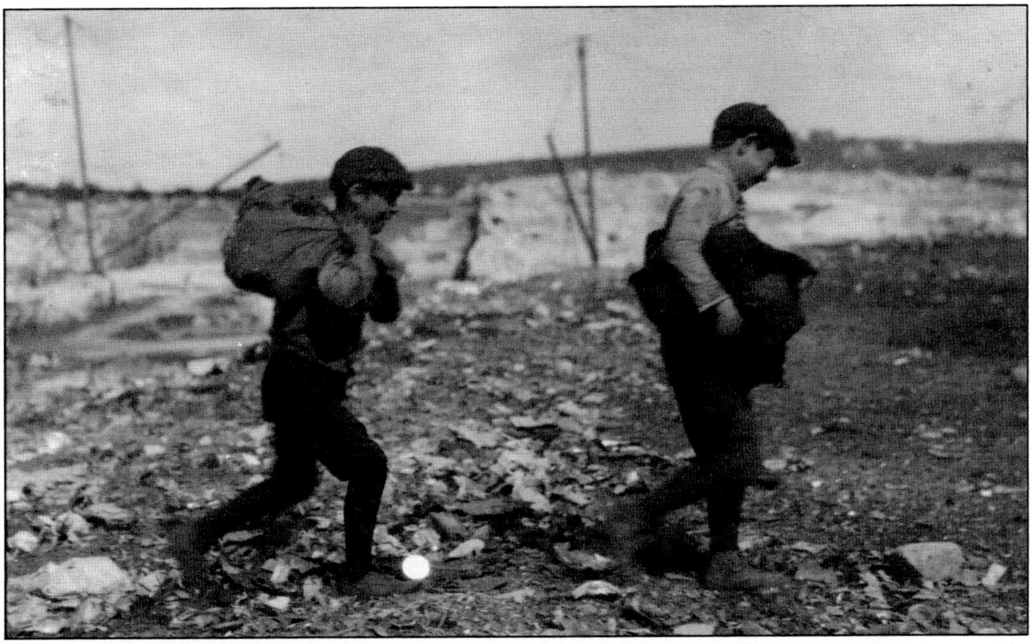

Two boys who spent the day scavenging at the dump in Fall River walk purposefully homewards, their sacks full of salvaged items for use at home or for sale.

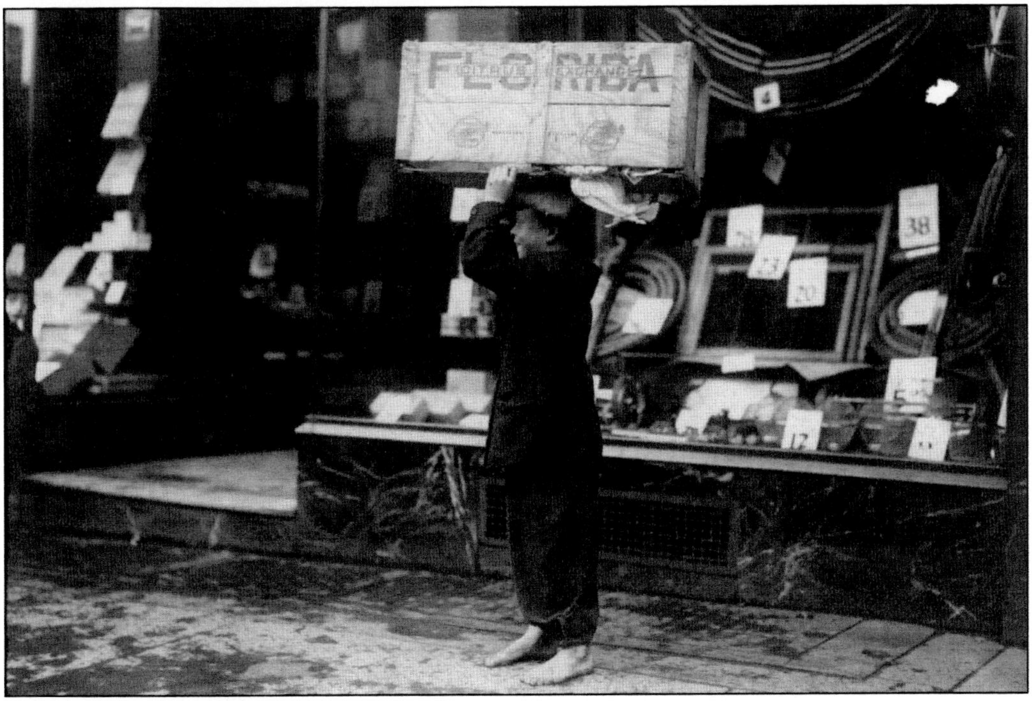

On September 19, 1874, the Granite Textile Mill in Fall River caught fire. Of the 19 workers killed, 9 were children under 12 years of age, including James Smith, James Newton, and Noah Poitros. Many other children were injured. In response, the Massachusetts Factory Act of 1876 banned children under 10 from working in mills. This June 1916 photograph shows a shoeless boy walking along a Fall River shopping street carrying a large wooden crate on his head.

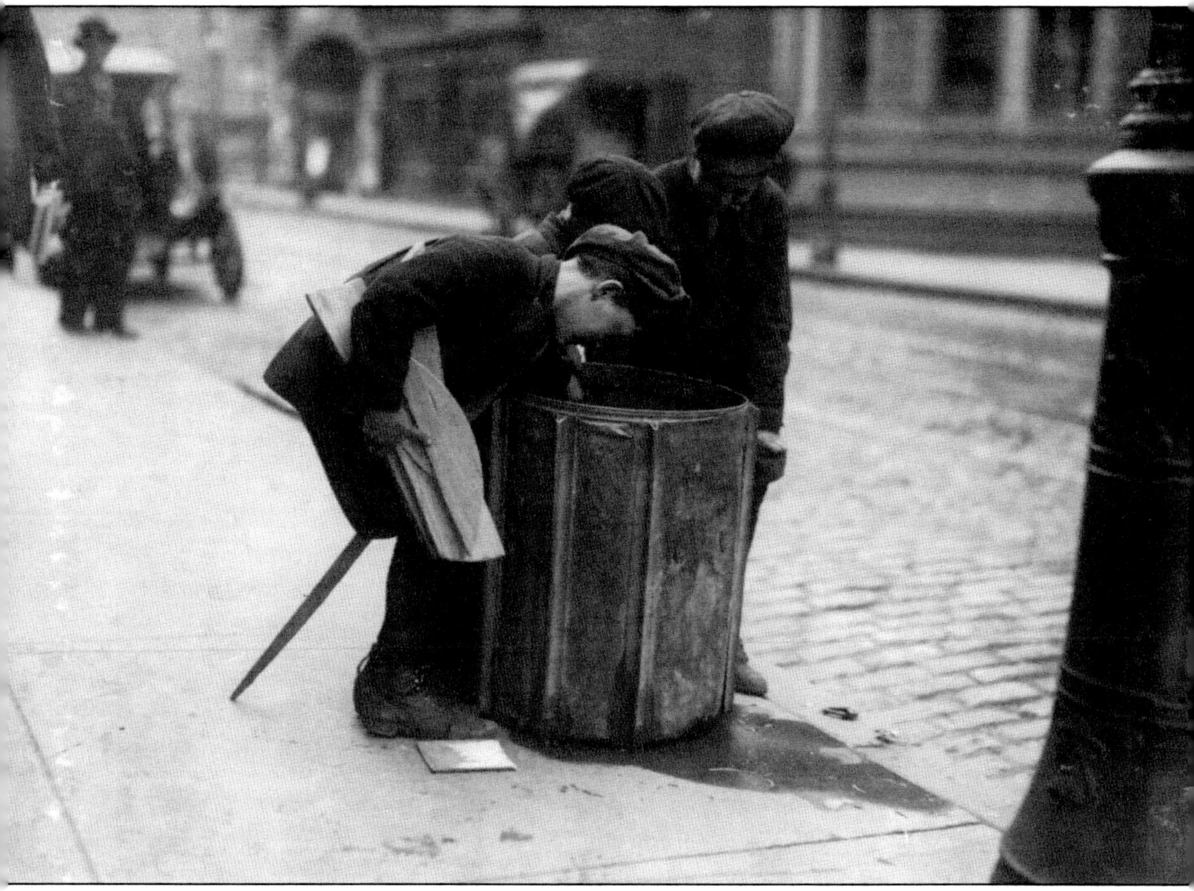

A Fall River street scene from June 1916 shows boys raiding garbage bins for pieces of wood and other usable or saleable objects.

Six

Factory Children

The American industrial revolution started in 1814 with the use of power machines to spin cotton into thread and weave the thread into cloth. Boston money greased the process in Massachusetts. In the age of waterpower, the early factories were built along the Charles and Merrimack Rivers. The Boston Manufacturing Company, incorporated by Francis Cabot Lowell and his fellow Boston merchants, was constructed at Waltham, where the Charles River drops 15 feet, generating enough waterpower for a few mills. After Francis C. Lowell died in 1817, his associates took his factory model to the powerful Merrimack River and built America's first industrial city, named Lowell in his honor. After Lowell came the textile cities of Lawrence, North Adams, and Holyoke. In the era of steam power, Fall River, New Bedford, and Taunton became textile cities. In the 19th and early 20th centuries, textiles were the leading industry of Massachusetts.

The Massachusetts shoe industry moved from craft to factory later than textiles. From the beginning, the shoe factories were driven by steam power. Lynn, Haverhill, and Brockton were the leading shoe towns. Boston and its surrounding towns became a great center for the making of organs and pianos. The Boston Rubber Shoe Company had its head office in Boston and factories in Malden. Patent medicines were made in Lowell, Lynn, and Boston. Mellin's Baby Foods and Walter Baker's chocolates were also made in Boston. Thomas Gustave Plant (1859–1943) built Queen Quality Shoe Company, the largest shoe factory in the world. The vast American Woolen Company and the United Shoe Machinery Company had their headquarters in Boston.

"There are in this Commonwealth upwards of 6,000 children of school age," wrote George Edwin McNeill, deputy state constable in 1917, "who are growing up ignorant, contrary to the accepted policy of the State, and in open violation of the letter and spirit of existing laws." Most of the children absent from school were driven by economic necessity to find jobs in the factories. "In the city of Boston alone," alleged McNeill, "there are a very large number of places wherein children are employed [especially] in large manufacturing towns, such as Lowell, Lawrence and Fall River." Child labor was endemic in the textile and shoe industries of Massachusetts as well as in hundreds of smaller industries in Boston and surrounding towns.

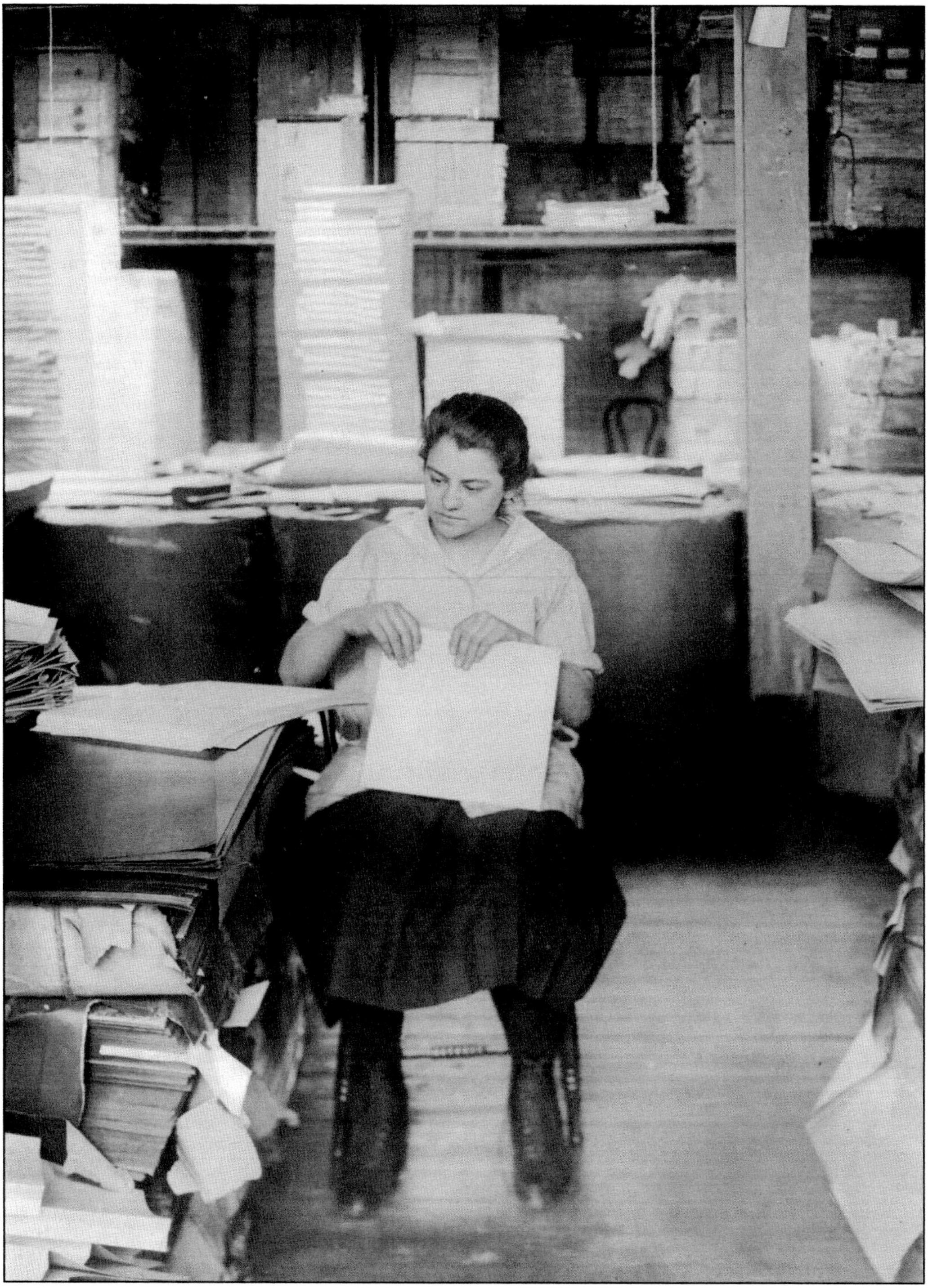

The National Child Labor Committee believed that children who left school early would land up in low-paid, repetitive work with little prospect of advancement. This 1916 photograph by Lewis Hine shows a young girl folding filing folders, one after another. Her workplace was the Boston Index Card Company at 103 Purchase Street in Boston.

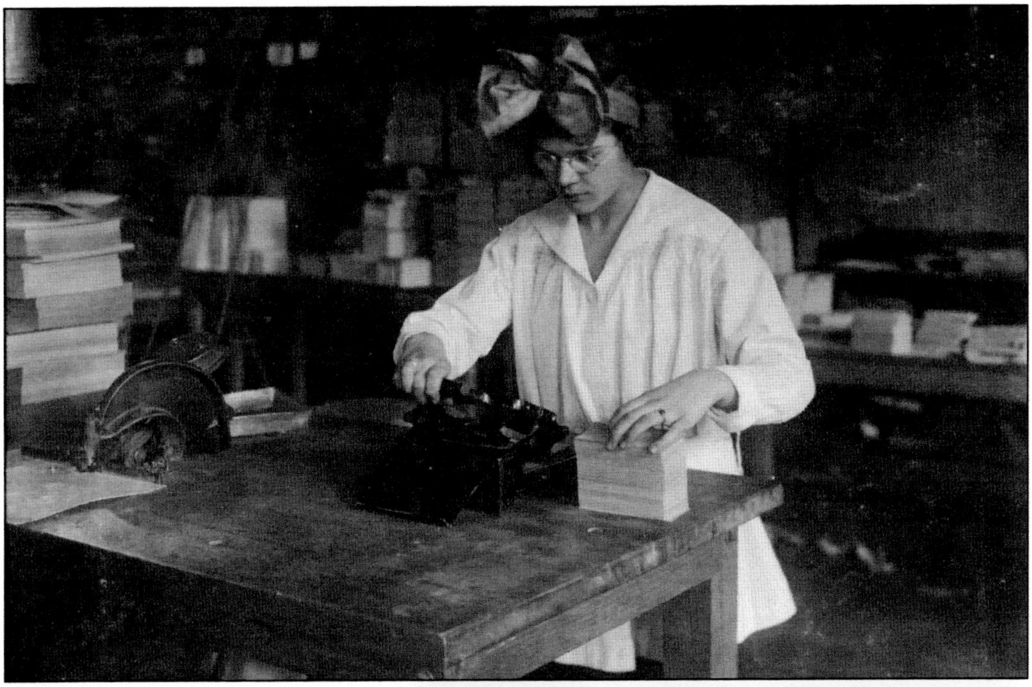

Working at the same company, a girl stamps addresses onto cards, one by one. Repetitive jobs like this were soon lost with the introduction of machines that did the work cheaper, quicker, and more accurately than low-paid children.

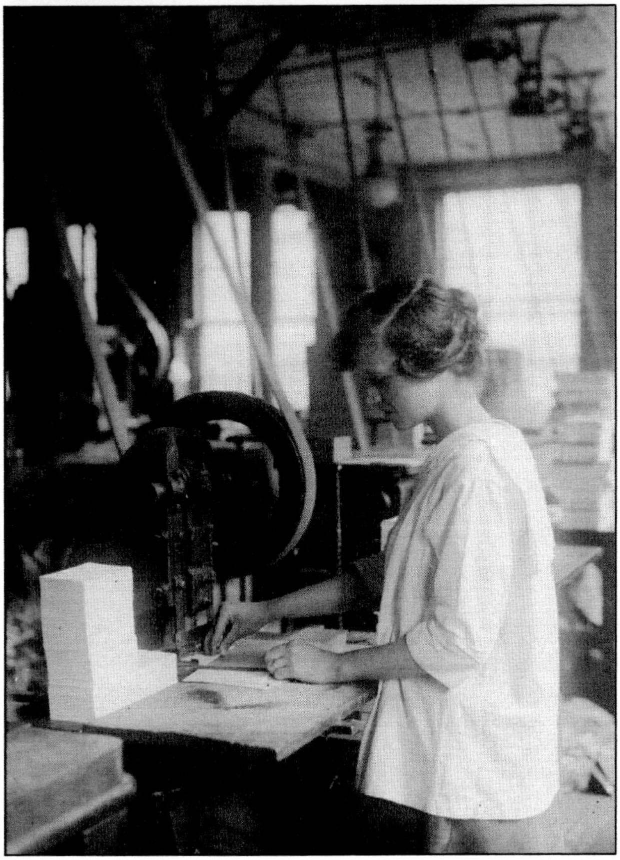

Here, a girl uses a stamping machine operated by steam power. Such machines were considered dangerous when used by children, with the risk of hair and clothing being caught up in the leather belting or fingers being crushed. The company advertised part-time jobs for women but hired girls of 14 and 15 full time.

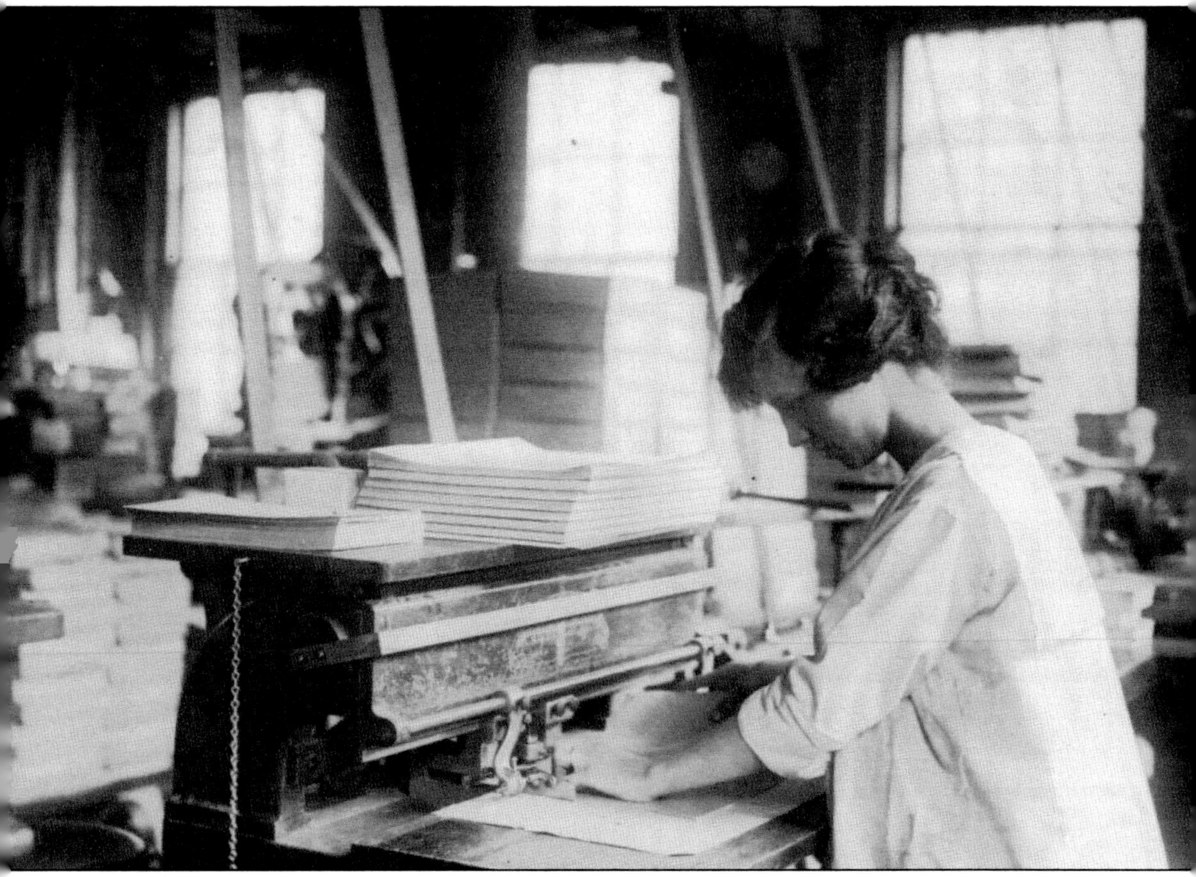

A girl operates a machine at the Boston Index Card Company in this 1917 photograph. The company made bank forms, ledger forms, signature cards, and bank statements. Known as BICCO, it was "America's Best." The company was at 113–115 Purchase Street, near Atlantic Avenue, now the site of a Boston firehouse.

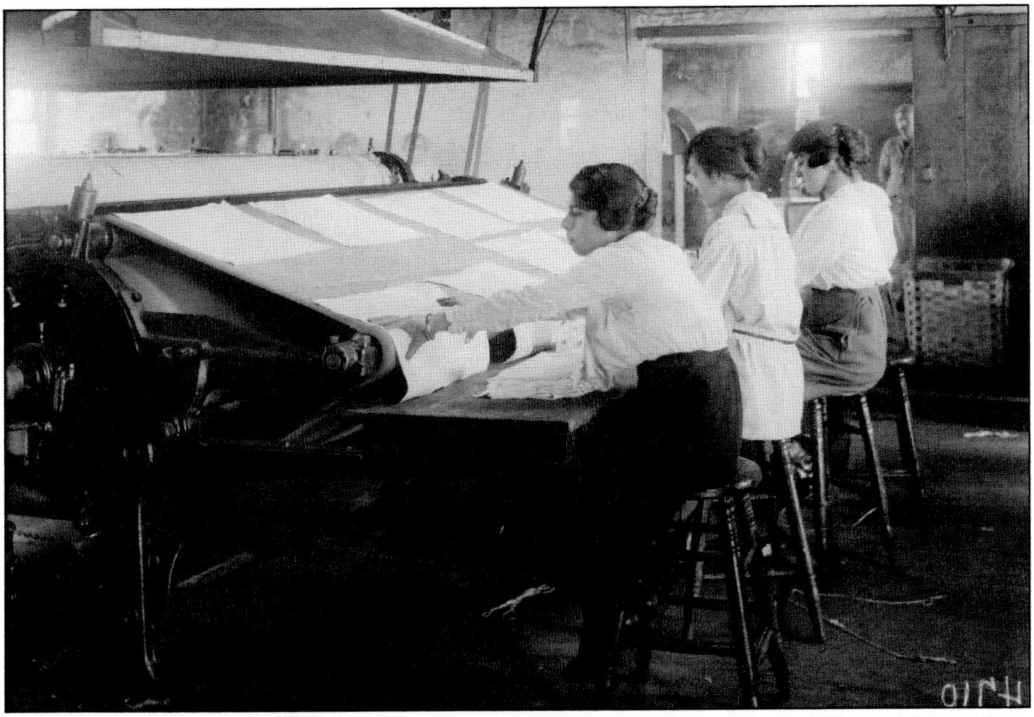

Three girls, all 15 years old, sit side by side, working in a laundry on Foster Wharf, folding cloth napkins and handkerchiefs emerging from a hot ironing machine in 1917.

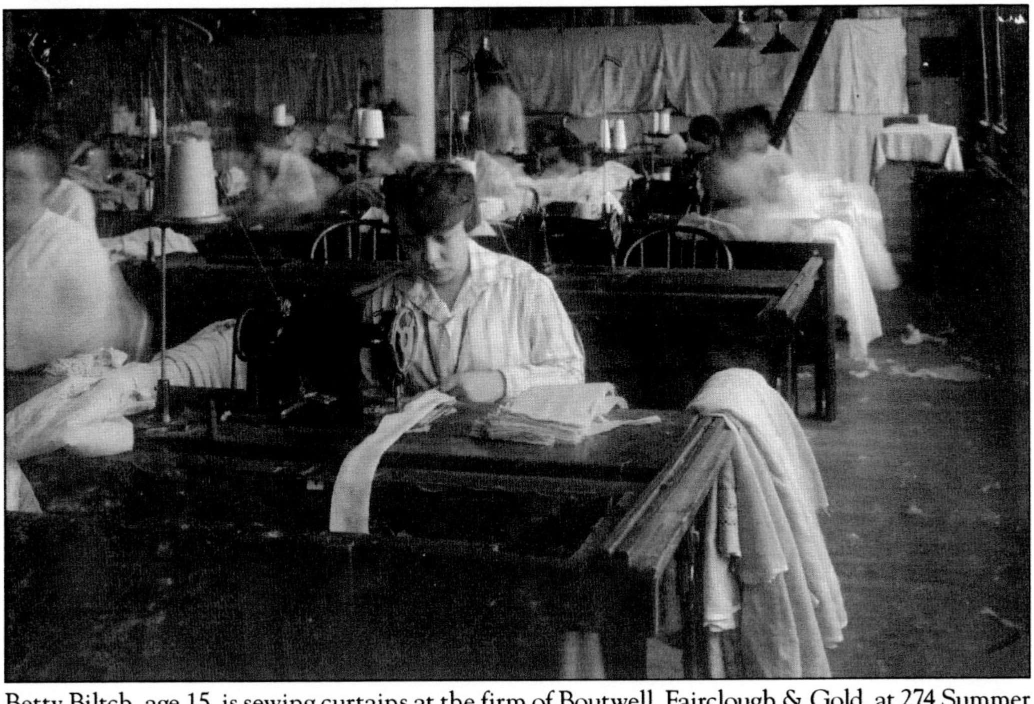

Betty Biltch, age 15, is sewing curtains at the firm of Boutwell, Fairclough & Gold, at 274 Summer Street, Boston, in 1917. The company was known for its draperies and lace curtains. Half the working girls in Boston were either in domestic service or in the needle trades.

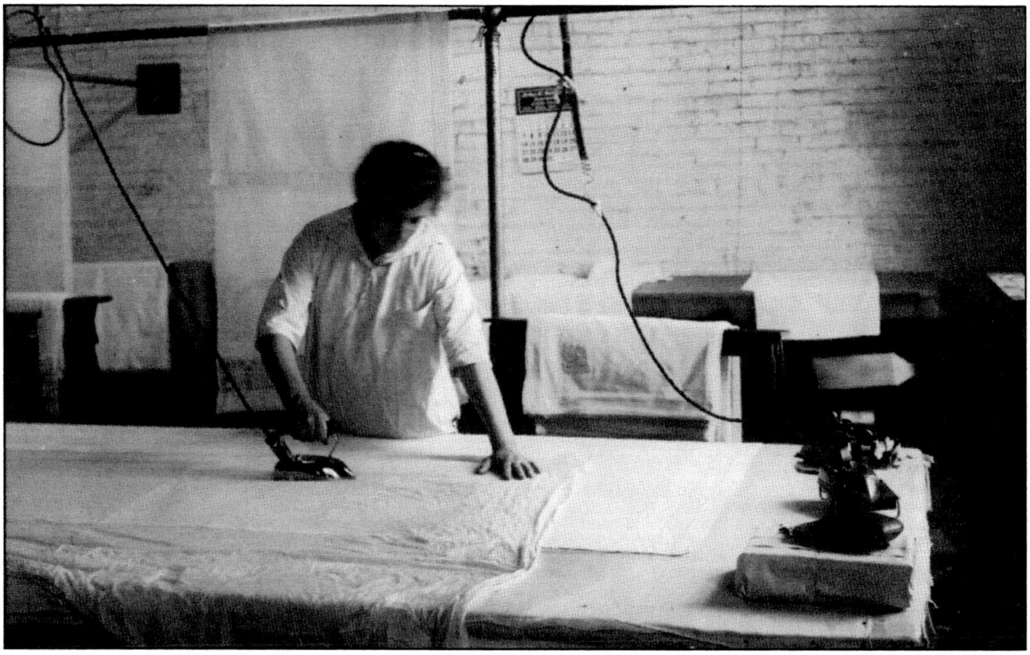

Sadie McGurin, age 15, irons curtains at Boutwell, Fairclough & Gold. In a survey of 588 girls, the Boston School Department found that 111 were shoe workers, 29 bundle girls, and 122 store messenger girls. Among an equal number of boys who left school early, 197 were messenger boys, 30 delivered telegrams, 24 were shoe workers, and 20 bundle boys.

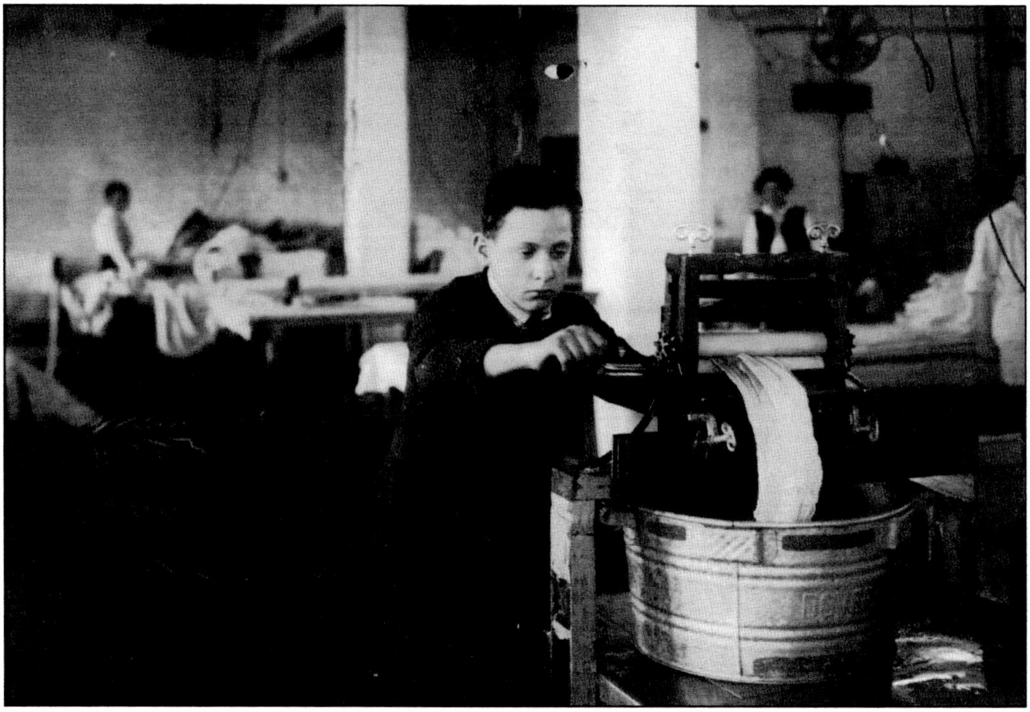

Edward McGurin, the 14-year-old brother of Sadie, operates a hand-turned wringing machine to dry curtains at the firm of Boutwell, Fairclough & Gold at 274 Washington Street.

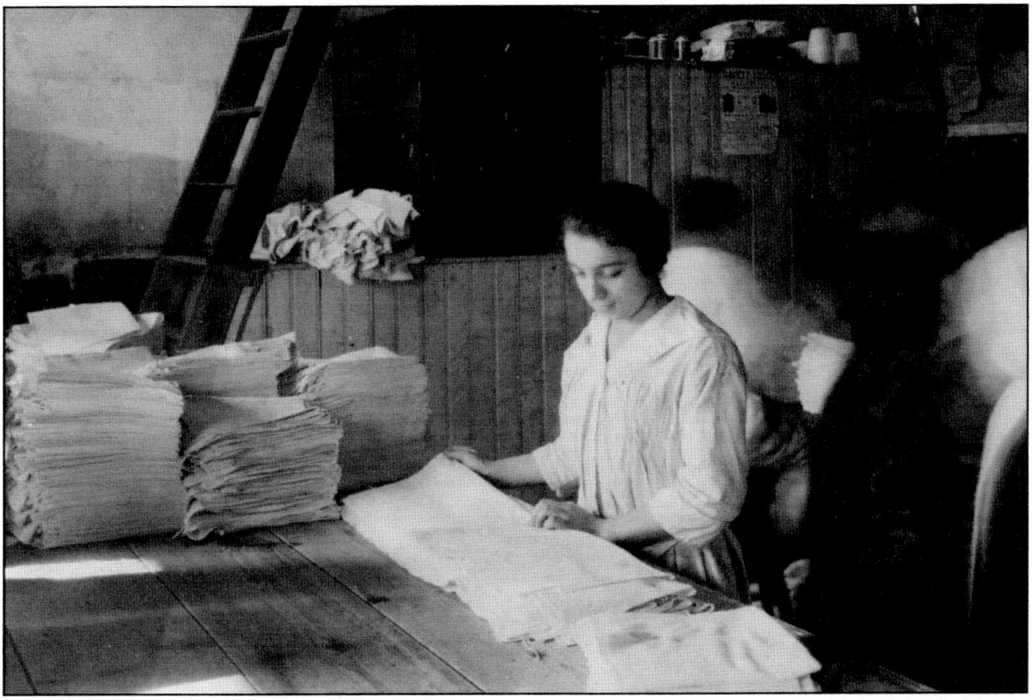

A 15-year-old girl folds towels at Charles Bonanno Steam Laundry, 12 Foster Wharf, Boston, in 1917. Bonanno's was one of dozens of laundries serving Boston.

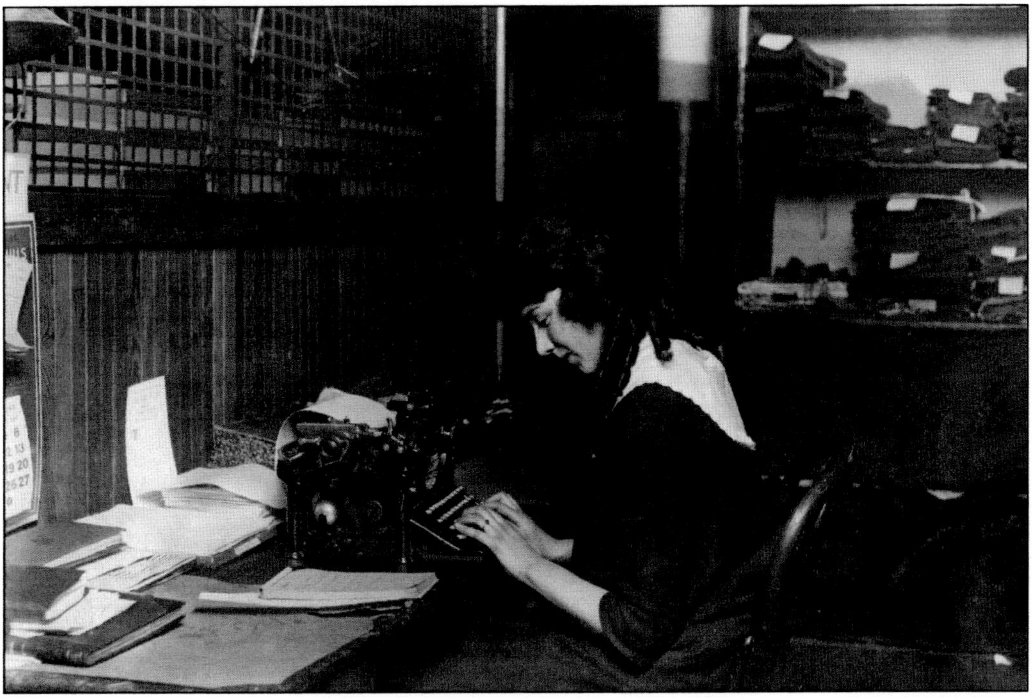

Ethel Selansky, a 15-year-old typist, is employed by the Standard Neckwear Company of 91 Essex Street, a few blocks from South Station. The company manufactured men's and boys' ties and cravats. This picture is from 1917.

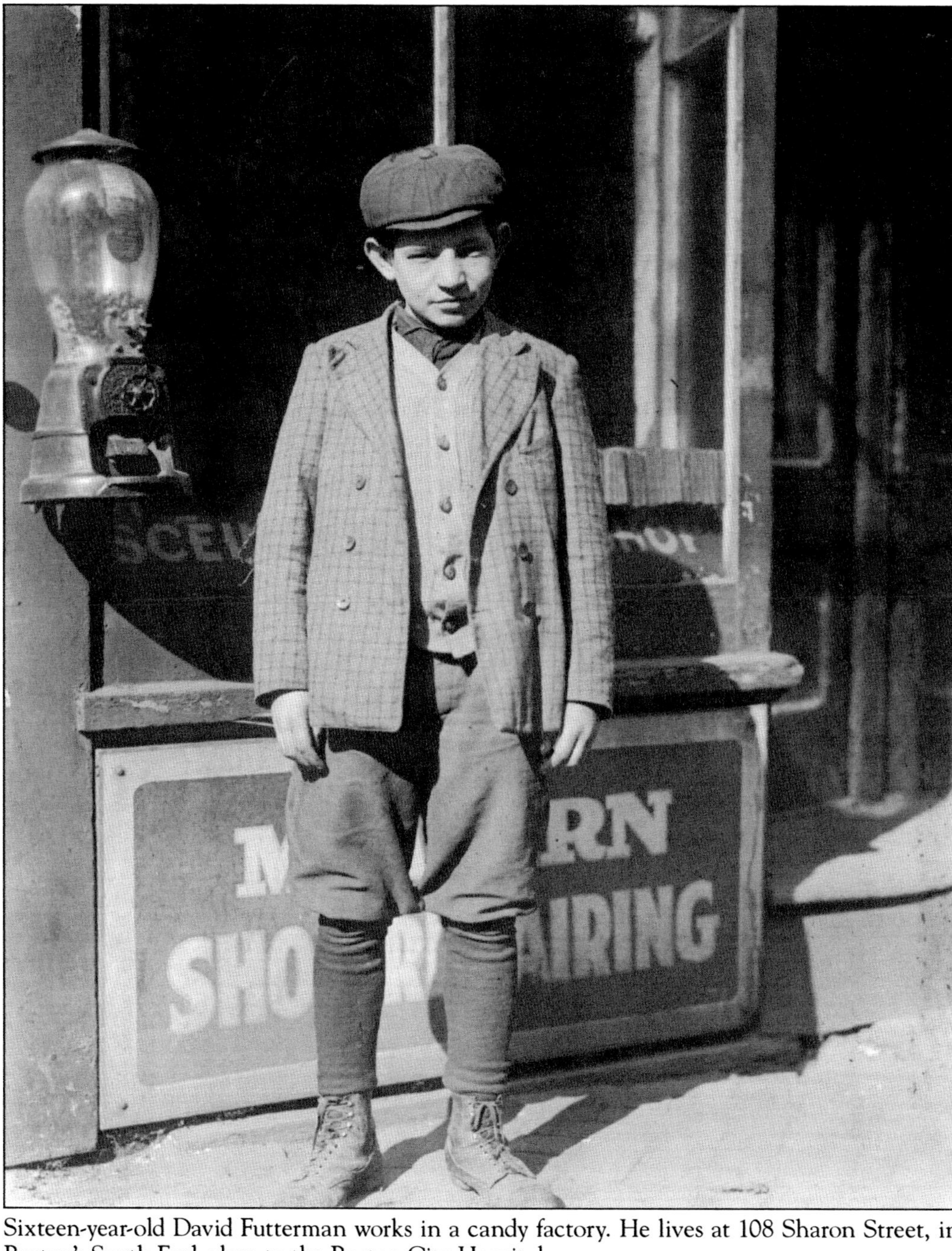

Sixteen-year-old David Futterman works in a candy factory. He lives at 108 Sharon Street, in Boston's South End, close to the Boston City Hospital.

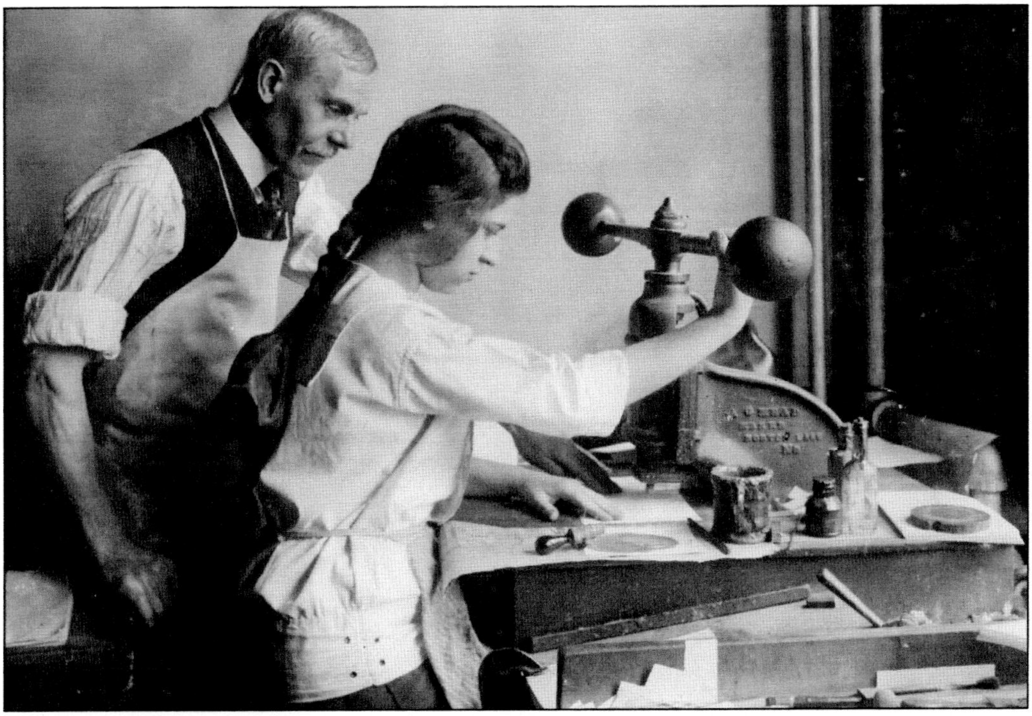

A 15-year-old girl is learning to use a hand-turned embossing machine in the shop of Harry C. Taylor at 61 Court Street, Boston, in 1917.

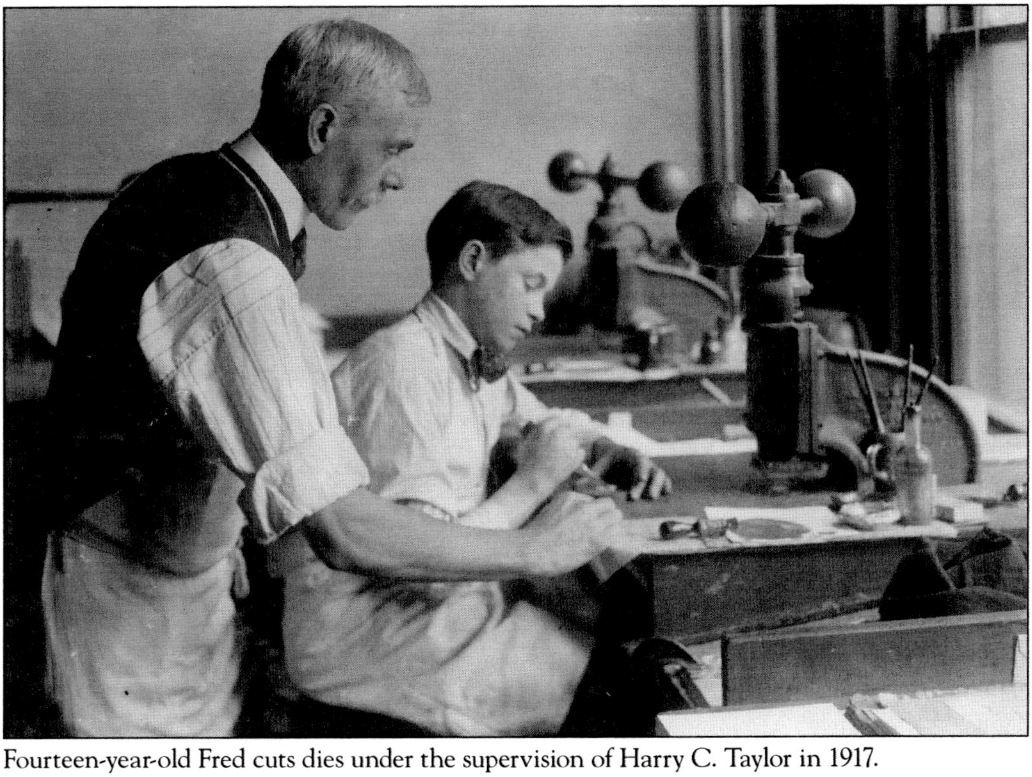

Fourteen-year-old Fred cuts dies under the supervision of Harry C. Taylor in 1917.

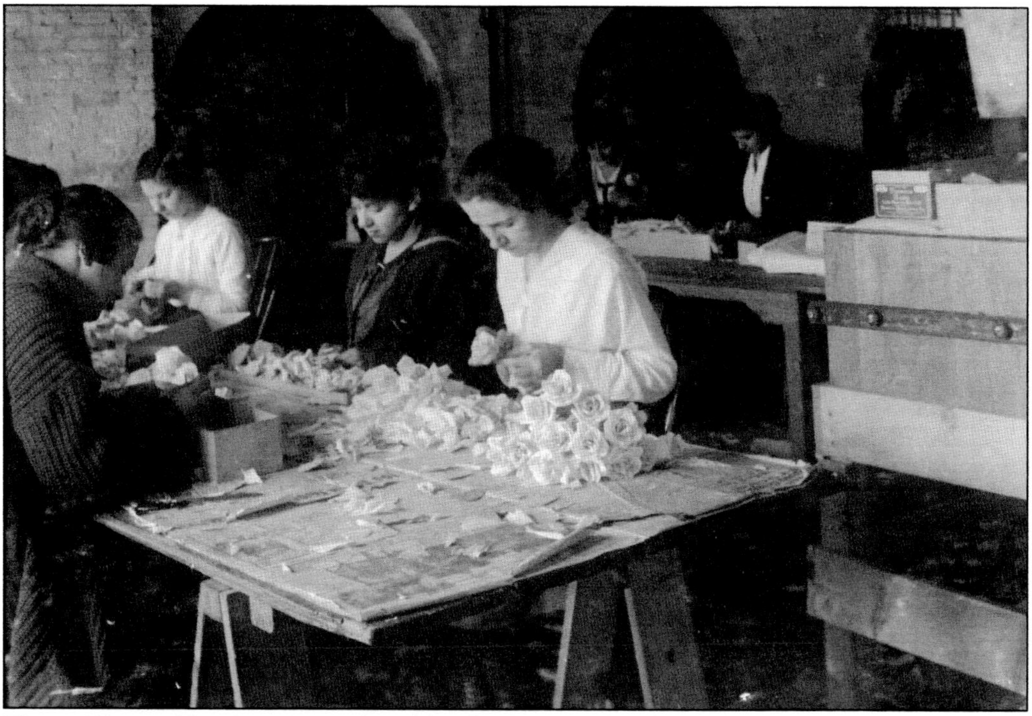

These 14-year-old girls were employed by the Boston Floral Supply at 347 Cambridge Street, Boston, making artificial flowers.

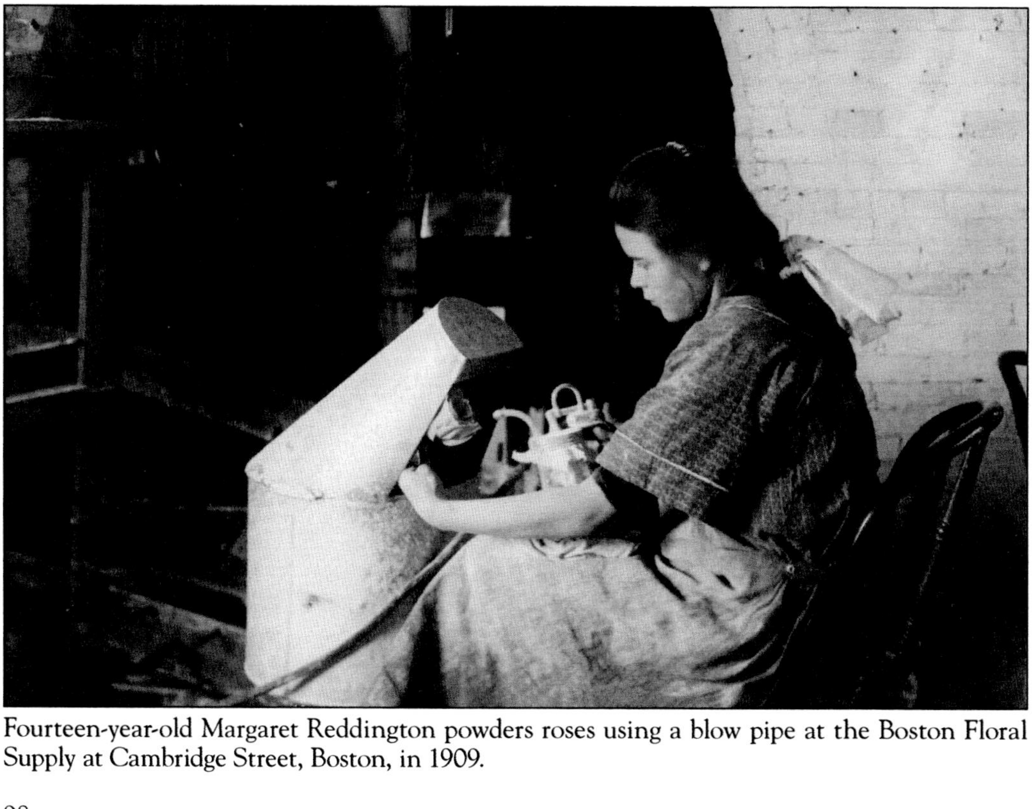

Fourteen-year-old Margaret Reddington powders roses using a blow pipe at the Boston Floral Supply at Cambridge Street, Boston, in 1909.

In this 1909 image, 15-year-old Margaret Chiampa is preparing artificial flowers for sale at Boston Floral Supply, 347 Cambridge Street, Boston.

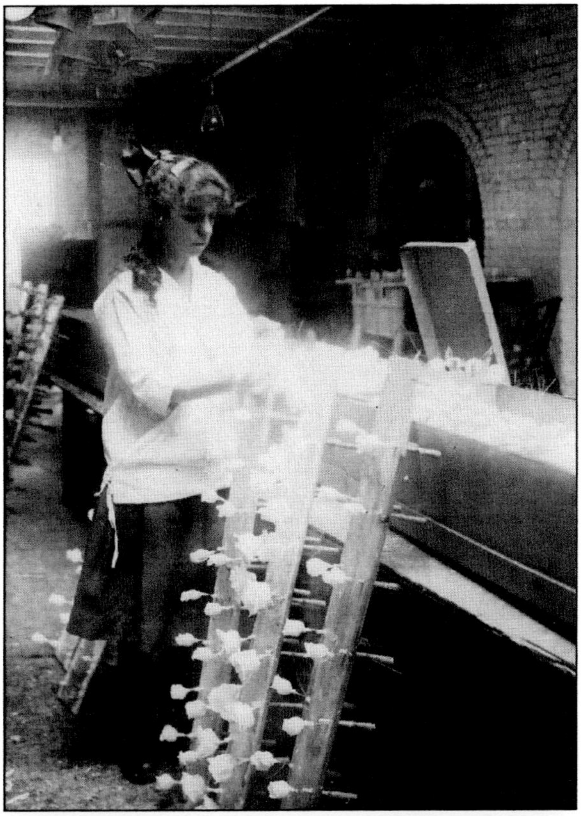

A 15-year old boy sorts cycas leaves at the Boston Floral Supply Company.

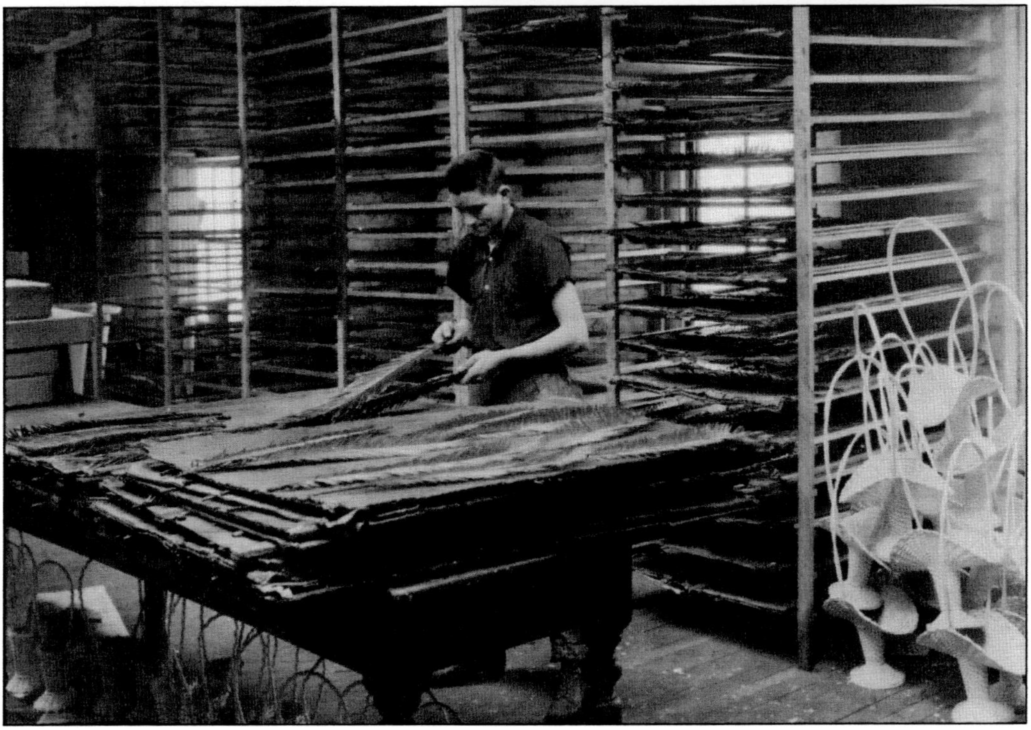

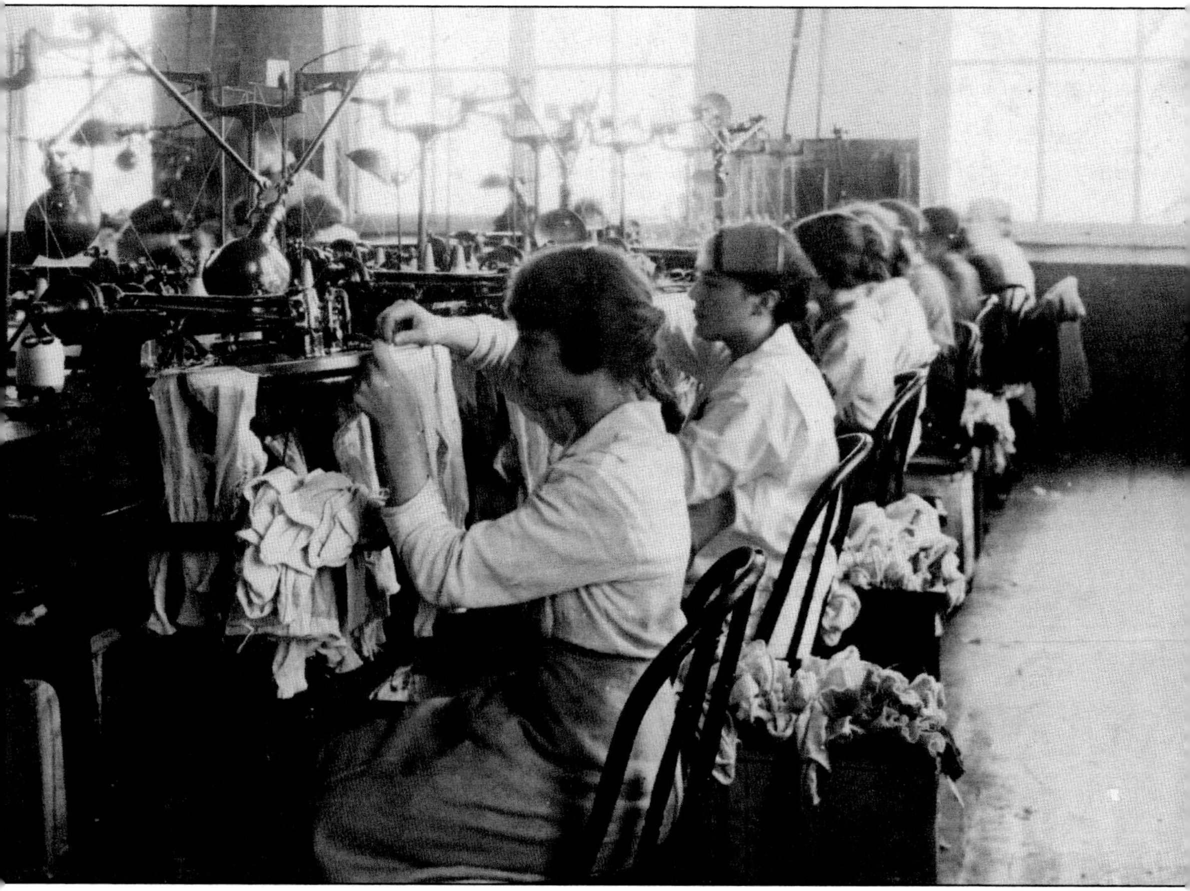

Knitting machines of the Ipswich mills, South Boston, are seen here. Immigrants from the English Midlands brought the craft of frame knitting to the United States. The knitting factories made mittens, socks, and knitted cloth. Knitwear factories were established in Needham, Lowell, Ipswich, Boston, and other Massachusetts towns. The knitting company opened in Ipswich in 1868 and expanded with branch factories in Lowell, South Boston (1913), and Belmont, New Hampshire. The company made seamless hosiery and moved in 1922 from steam to electric power.

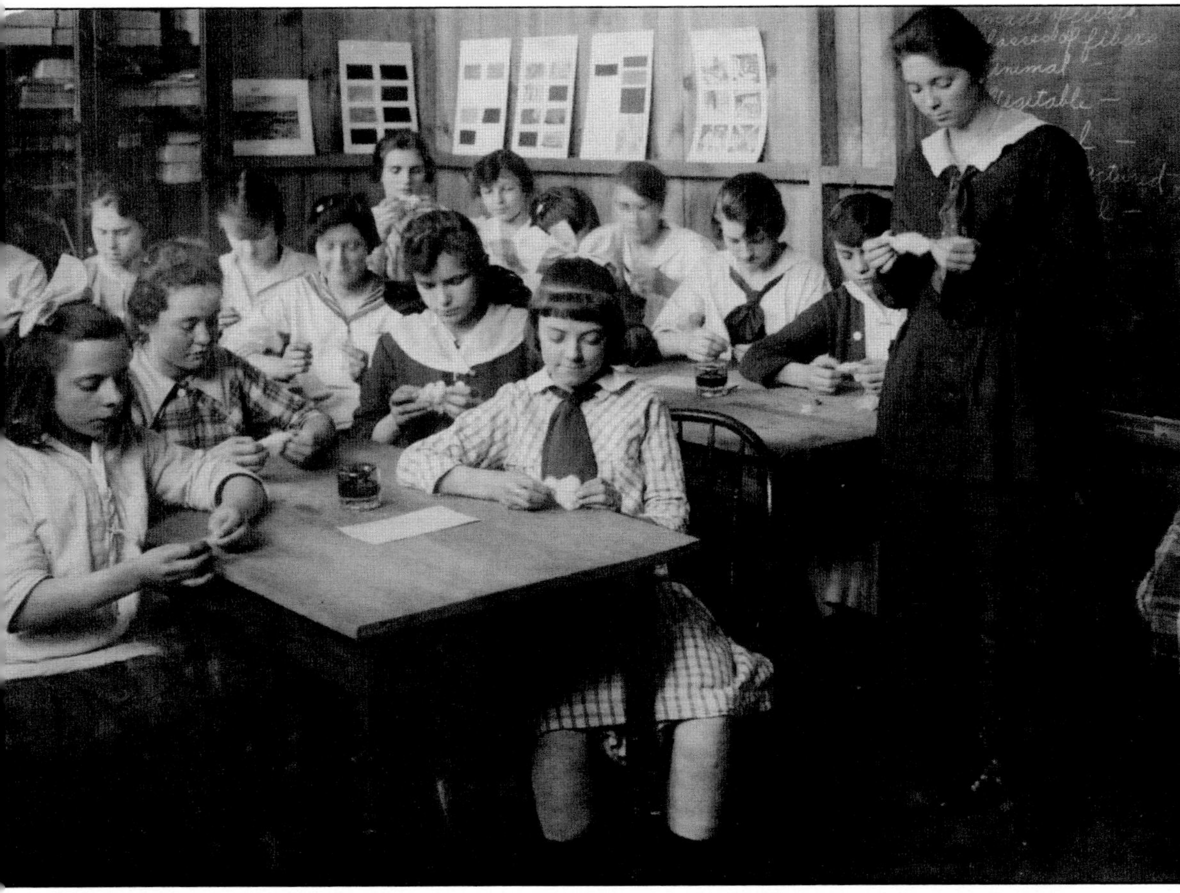

Shown here are continuing education classes in 1917 at Ipswich Mills in South Boston. Because so many children were leaving school at 14, the Boston School Committee, under Chapter 805, Act of 1913, set up compulsory continuation education classes at factories for children 14–16 who worked in the leather and textile trades or in department stores. After work, the children received at least four hours of instruction a week. Employed girls shown here studying textiles also studied arithmetic, reading, and writing. The goals of continuing education were to equip working children with skills for advancement and to better perform the duties of citizenship.

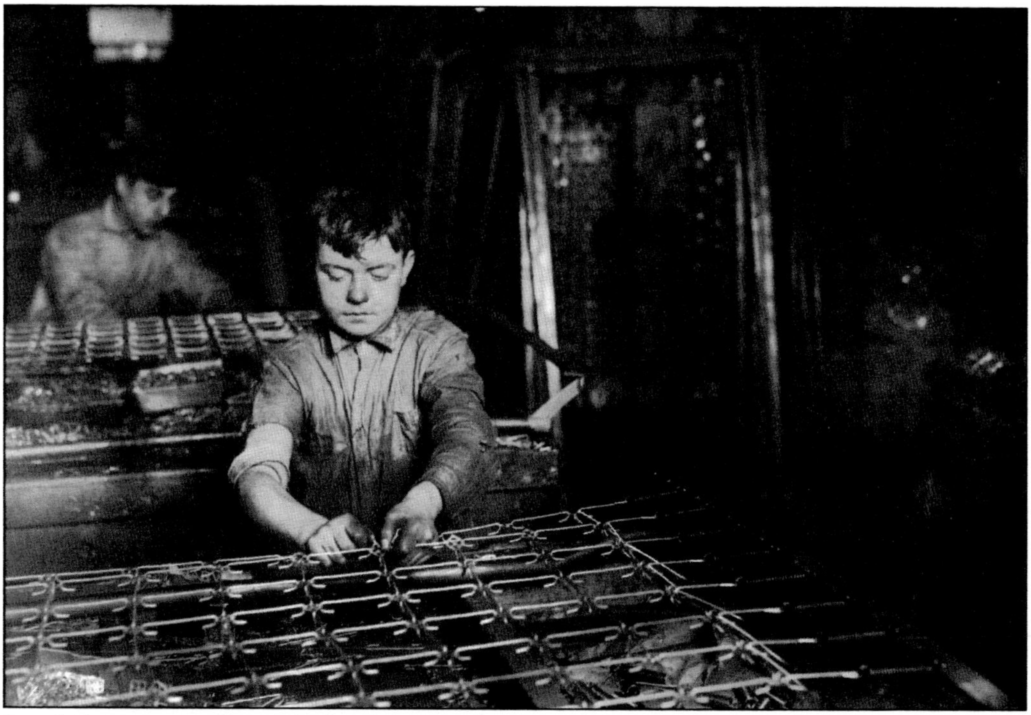

Boys link springs in a Boston bed and mattress factory in this 1917 image, possibly taken at the George W. Bent Mattress Company. Founded in 1882, it grew to be the largest mattress company in New England, employing 300 workers, many of them boys. The company also made folding beds and furniture for hotels and institutions. Company offices and the factory were at 934 Causeway Street.

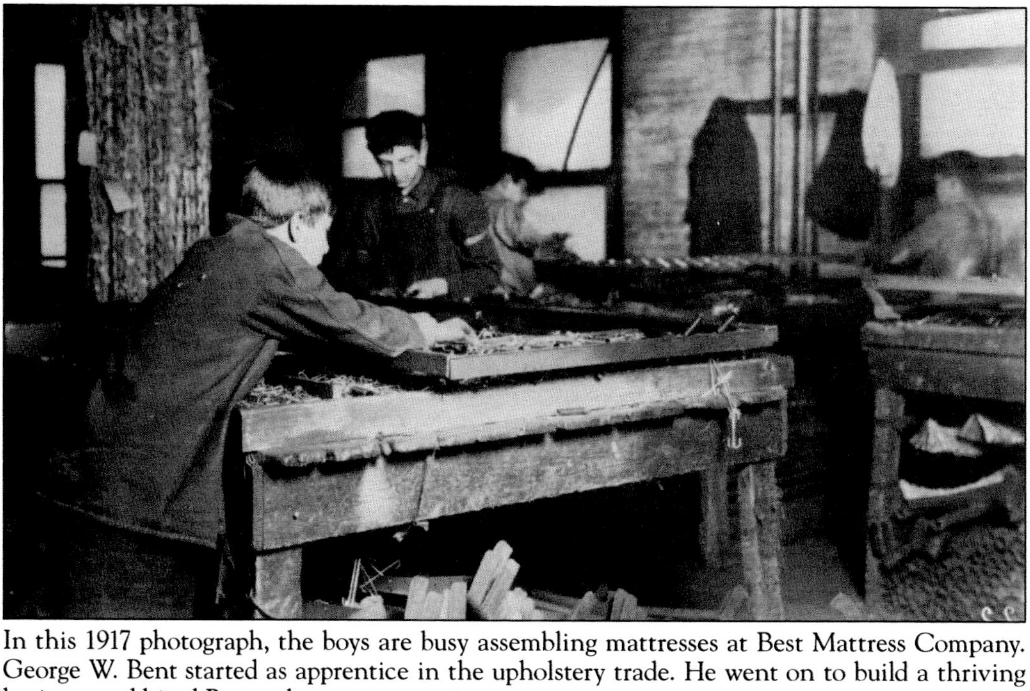

In this 1917 photograph, the boys are busy assembling mattresses at Best Mattress Company. George W. Bent started as apprentice in the upholstery trade. He went on to build a thriving business and hired Boston boys as apprentices.

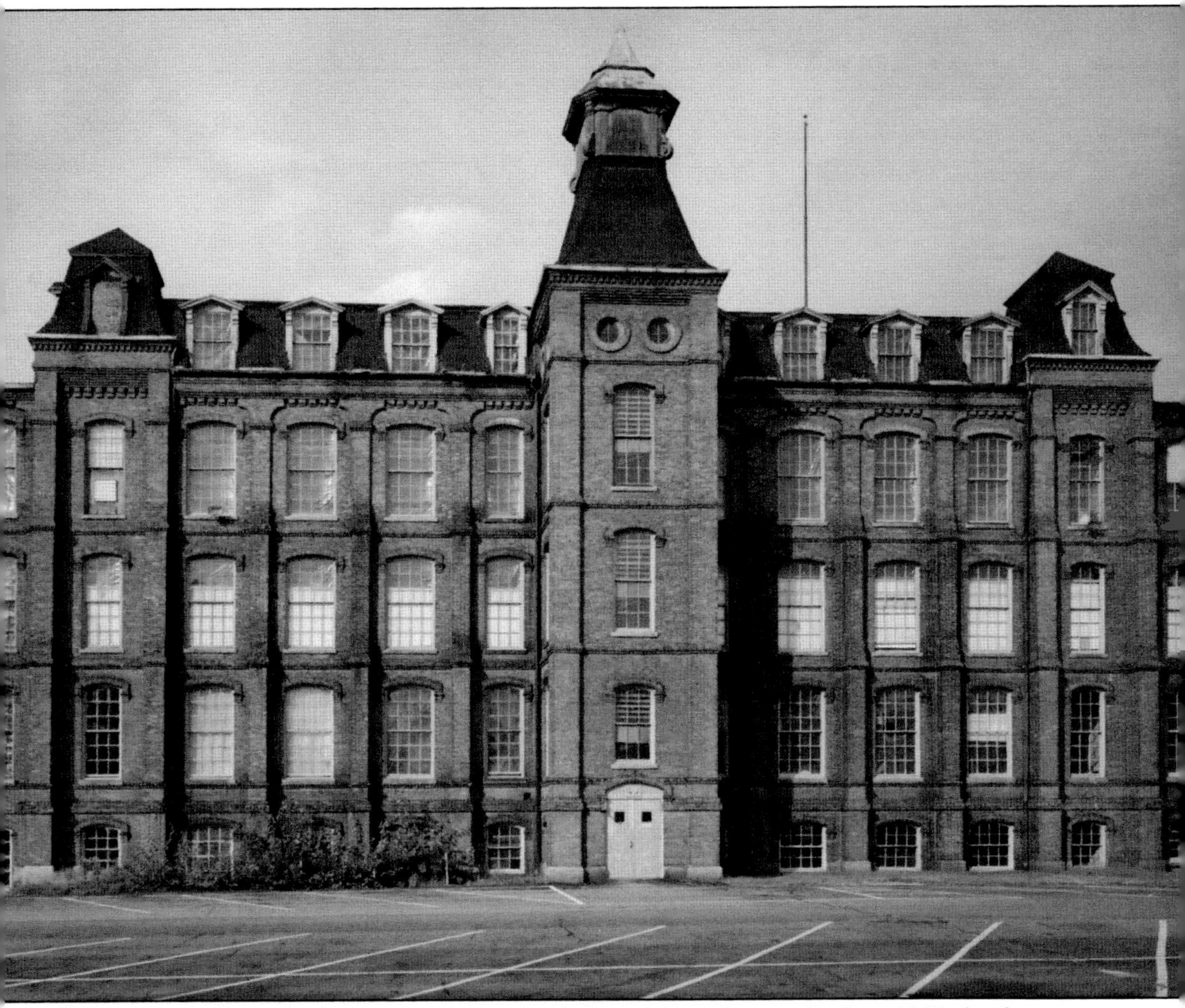

Silver Lake Cordage Company, Nevada Street, Newton, Massachusetts. Built in 1866, this factory was one of America's largest cordage companies. In 1870, James Tolman, a 23-year-old graduate of the Massachusetts Institute of Technology, was appointed superintendent. Later, he served as president and built Silver Lake into one of the world's largest manufacturers of braided cord.

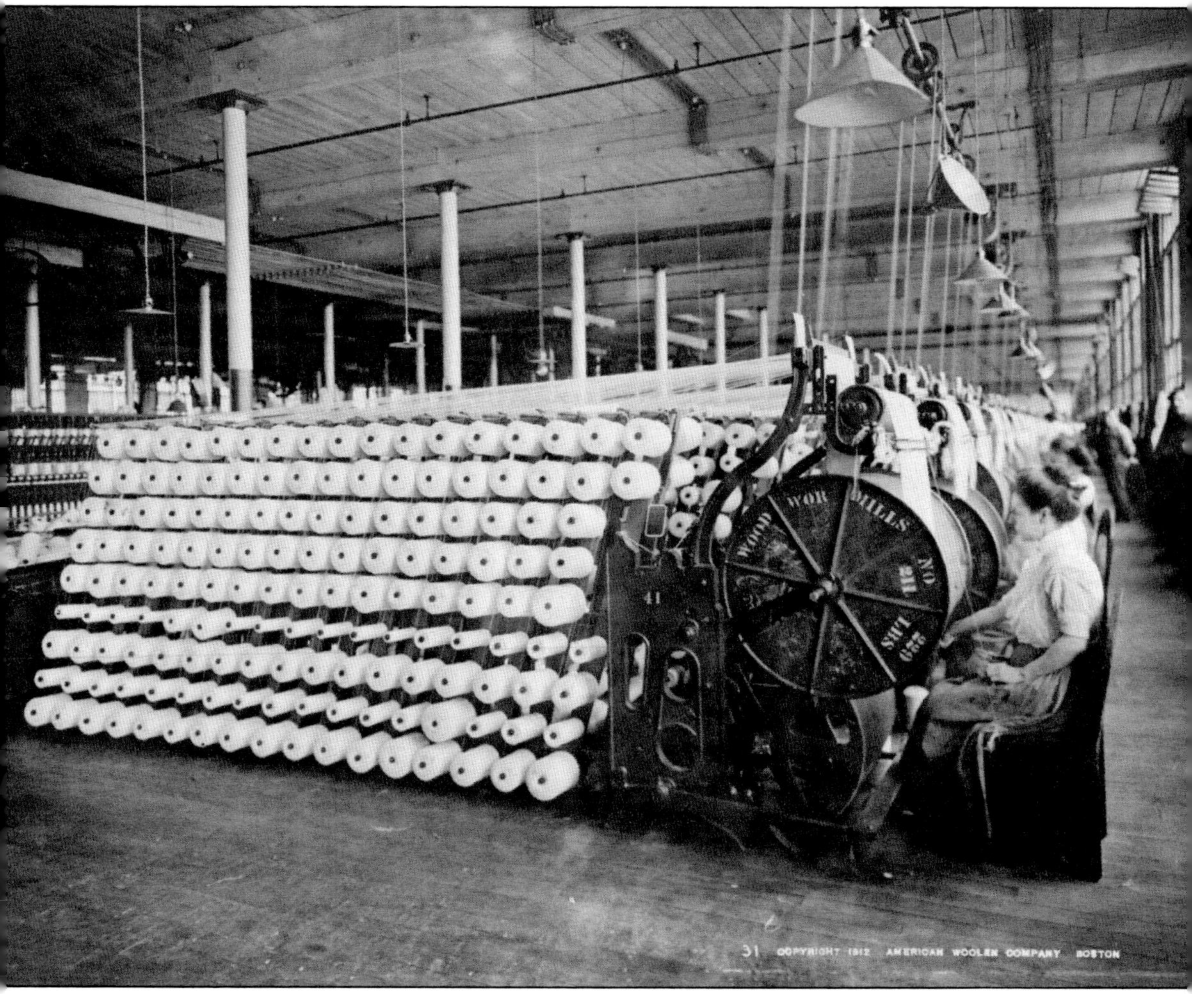

Massive looms are at work at the Wood Mill of the American Woolen Company, Lawrence, in 1912. Run by William Madison Wood (1858–1920), the company headquarters were at 245 State Street, Boston, controlling 58 mills, mainly in New England, and employing 40,000 workers. The American Woolen Company filled 1/4 of the nation's needs for woolen cloth.

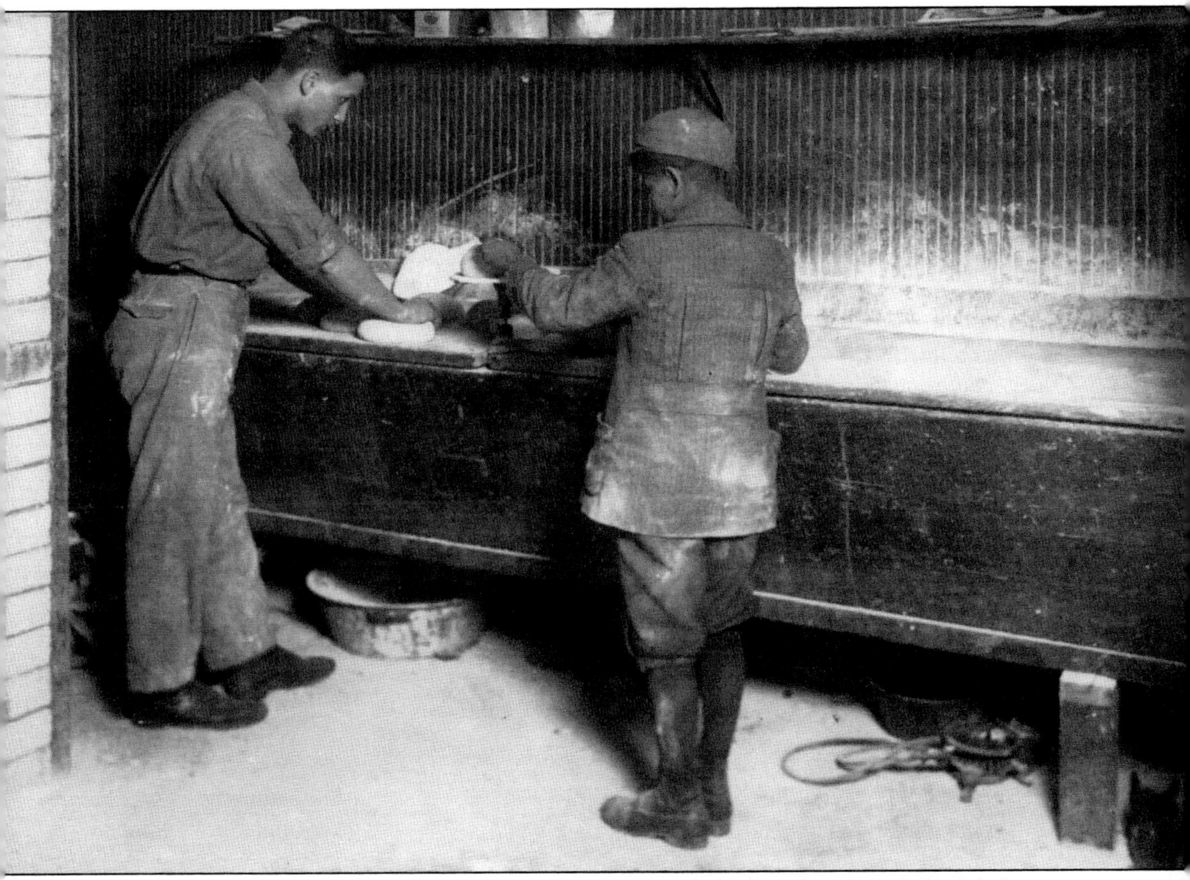

Vincenzo (age 15) and his brother Angelo Messina (age 11) bake bread at their father's bakery in Cambridge, Massachusetts. The boys also helped sell baked goods in the shop.

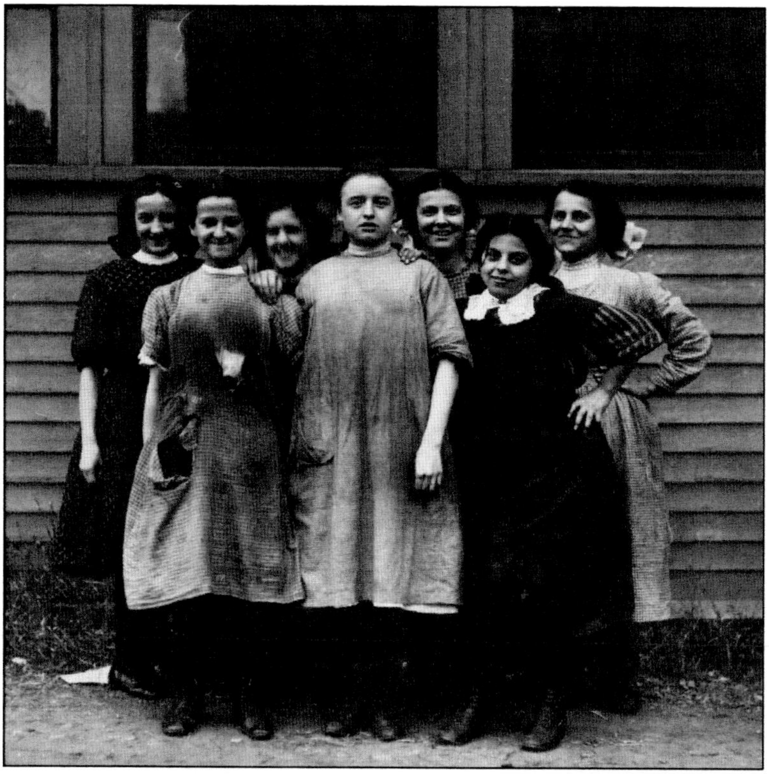

This photograph shows a group of girls who work at the Cass & Daley shoe factory in Salem, Massachusetts. Cass & Daley opened in 1893 making medium-priced boys' and men's shoes. The company had a long history of labor troubles, with strikes over conditions and wages common.

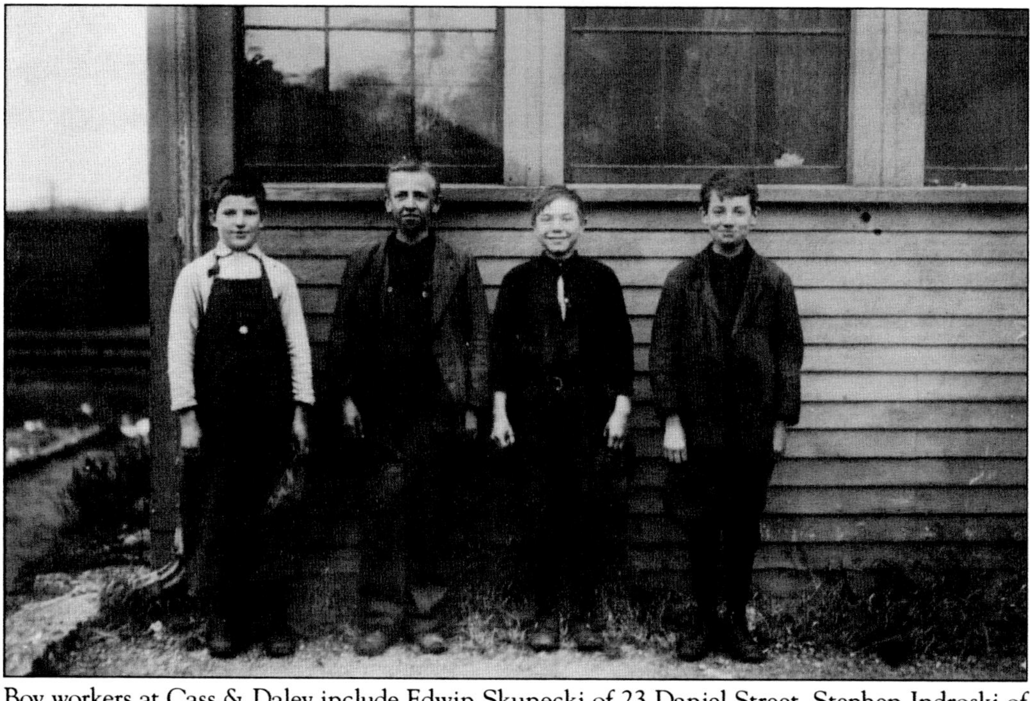

Boy workers at Cass & Daley include Edwin Skunecki of 23 Daniel Street, Stephen Indroski of 19 Turner Street, William Prasecki of 26 Peabody Street, and Brony Gelski of 45 Union Street, Salem, Massachusetts.

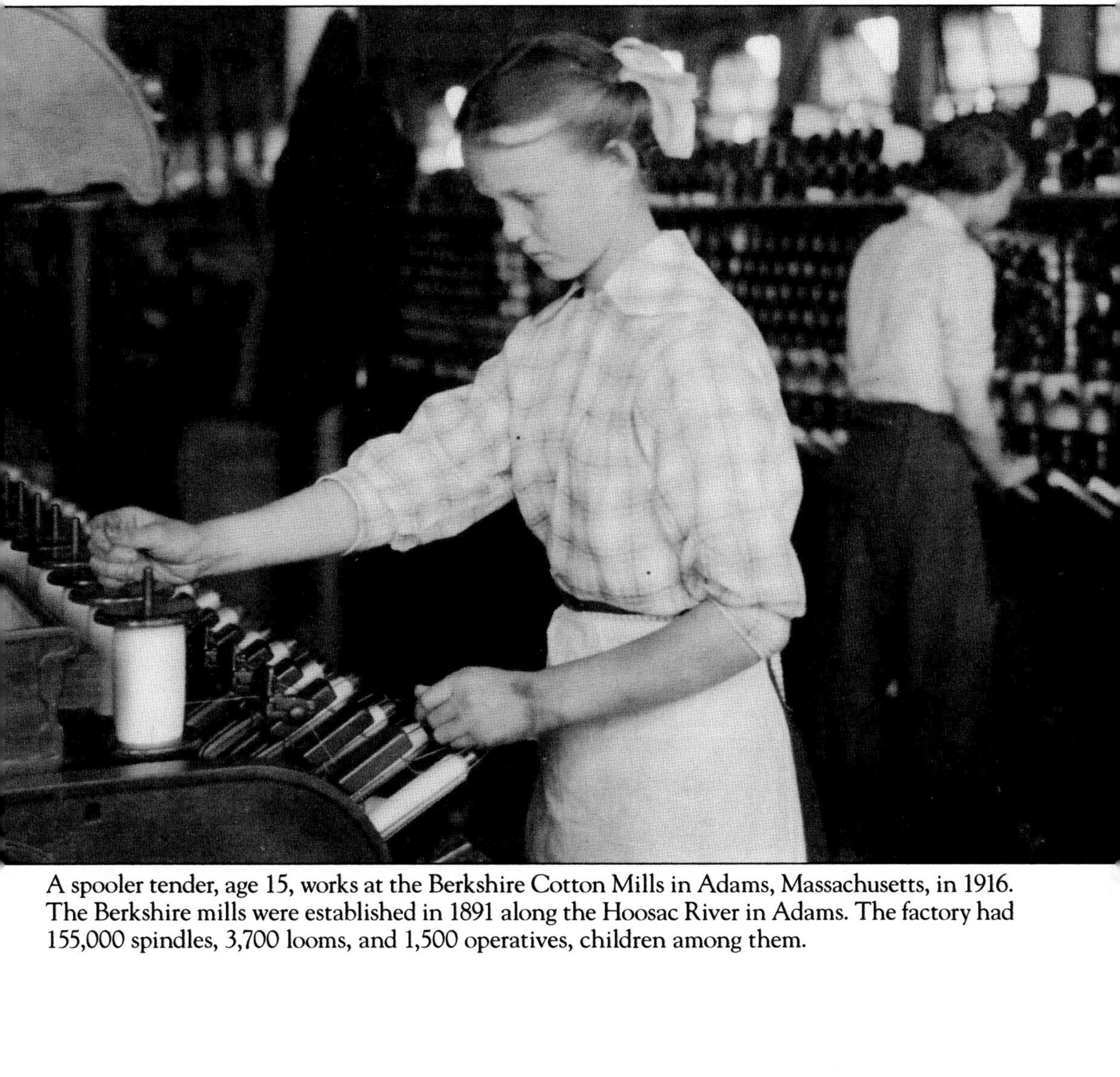

A spooler tender, age 15, works at the Berkshire Cotton Mills in Adams, Massachusetts, in 1916. The Berkshire mills were established in 1891 along the Hoosac River in Adams. The factory had 155,000 spindles, 3,700 looms, and 1,500 operatives, children among them.

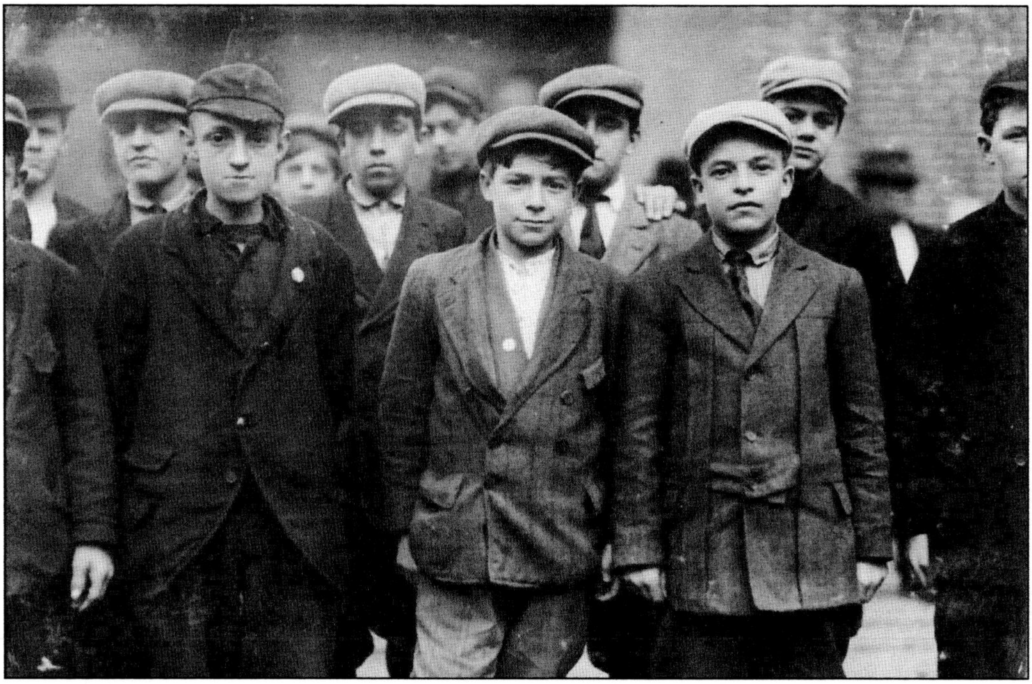

In October 1911, Lewis Hine visited Lowell, America's first textile city. In this gathering are Alexander Durante of 35 Tucker Street and Joseph Courtois of 33 Tucker Street. The boys appear younger than 14 years old.

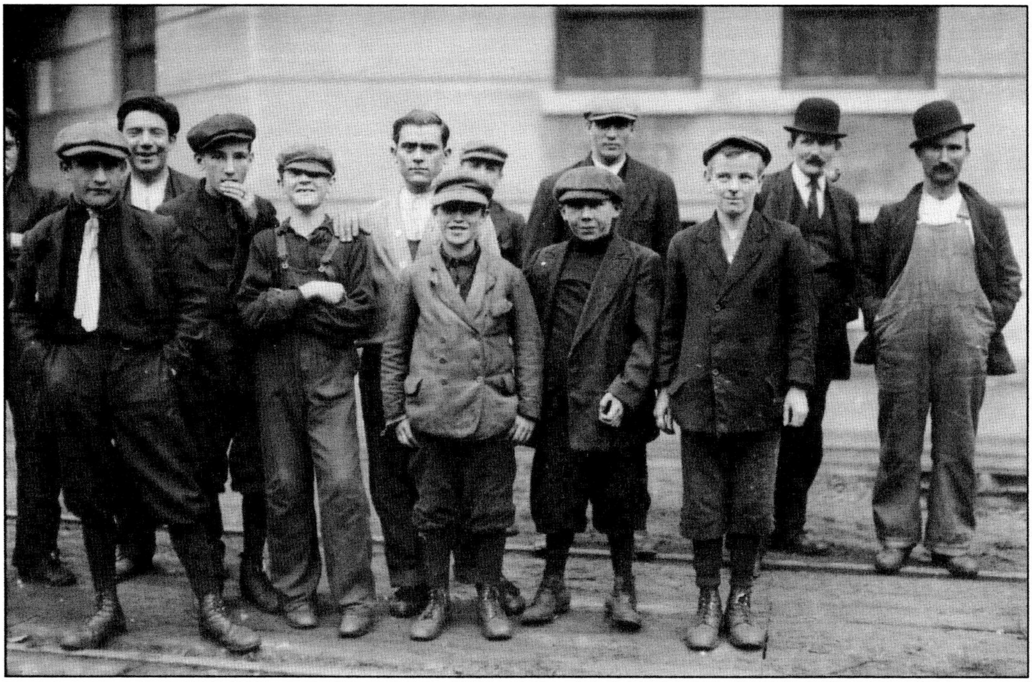

Wearing caps or bowler hats, this group of Lowell workers was photographed near the mill gate in 1911. Among the smaller boys were Dennis Cavanaugh of 24 Bassett Street and Alexander Stankiewicz of 3 Fayette Street, Lowell.

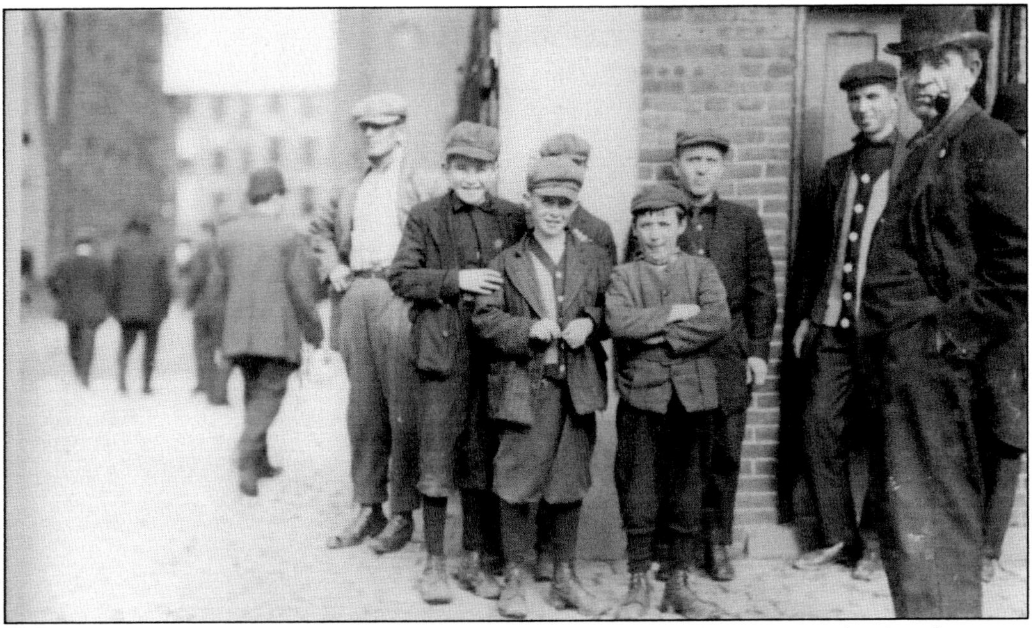

This October 1911 photograph was taken outside the gate of the Merrimack Manufacturing Company in Lowell. The smallest boys in the group are Robert Magee of 270 Suffolk Street, Michael Keefe of 32 Marion Street, and Cornelius Hurley of 298 Adams Street in Lowell. The Merrimack Mill dates to 1823 and was the first textile mill in Lowell; it used waterpower.

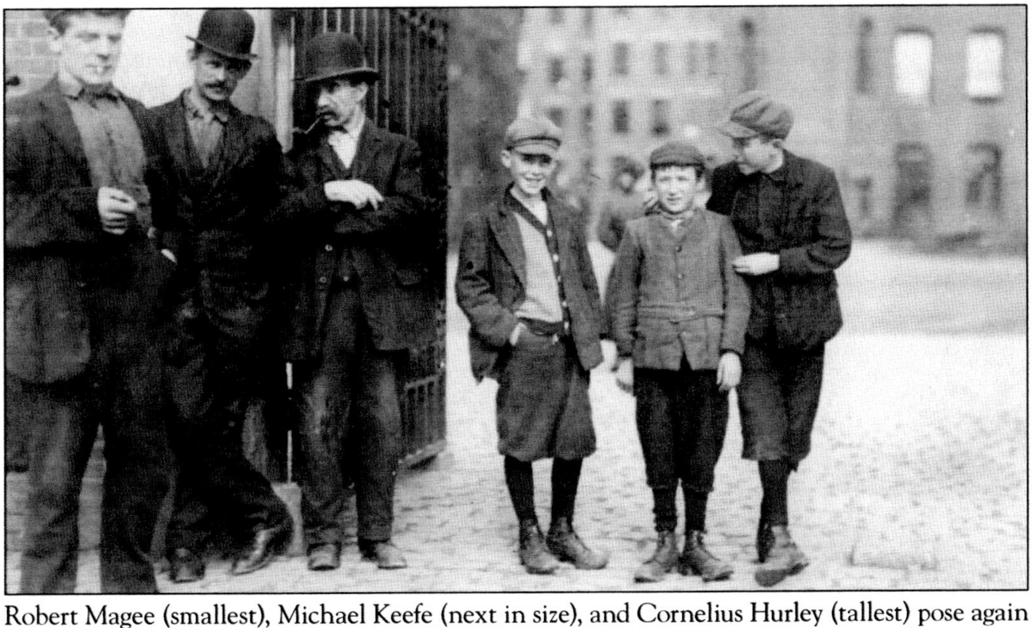

Robert Magee (smallest), Michael Keefe (next in size), and Cornelius Hurley (tallest) pose again at the main gate of the Merrimack Mill in 1911. All the boys appear too young to be working legally in a Massachusetts textile mill. In 1900, the Merrimack Manufacturing Company opened a subsidiary in Huntsville, Alabama, employing even more child labor. The Lowell mill succumbed to the lower manufacturing costs in the South and closed in the 1950s; the building was demolished in the 1960s.

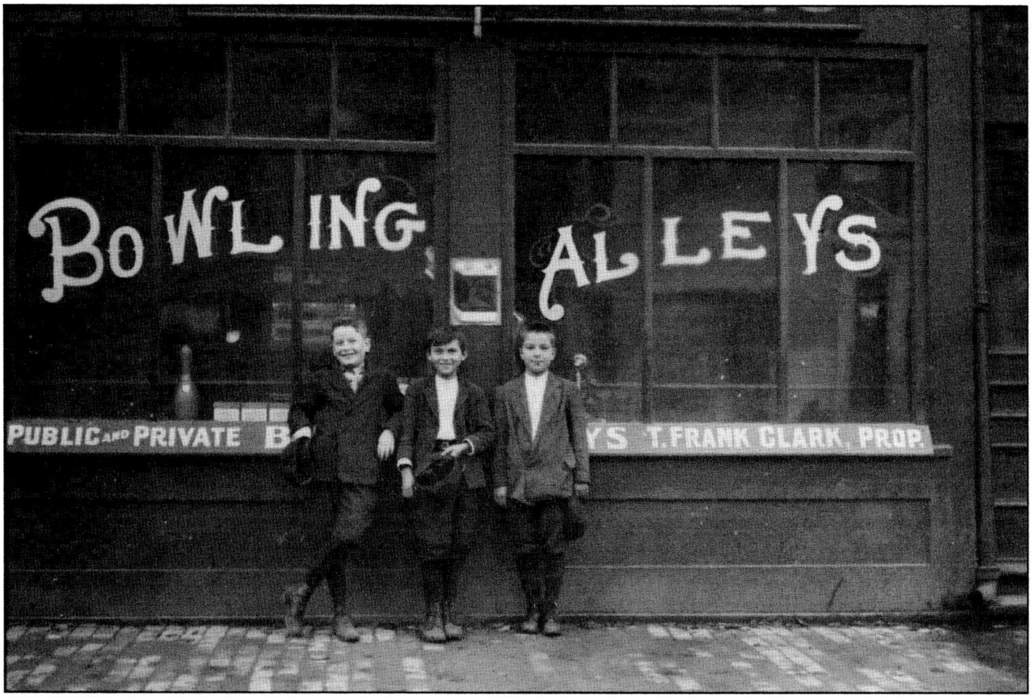

Shown here are boys who work at Les Miserables Bowling Alley in Lowell. From left to right are Frank Jarosse of 7 Fayette Street, Joseph Phillip of 5 Wall Street, and Willie Payton of 196 Fayette Street. Their job is to retrieve the fallen pins and replace them for the next game. Automatic electric ball machines took away these jobs. This picture was taken by Lewis Hine in October 1911.

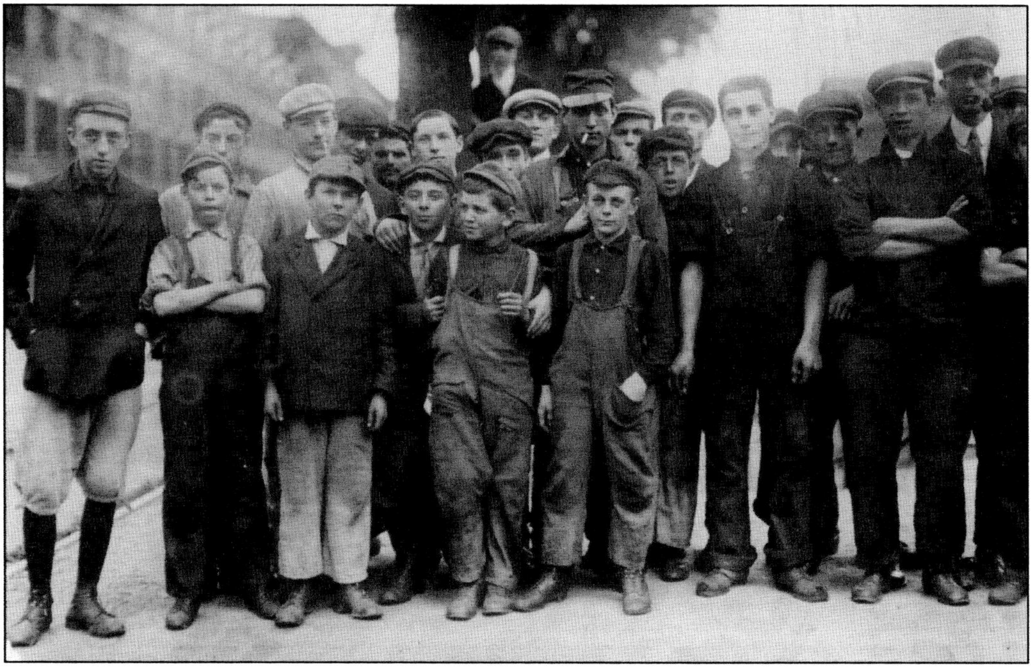

Boys and grown men pose outside the Washington Mills in Lawrence, Massachusetts, in 1911. Lawrence was known as Immigrant City, attracting workers from all over the world.

In this c. 1910 photograph, girls leave the Pacific Mills, located in Lawrence, Massachusetts. Built in 1853, Pacific Mills had 200,000 spindles by the time of this photograph. The mill was later owned by James and Frederick Ayer, who made their fortunes manufacturing patent medicines in Lowell. After James died, brother Frederick, with William Wood, bought struggling mills to form the vast American Woolen Company.

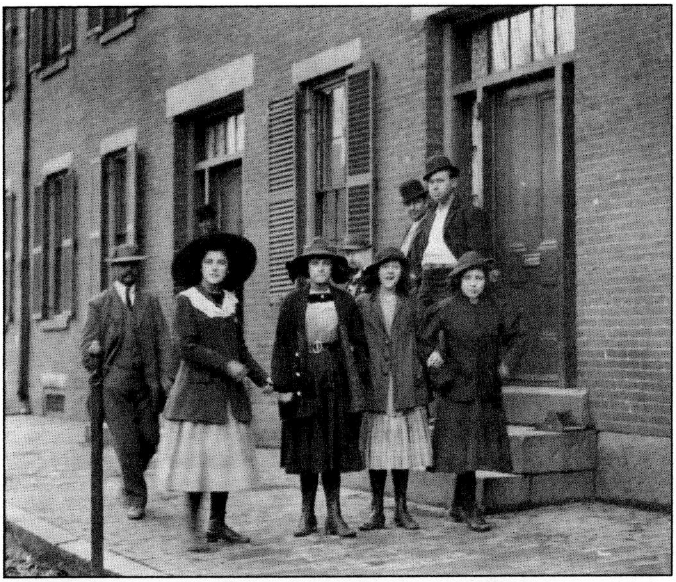

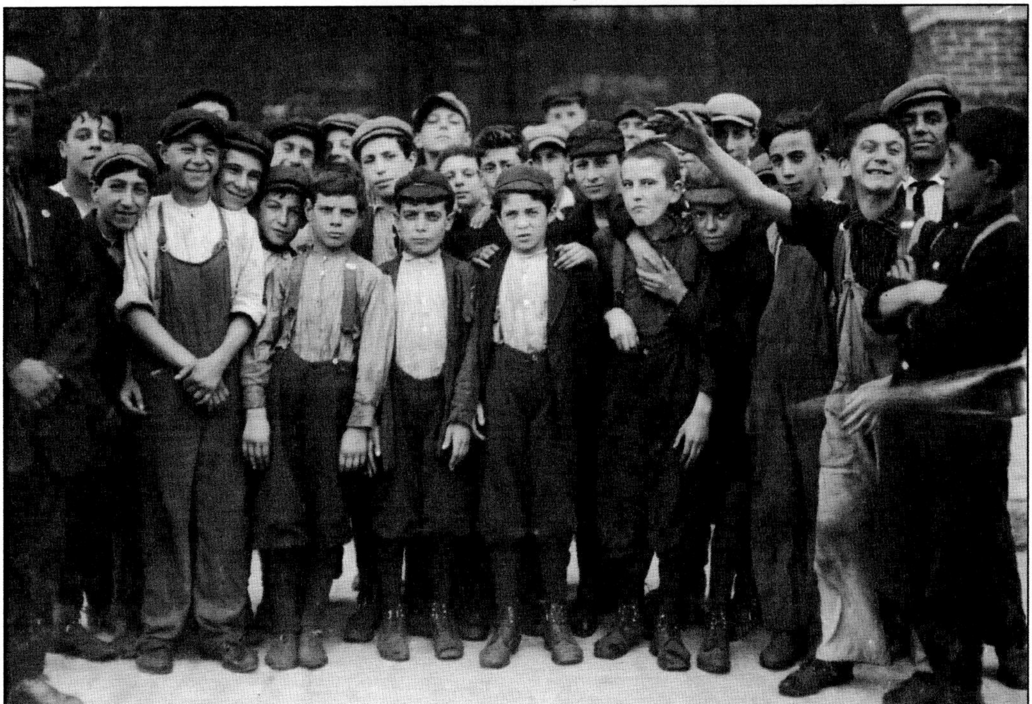

A large group of Lawrence mill boys, aged 12–15, work despite state laws prohibiting mill employment for children under 16. The boys and their parents may have lied about their age or the inspectors were lax. This group of boys included, among others, John Gopen of 189 Elm Street, Joseph Stonge of 73 King Street, Billie Welch of 178 Union Street, Tim Carroll of 310 Salem Street, Michael Devine of 64 South Broadway, Jacob Black of 15 Bradford Boulevard, Binnie Greenfield of 281 Park Street, Andrew Pomeroy of 76 South Broadway, Louis Gross of 39 Myrtle Street, Arthur Davois of 244 Salem Street, Joseph Latham of 165 Willow Street, Salvatore Quatirtto of 48 Union Street, and Sam Gangi of 82 Pleasant Valley Street.

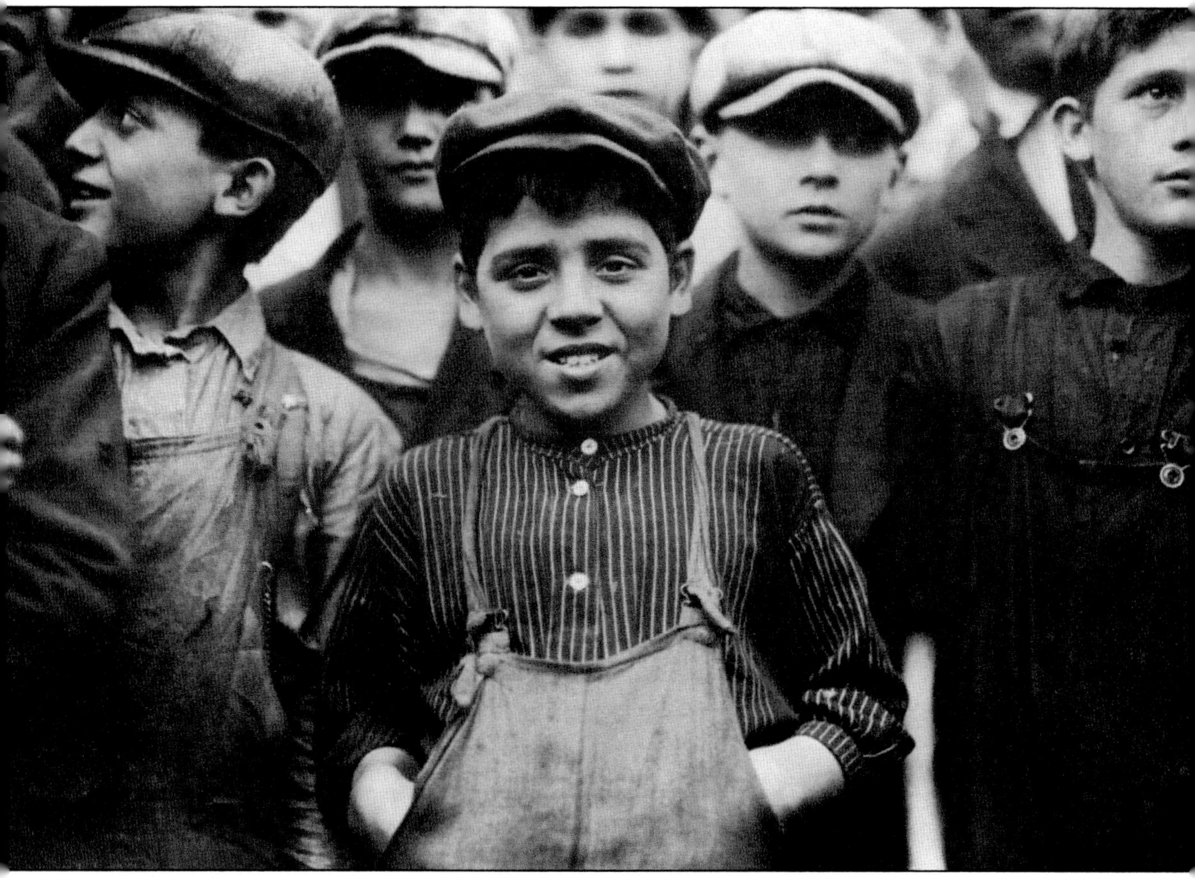

The smallest boy in the group is Secondino Libro, about 11 years old, of 34 Walnut Street, Lawrence, Massachusetts. This picture, taken in 1911, shows other boys who work at Washington Mills No. 4 spinning room.

Despite state laws forbidding the practice, children in the early part of the 20th century continued to work in Massachusetts textile mills as cleaners, doffers, and bobbin boys and girls—the lowest paid jobs. The pattern was repeated in the South as mills moved to find cheaper labor.

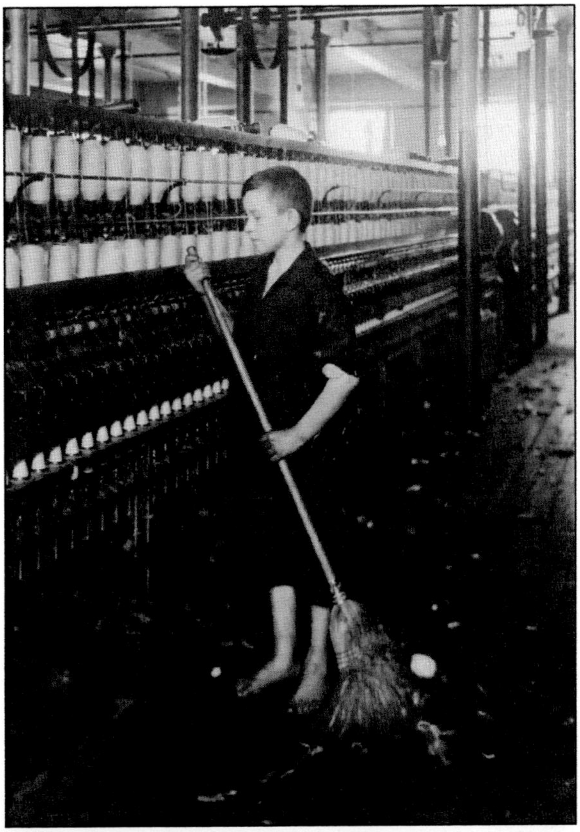

The Connecticut River provided ample power to run cotton mills. In Chicopee, money from Boston developed the Chicopee, Perkins, Dwight, and Cabot mills. This 1911 image shows Andrew Stefanik, of 4 Exchange Street, working as a bobbin boy.

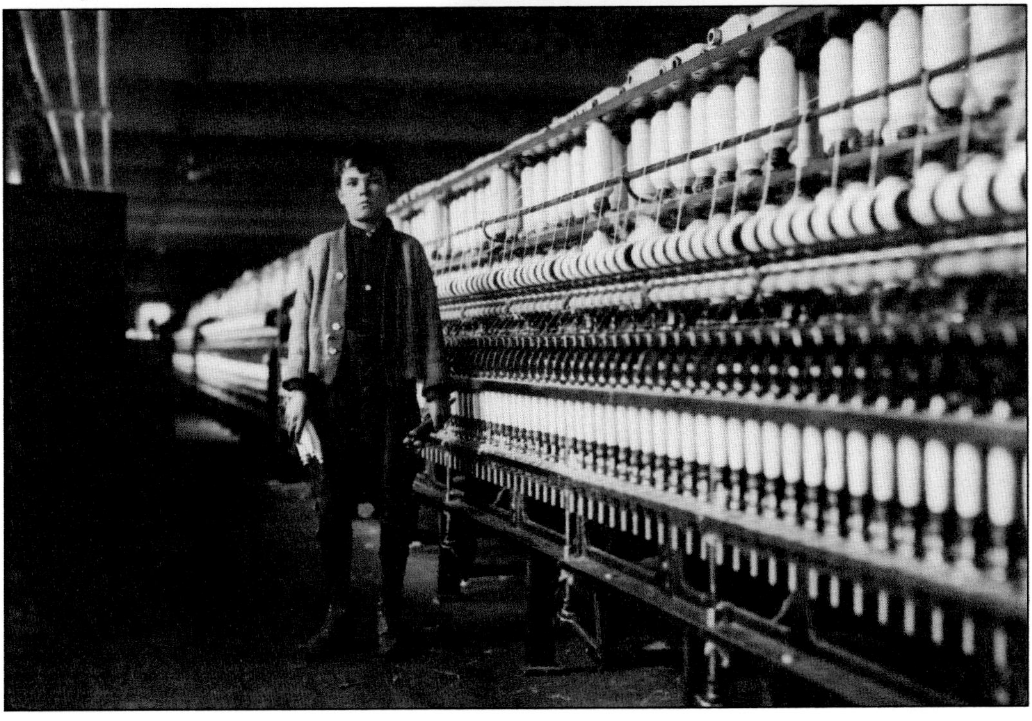

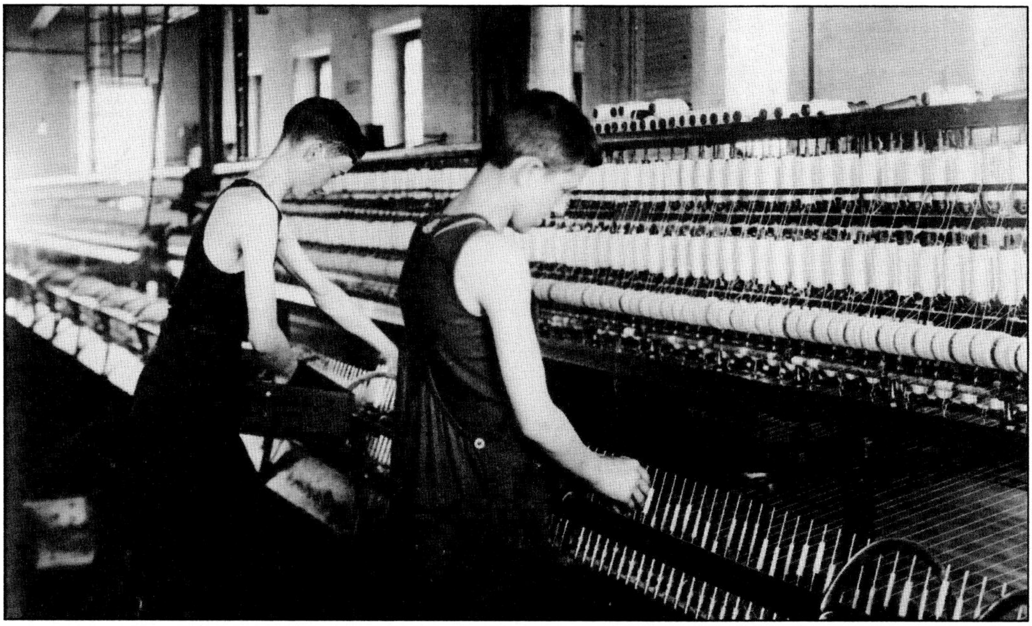

The King Philip Mill at 372 Kilburn Street, Fall River, opened in 1871. The Fall River textile mills were established after Lowell and Lawrence and soon out-produced the competition. This picture shows Thomas Nicholls, at left, who lives at 54 Kilburn Street and works at the mill in the mule spinning room.

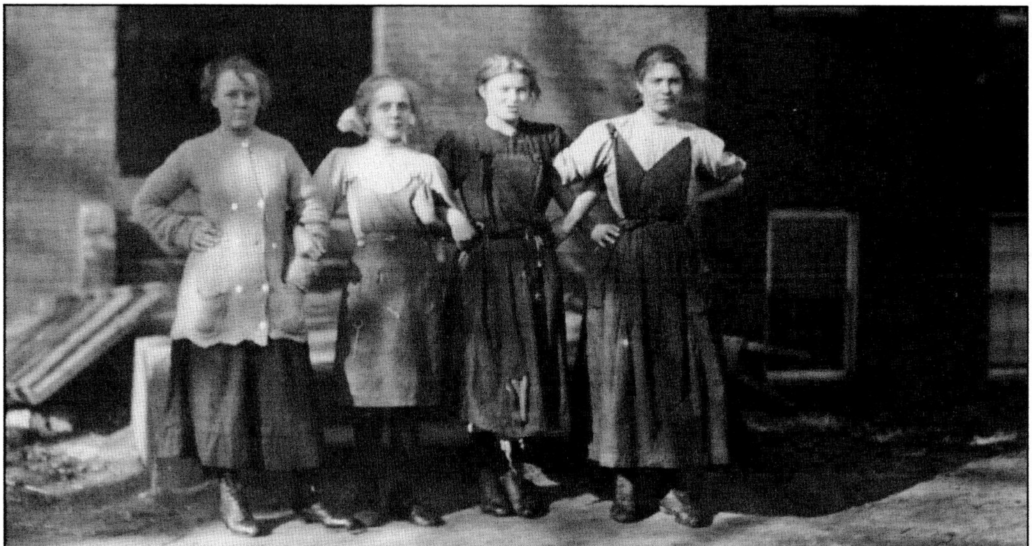

Seen here are girl workers from the spinning room at the Dwight Mill in Chicopee. The shortest of the girls is Sophie Motralske of 3 Lawrence Street. Dwight became the largest company in Chicopee, absorbing the Cabot and the Perkins companies. At its prime, Dwight of Chicopee employed 1,475 workers, 1,030 of whom were girls or women. Protesting the restrictive labor rules in Massachusetts, Dwight Manufacturing Company opened a subsidiary in Alabama City, Alabama, in 1895. The company moved the jobs and the use of child labor from New England to the South. Other Massachusetts mills soon followed Dwight's example. The Dwight Manufacturing Company of Chicopee closed in 1927.

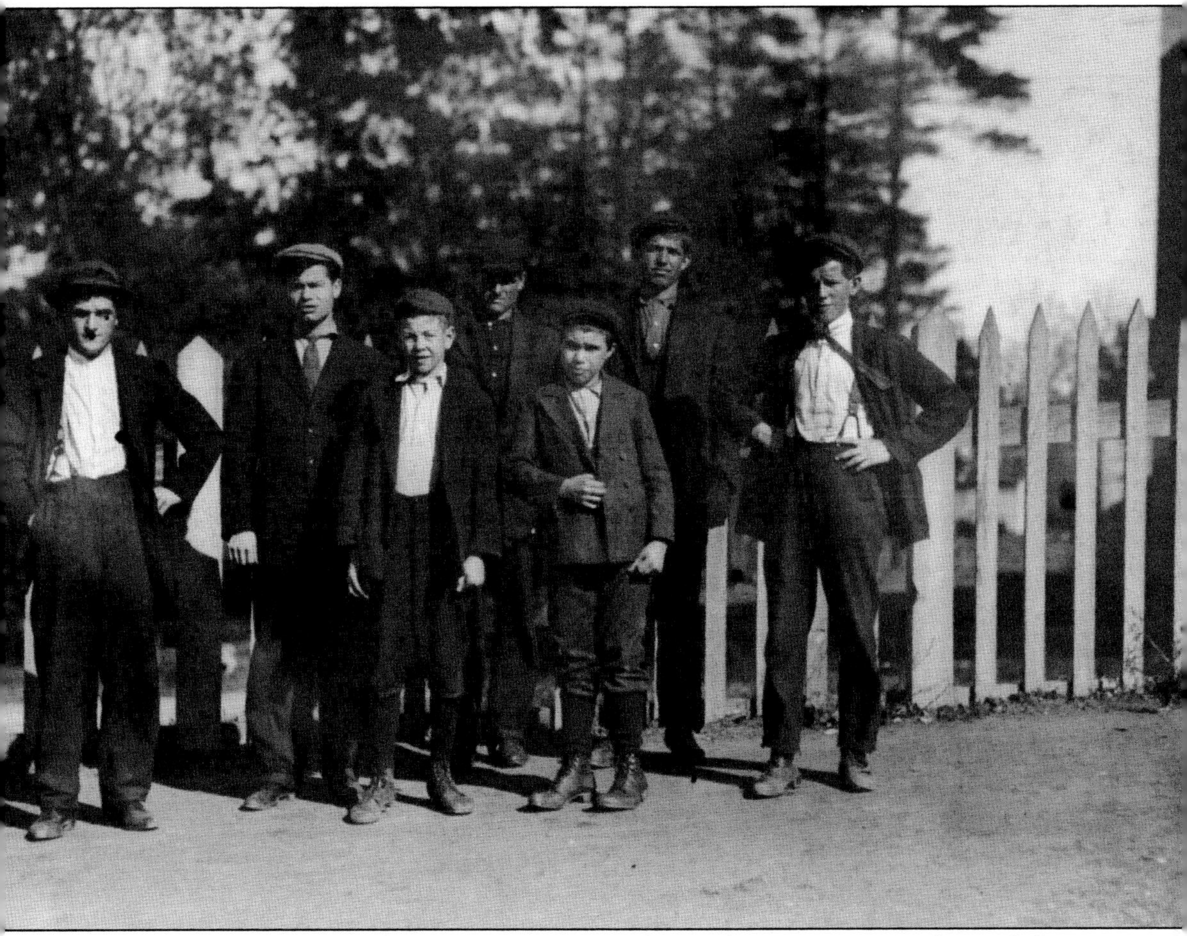

Boys work at the R.H. Long Shoe Factory in Framingham. The company manufactured shoe machinery, made shoes, and sold shoes in company-owned retail stores across the nation. During World War I, R.H. Long had a contract to supply boots for the British army. Richard Long ran for governor of Massachusetts but was soundly beaten by Calvin Coolidge, future president of the United States. Long's Bay State automobile company of the 1920s ended in failure.

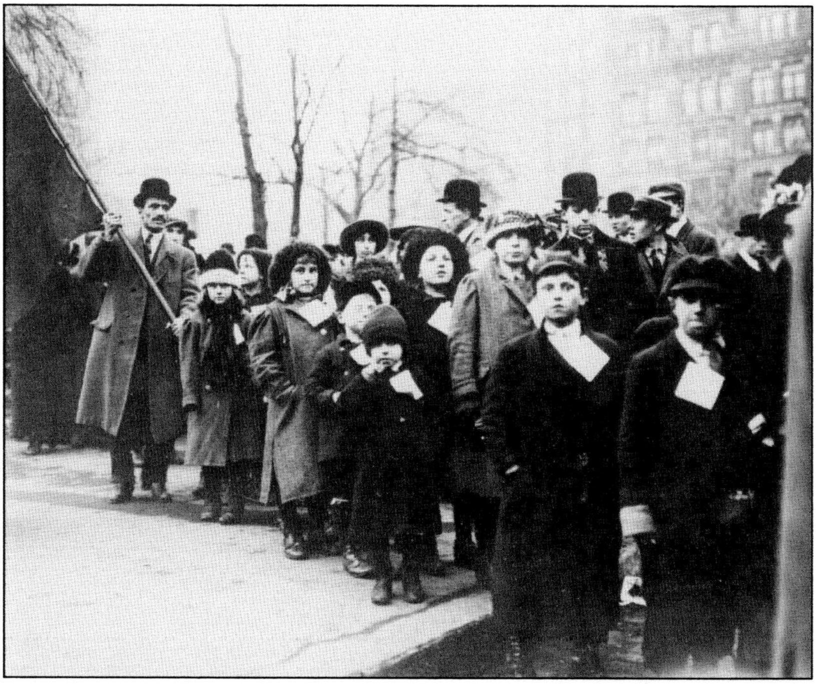

During the 1912 Bread and Roses Strike, hundreds of children were evacuated to sympathetic families in other states. This picture shows children of Lawrence strikers about to board trains to live with sympathizers in other states for the duration of the strike.

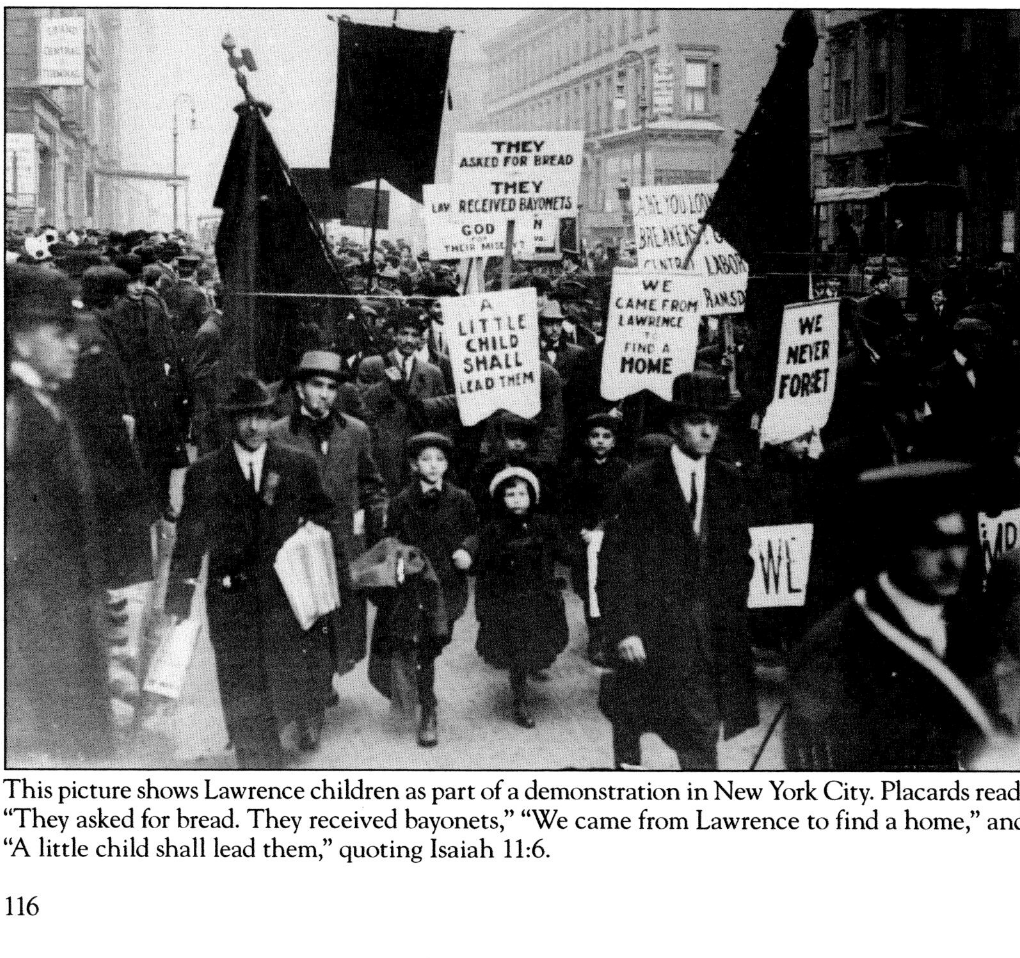

This picture shows Lawrence children as part of a demonstration in New York City. Placards read, "They asked for bread. They received bayonets," "We came from Lawrence to find a home," and "A little child shall lead them," quoting Isaiah 11:6.

Seven

FARMING AND FISHING

The returns from agriculture were so meager in colonial Massachusetts that a farmer could not afford to hire outside labor. Instead, he depended on his wife, sons, and daughters to care for the house, make cloth, feed the animals, chop wood, grow fruits and vegetables, and perform the myriad of other farm activities. Children began helping their parents at age five. By age 14, they were skilled enough to produce more than the cost to maintain them. Massachusetts land was hilly, filled with stones, and the soil was poor. To support its great textile and shoe industries, Massachusetts imported the bulk of its wool, cotton, and hides from other states or from abroad. These raw materials were shipped to Boston Harbor and stored in the large warehouses on Summer Street. From Boston, the goods were sent by rail to the manufacturing towns to be processed into textiles and footwear. The finished goods were transported to Boston and sent to other states or shipped for export. Increasingly, Boston became the center of finance and insurance.

The waters off the Massachusetts coast were once rich in fish. Boats went out from Boston, Marblehead, Salem, and Newburyport carrying seasoned fishermen teaching their sons the ways of the sea. From New Bedford, whaling ships carrying apprentice seamen left on voyages to the Pacific Ocean that lasted many months. Whales were harpooned and killed, the blubber boiled down to oil.

By the start of the 20th century, Massachusetts's farming, fishing, and factories were in trouble. The small Massachusetts farms could not compete against the bounty of the Midwest, whale oil was replaced by petroleum, and the great textile and shoe industries were failing against competition from the South and the Midwest. The agricultural product in which Massachusetts excels is growing cranberries. Native Americans harvested cranberries for food, medicine, and for ceremonies. The early settlers learned to appreciate cranberries for sauces added to game and poultry. Whalers and merchant ships carried barrels of cranberry juice as protection against scurvy. The harvesting of cranberries in Massachusetts begins early September and continues until mid-October. Before the 1950s, cranberries were picked by hand or raked. Today, growers flood the bogs to loosen the cranberries, which float to the surface to be collected and then are processed into juice, jam and jelly, or dried.

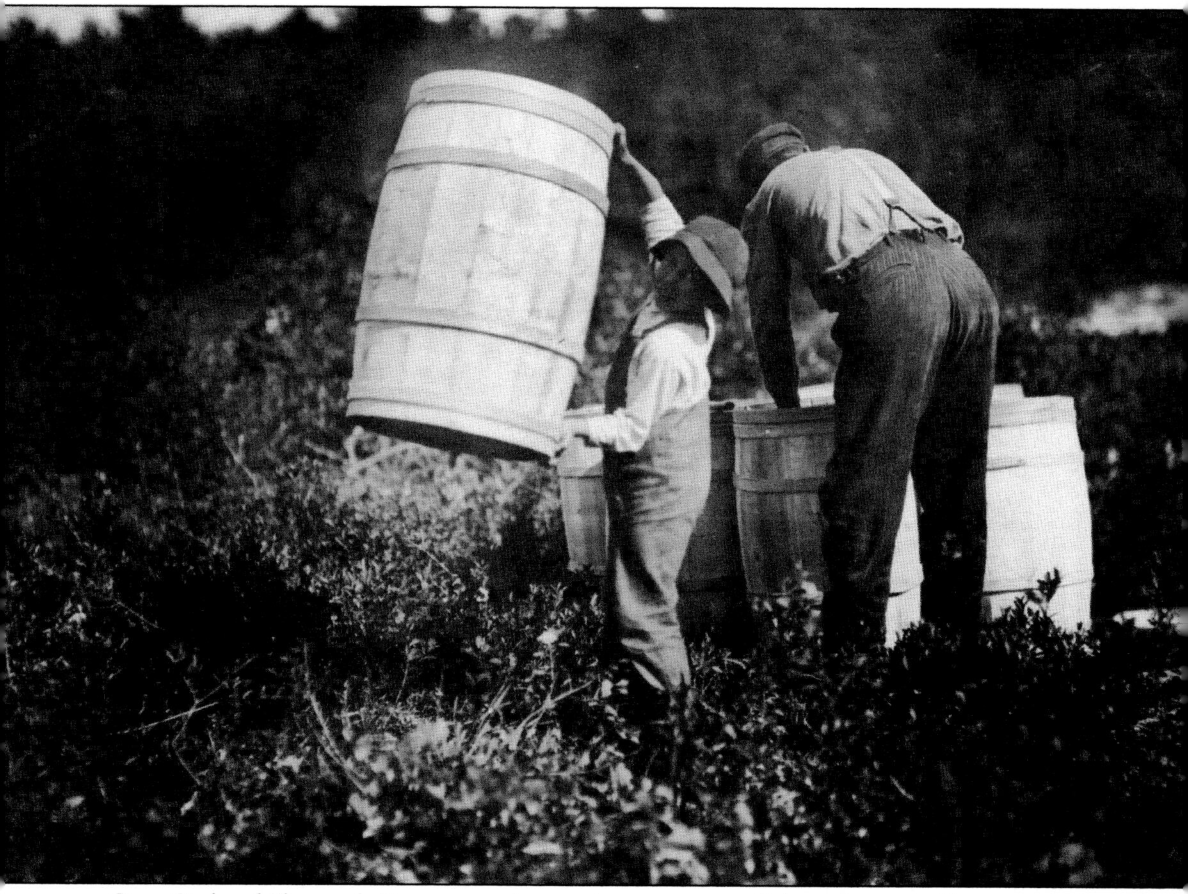

Cape Cod and Plymouth County are the cranberry centers of Massachusetts. This picture shows Robert Saunders, age 11, helping his father collect the cranberries and place them in large barrels in 1911. At that time, the berries were picked by hand or manually raked, requiring much crouching and bending to the ground. The picking season started early September and lasted until mid-October, making children start the school year late.

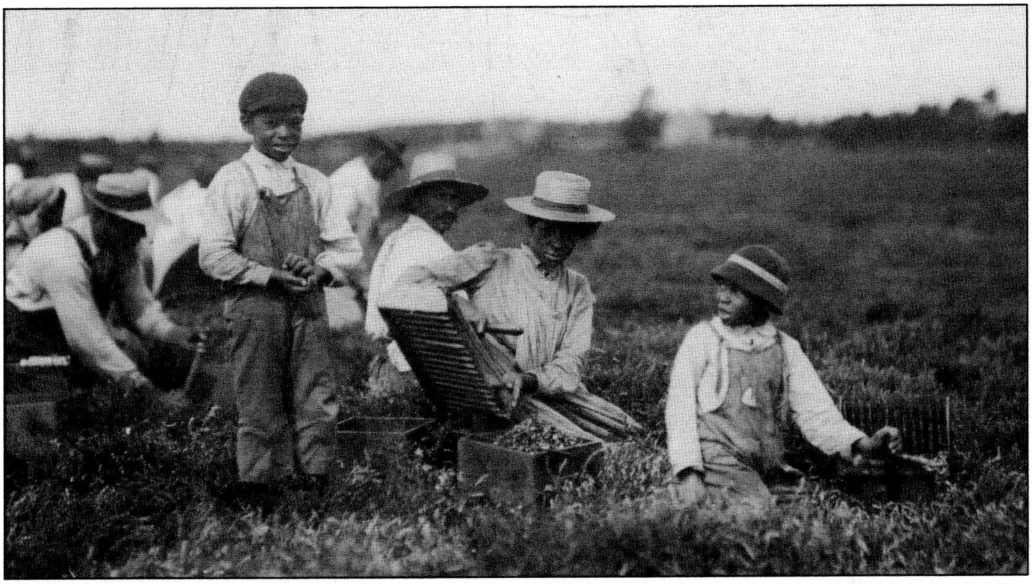

Arthur Fernandes, age eight, picks cranberries by hand, while his nine-year-old brother Charlie uses a scoop. The Fernandes family is probably of Cape Verde origin. Yankee merchant ships and whalers frequently stopped at the Azores islands to take on supplies and sailors. These men were the founders of the Portuguese-speaking Azores community of New Bedford. This image was taken by Lewis Hine in September 1911 at the Hollow Branch Bog in Wareham.

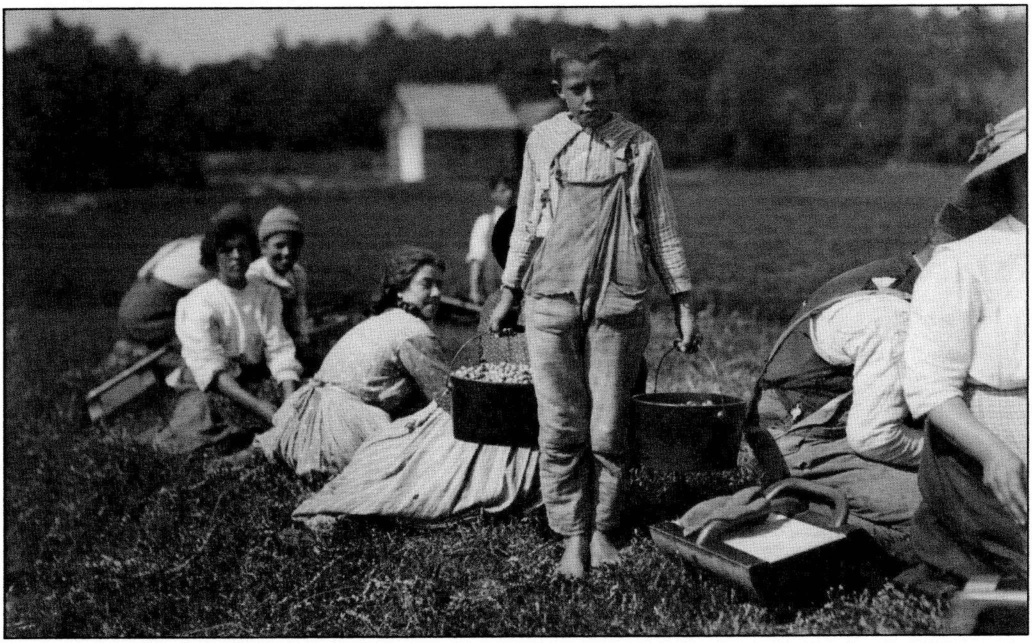

Manuel Robello, age 10, fills his buckets with cranberries, working at the Baker bog in Falmouth, Massachusetts. Manuel lives with his family in Teaticket, some five miles from Falmouth. Isaac F. Baker, born in Falmouth in 1838, owned a dry goods and grocery store before switching to the more lucrative cranberry growing. The agricultural school at Harwich started classroom instruction on November 1 "because of the cranberry harvest and scallop fishing." This photograph was taken by Lewis Hine in September 1911.

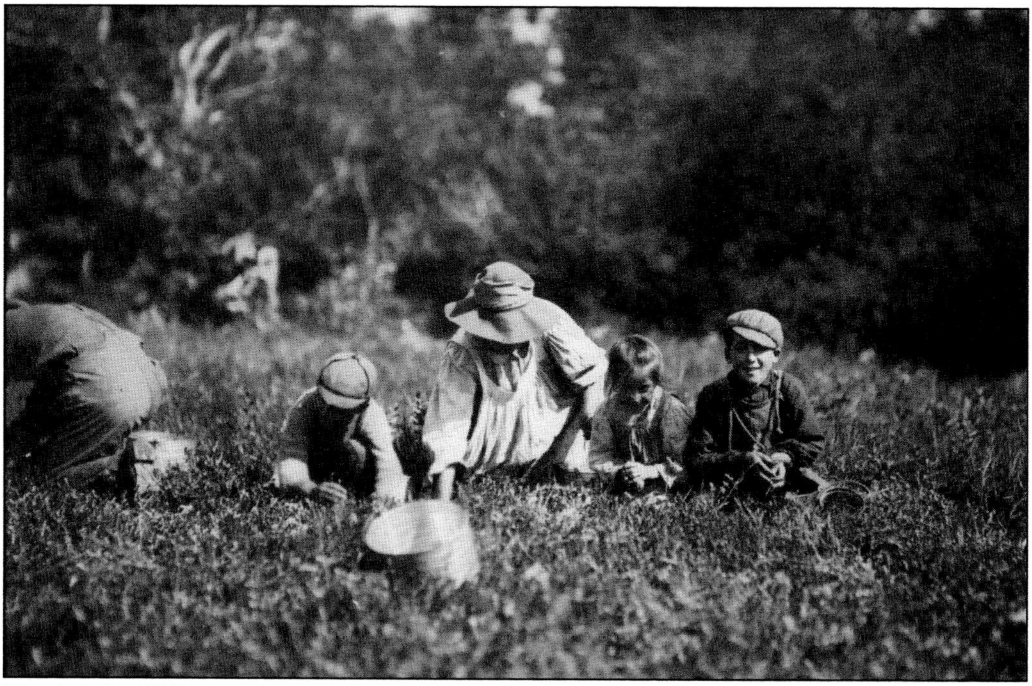

The family of Thomas Vegas works on a cranberry bog in Falmouth in September 1911. Coming from New Bedford, whole families of cranberry pickers work in the nearby bogs as contract labor, keeping the children out of school until mid-October.

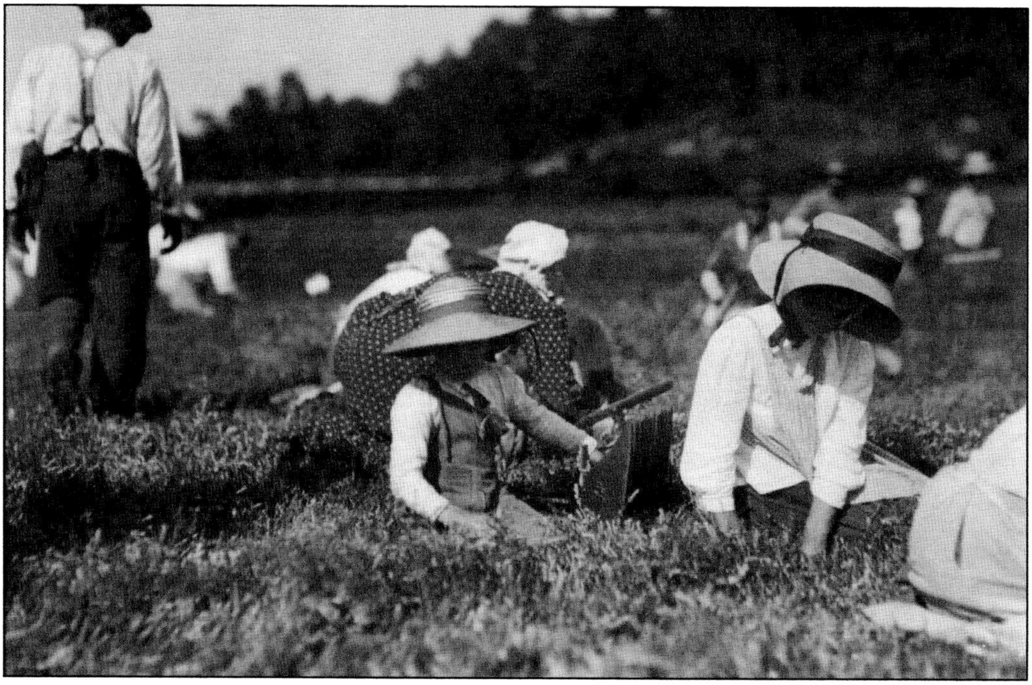

Employing children in Massachusetts as cranberry pickers continued into the 1920s, when Sen. Henry Cabot Lodge proposed an amendment to the US Constitution for a national ban on child labor. Hiring families of pickers for fruits and vegetables was standard practice across the nation.

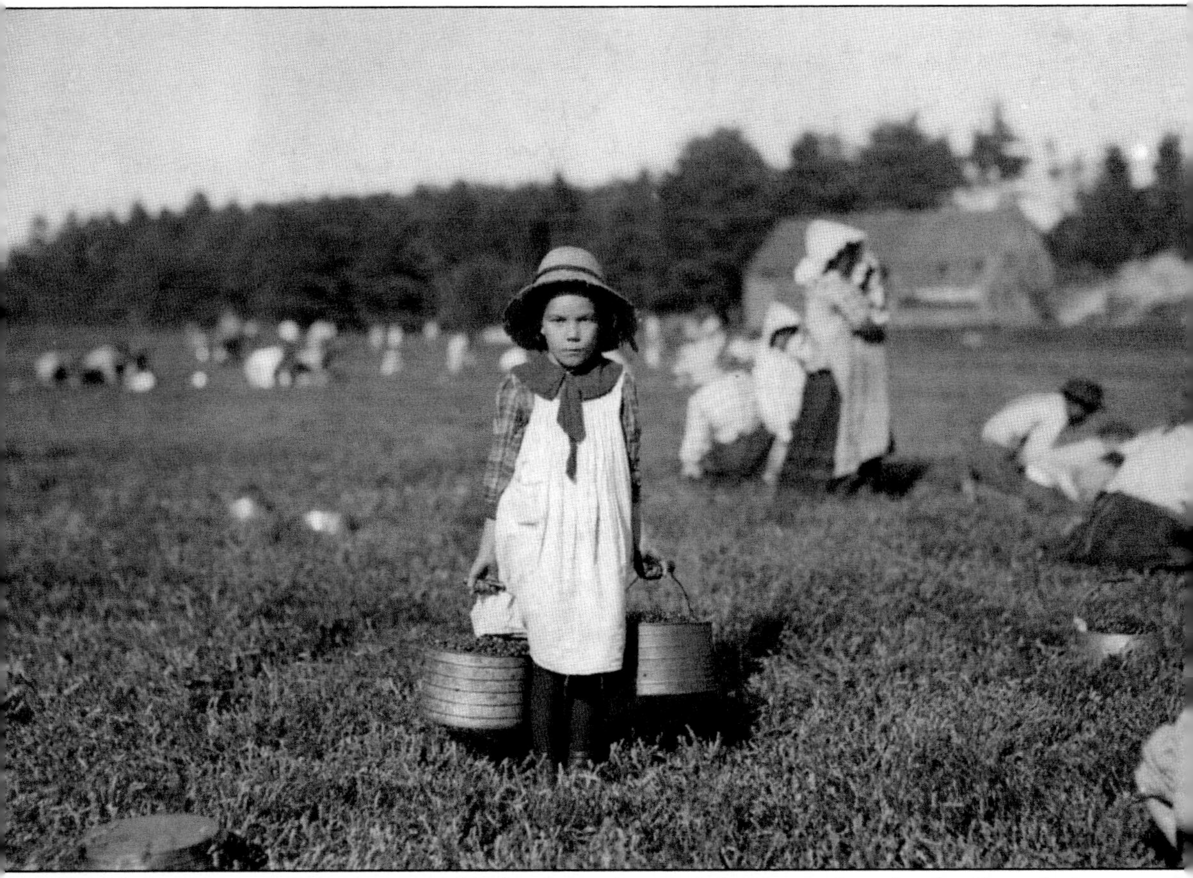

Merilda, age seven, carries containers filled with cranberries. Like many others, her family worked the Eldridge cranberry bog in Rochester, Massachusetts, in September 1911. Ancestors of the Eldridge family settled on Cape Cod as early as 1645. At one bog, Lewis Hine counted seven children, aged 6–12, among the 57 workers.

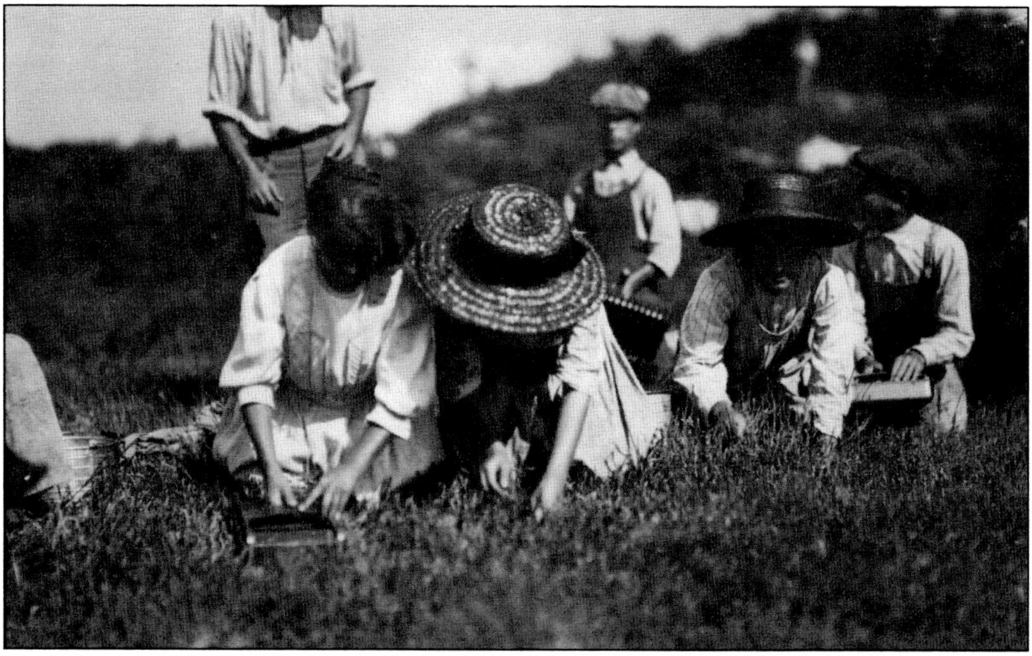

The bogs required 150–200 pickers; whole families, men, women, and children, worked a cranberry bog until all the berries were gathered in. Employed as contract labor, they worked nine hours a day and lived in shacks during the picking season, returning to their homes in New Bedford and other towns when the work was done.

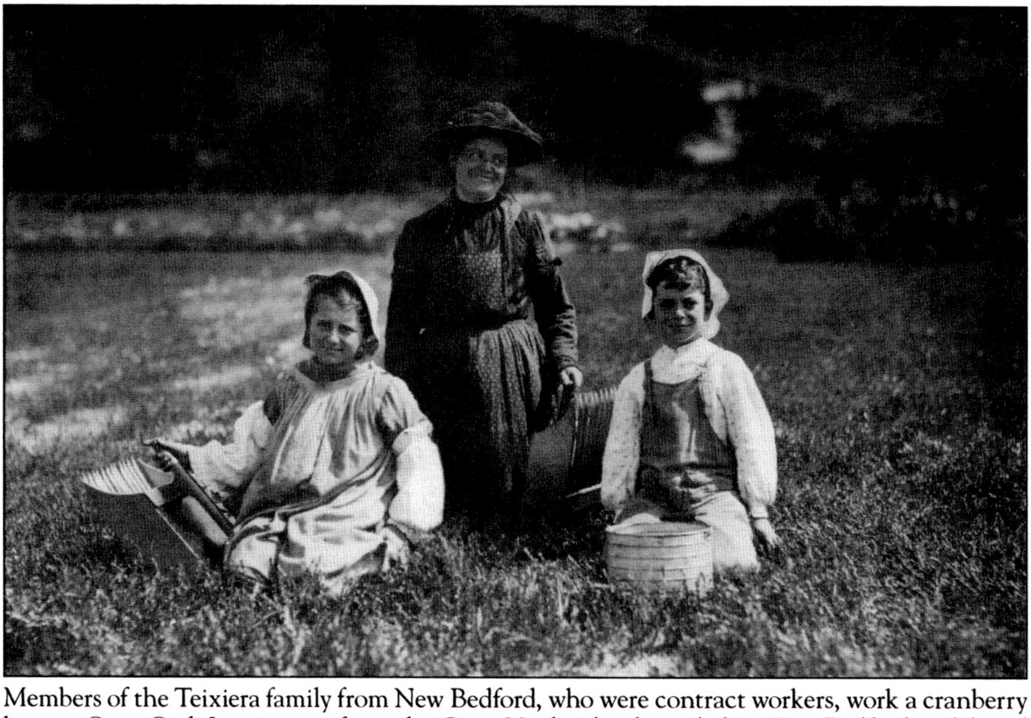

Members of the Teixiera family from New Bedford, who were contract workers, work a cranberry bog on Cape Cod. Immigrants from the Cape Verde islands settled in New Bedford and found work fishing, in the textile mills, and on the cranberry bogs.

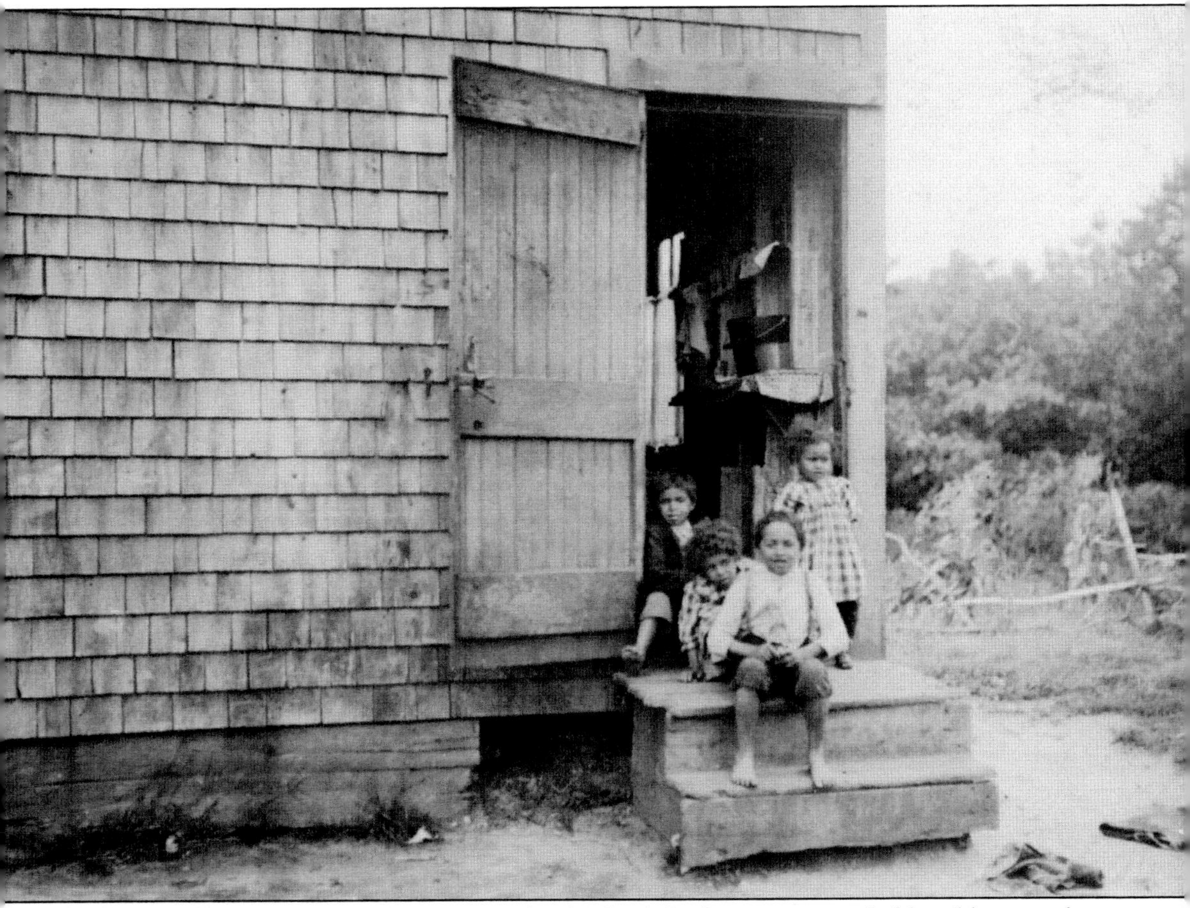

Four little children are left on their own in the shack while their parents and older siblings work at the Makepeace Cranberry Bog in Wareham, Massachusetts.

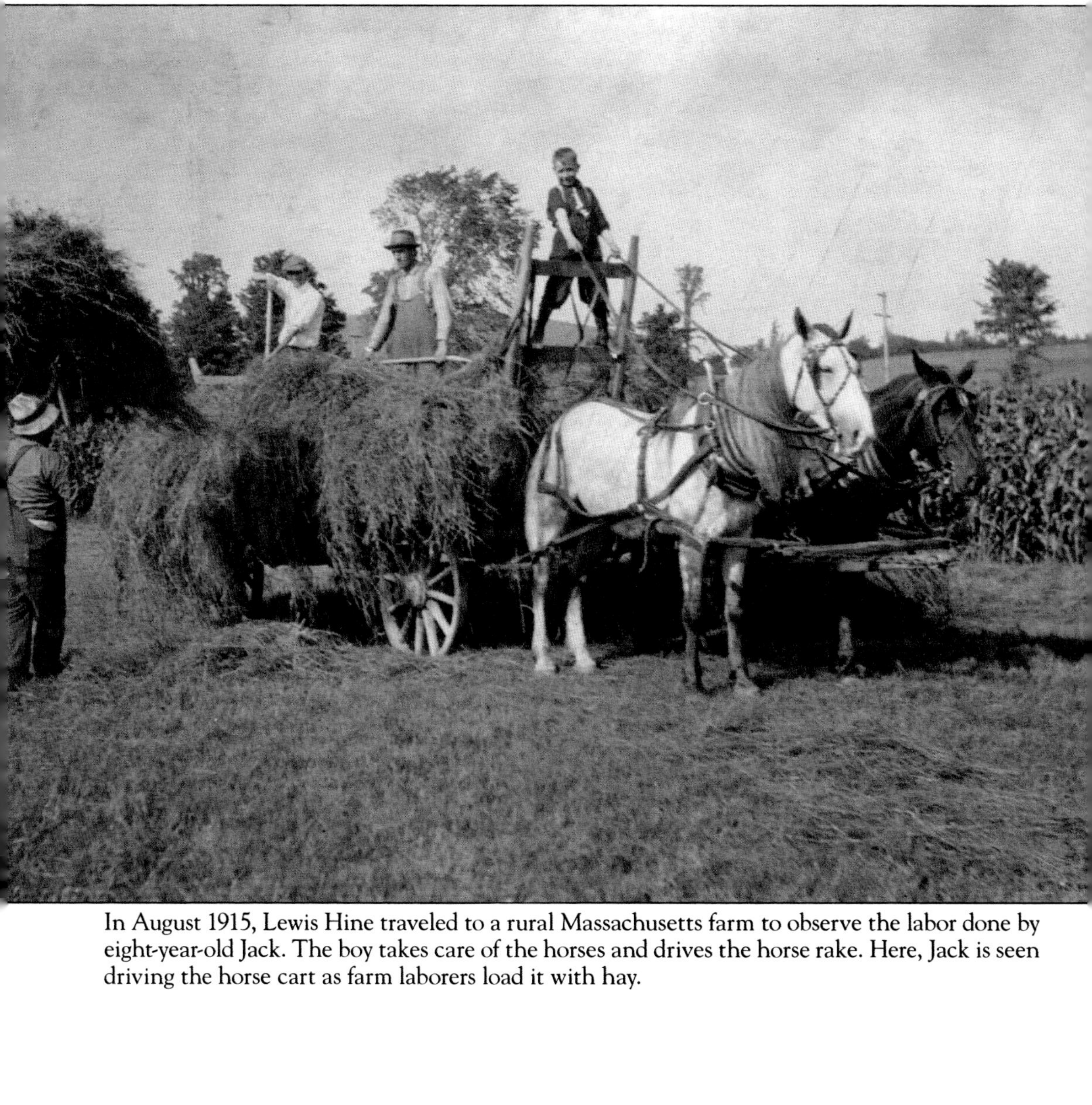

In August 1915, Lewis Hine traveled to a rural Massachusetts farm to observe the labor done by eight-year-old Jack. The boy takes care of the horses and drives the horse rake. Here, Jack is seen driving the horse cart as farm laborers load it with hay.

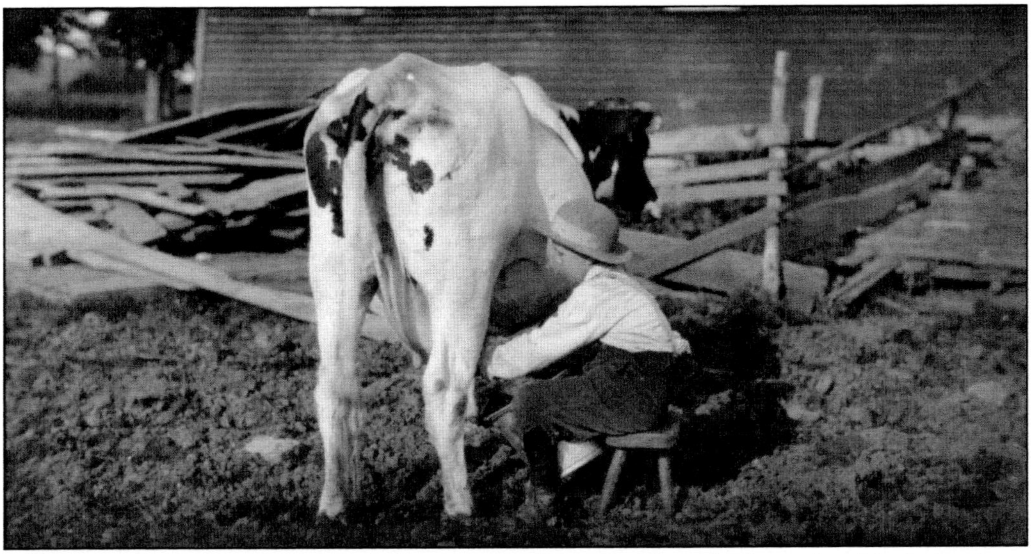

Jack milks the cows and carries the heavy containers of milk to the barn. It is likely that he is the farmer's son and expected to help with a variety of tasks around the farm, particularly during school vacations. To encourage farming, Massachusetts established agricultural schools in Boston, Brimfield, Orange, Plymouth, Worcester, and Springfield.

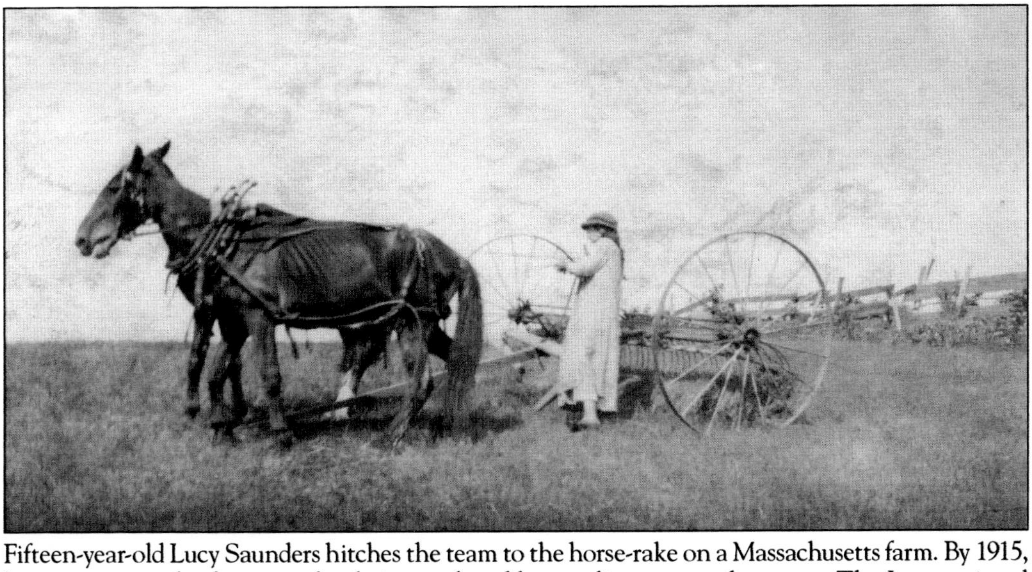

Fifteen-year-old Lucy Saunders hitches the team to the horse-rake on a Massachusetts farm. By 1915, horsepower on the farm was fast being replaced by gasoline-powered tractors. The International Harvester and John Deere companies did much to remove the heavy work, and child labor, from the American farm.

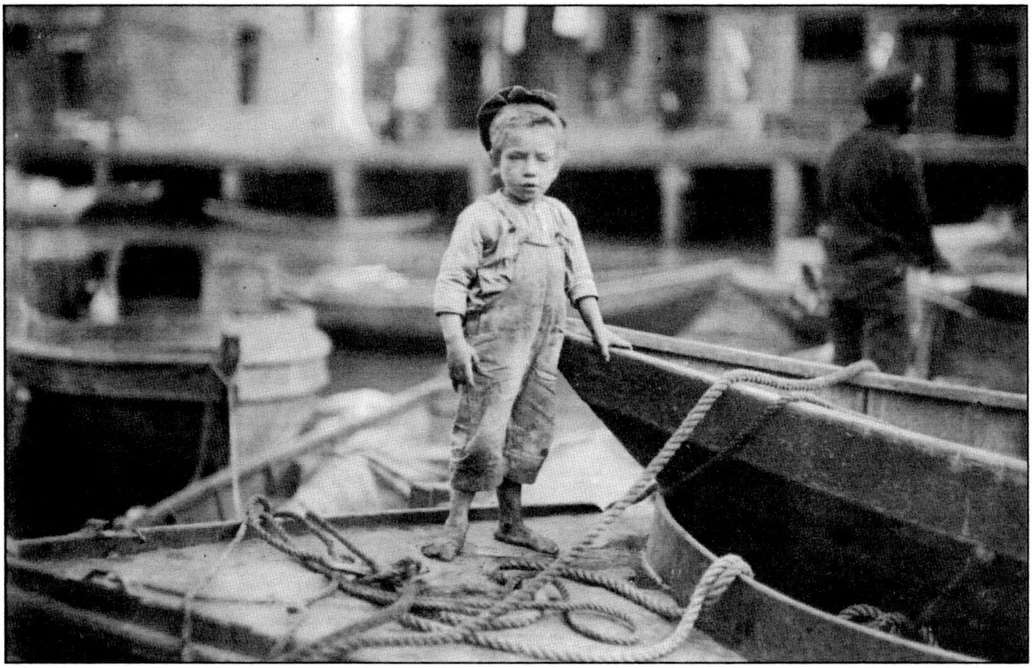

The son of a Boston fisherman learns his father's trade. At the start of the 20th century, Boston had a thriving fish industry. Boston Harbor held many fishing boats, returning to T wharf with their catch at the day's end. The boats were met by horse-drawn wagons from the dozens of wholesale fishmongers and retail stores.

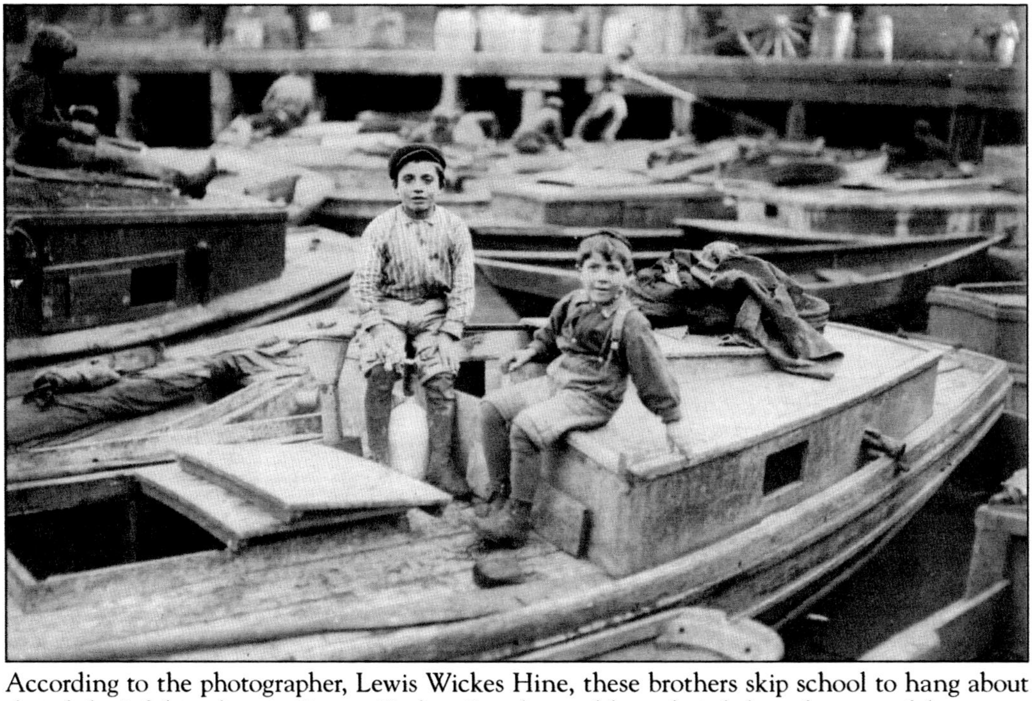

According to the photographer, Lewis Wickes Hine, these brothers skip school to hang about their father's fishing boat in Boston Harbor. Boys learned from their fathers the ways of the ocean; many became fishermen when they grew up.

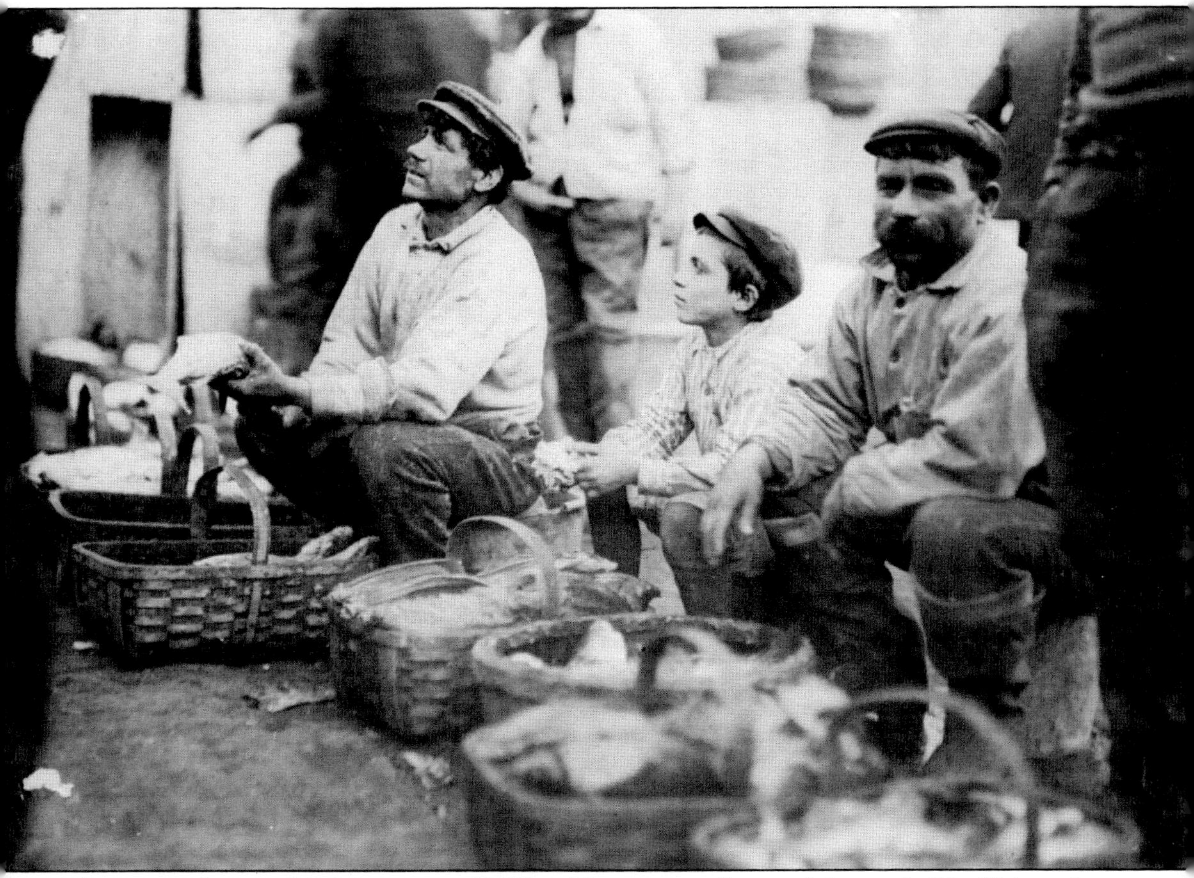

A boy sits with two adult fishermen at T Wharf, hoping to sell part of the catch. The T-shaped wharf extended into the harbor at the end of Long Wharf and was used by fishermen to off-load the catch.